the fable of the world

THE FRENCH LIST

gérard mairet

the fable of the world

A PHILOSOPHICAL INQUIRY INTO
FREEDOM IN OUR TIMES

TRANSLATED BY PHILIP DERBYSHIRE

LONDON NEW YORK CALCUTTA

Seagull Books 2010

Gérard Mairet, *La Fable Du Monde*: *Enquête philosophique sur la liberté de notre temps*
© Editions GALLIMARD, Paris, 2005

English translation © Philip Derbyshire 2009
First published in English by Seagull Books, 2010

ISBN-13   978 1 9064 9 719 4

British Library Cataloguing-in-Publication Data
A catalogue record for this book is available
from the British Library

Typeset by Seagull Books, Calcutta, India
Printed in India at Leelabati Printers, Calcutta

Contents

It is always a matter of great satisfaction (indeed of pride) for an author to see his work translated. For me, there is a very particular satisfaction in being able to make this work available to a wider Anglophone readership. The book is the result of a number of years of study and research and follows from various works of political philosophy, all having in common a critical reflection—in every sense of the word—on the subject of sovereignty. As we know, the philosophical elaboration of sovereignty was the work of Hobbes, who to a certain extent is the legatee of Bodin's invention of the concept. This is no doubt the reason why in the course of the 1980s I translated *Leviathan* into French—it is impossible to be serious about sovereignty without spending a great deal of time with Hobbes!

If I allow myself to recall one of the constitutive moments of my reflection in *The Fable of the World*, it is because something akin to the spirit of Hobbes is present here. Not that I am proposing a Hobbesian philosophy of the world, but that what inspired Hobbes in his time of troubles—can we rationally envisage peace?— is what motivates this *Inquiry into Freedom in Our Times*. So even if I am not

Hobbesian, my posture is. I do not think, as Hobbes does, that freedom is a 'specious word'. The question rather is that of evaluating the meaning of the word, and this evaluation is precisely the task of today's political philosophy, just as it was of yesterday's.

The book is not only marked by the time I spent with *Leviathan* but is also, so to speak, split between Hobbes and Locke. There is a discovery in the *Two Treatises of Government* which has intrigued me for two decades: what Locke calls the *'federative power'*. Here again, my research, though seasoned with Locke's thought of the federative, is not that of a disciple. I am not Lockean. But the thought of the federative is undeniably present in the book.

The task of this work, like those that preceded it, is just to extract myself from the constitutive thought of political modernity as it has been structured in great part by Hobbes and Locke. True, the 'modernity' in question—in effect, sovereignty—cannot be reduced to the thought of these two authors. But anyone interested in the modern State can have no understanding of it without meditating on their writings. At any rate, this fable attempts to surpass these and other authors, in the same way that the steam engine surpasses the horse—it wouldn't occur to anyone to claim that the horse had failed. It is the same with the political philosophy of the past. Contemporary language is right to talk about 'horsepower', and this is enough to ridicule the pretension that the modern, the contemporary, is more valuable than the ancient. If Rousseau replaces Hobbes, this does not mean that Hobbes is wrong but that the times have changed. Rather than a 'surpassing', it may be better to talk of a 'replacement'. One author takes the place of another, but only because the new has arrived at another moment of historical time. Our time is no longer that of Hobbes, Locke or Rousseau.

The claim I make here is that our time is witnessing the culmination of sovereignty, especially in Europe. If this proposition has any meaning, it is the one established by the present work. To do so, I have tried to understand what sovereignty is. It is not reducible to 'decision' or to 'supreme power' and these so-called definitions are in fact falsifications of the concept—identifying sovereignty with war. They have their origin in Carl Schmitt, a Nazi thinker, who, let us note in passing, today enjoys a new and posthumous reputation. I have shown, rather, that sovereignty is the process, characteristic of political modernity, which establishes freedom in the form of a particularism of a people, of a nation. The thesis of this fable is that this process has come to an end—that is, it has come to end only in Europe. In other words, the fable of sovereignty has come to an end in the place where it originated and was first put to work. If this claim is historically meaningful, it is important for political philosophy to take its measure, to rethink freedom in this period when sovereignty has reached its culmination.

There are two necessary dimensions to the constitution of this thought, since it is a question of conceiving a higher form of freedom: the henceforth obsolete character of the old 'Atlantic Freedom', and the cosmopolitan constitution of Europe, which consists of federating not peoples but the freedoms conquered by great struggle during the course of the period we call 'modernity'. On the important question of the *European federative*, this English edition has allowed me to clear up the ambiguities that might have been present in the original French, explaining the principle and clause of the *res publica* founded not on sovereignty but on its abandonment within a *European jus gentium*[1] whose elaboration remains the political task of our time.

All of this would not have been possible without the painstaking work, the philosophical competence, in a word the excellence, of Philip Derbyshire's translation, and I take great pleasure in thanking him here.

Gérard Mairet
Les Grands Millets, 25 April 2009

1 See Conclusion in this volume.

Where possible I have used extant translations for the materials that the author cites. Where for various reasons this has proven difficult, I have made my own translations from the French versions that the author has used. This should be clear in the references.

Philip Derbyshire

This World, Philosophy and 'Examples of Things Past'

The essential propositions of political philosophy in the modern period are properly unintelligible unless they are related to the central principle that organizes them—*sovereignty*. In fact, it is this principle that is in question today, and with it the philosophy that is the foundation of our republics. This interrogation (*mise en question*) throws them into obvious question (*mise en cause*) without producing a place to regroup. For five centuries, the (political) history of Europe ran in tandem with the development of political philosophy, as if the genesis of the historical State in Europe followed the rhythms of philosophical utterance. Just as political action was ordered through the institution and consolidation of sovereignty, political philosophy structured its principles of government on the basis of that concept—to think politics was to think sovereignty. Today, it is no longer a question of thinking the structure of sovereignty but, rather, its culmination and supersession—sovereignty, born in Europe, is being transcended before our very eyes.

Political philosophy—thought that thinks freedom—seeks to establish the conditions of the just life: since these were found in the organization of civil life centred on sovereignty, in these times of its supersession, philosophy is content merely to repeat assertions about the will of the people, the indivisibility of the republic, the dictatorship of the proletariat or the rights of Man. These things have had their day, not because they have entirely vanished from our lives and minds but because they cannot be the foundation of the free existence of the multitude. This is regardless of whether their historical embodiment led to their own, at times criminal, contradiction, or whether they opened up the road to the free life while being incapable of attaining it. Why, then? It is perhaps because these categories referred to a world which our present is consigning to the past. This is not to say that the problem—the conditions of the free life—has entirely disappeared from the surface of the *orbis* or even just from Europe. But it is to say that sovereignty cannot, even provisionally, provide the solution that humanity requires—in Europe or anywhere else. So philosophy has a twofold task. The first is to show how sovereignty has come to its culmination and what that means. The second is to formulate those *serious* propositions which might orient contemporary political debate. The philosophically serious is generally indebted to a *doxa* which must be overcome. In this case, the *doxa* consists of repeating the old falsehood—that sovereignty can be reduced to the decision in the state of exception. Here, not the least weakness is that this gives a pre-modern understanding of the notion, for, reduced to this appearance, it no longer presents any historical or philosophical specificity. It is, so to speak, sovereignty from before the age of sovereignty. Another aspect of the *doxa* which has failed to prosper in its various elaborations would downgrade sovereignty in favour of multiple *dispositifs* of power, without seeing that this multiplication is just the effect of the metastases of sovereignty itself. Whatever it might be, sovereignty is at the forefront of contemporary thought, because the political and moral structures whose emplacement in the modern State it makes possible, are henceforth incapable of producing what they once did, particularly, but not exclusively, in Europe—*a certain state of freedom.*

It is thus a question of grasping how and to what extent sovereignty is no longer philosophically conceivable as the structure of freedom, nor as the bearer of the future. Our inquiry is concerned with the European world, since sovereignty must first be understood as the form of individuation of historic nations—it is the basis of the particular shape of freedom as this is experienced in a particular people. Thus grasped, and understood as something more than the final exercise of power, which is merely the tip of the iceberg, sovereignty has reached its culmination. We say that an organism has reached its culmination when its constitution is complete and it has reached the full extent of its growth. Similarly, sovereignty must be seen as having reached its culmination, since it has ceased to develop and no longer produces the effects of freedom that it once did. In Europe, there is no further growth of freedom for the politics of sovereignty since it cannot surmount the limitations of the order of particularism—for the very reason that it is, properly, its foundation. In this sense, then, to the extent that we look at the question of the world from the political angle of morality, the modern fable of the world has come to an end, as we shall see.

However, we should first note that the deployment of sovereignty over the surface of the *orbis* was achieved through the philosophical production of a notion of evolution, thought in terms of a universal history. This production is itself an element (that we might call 'ideological') of the worldwide growth of sovereignty. In other words, States were instituted among human beings by dividing them according to the materiality of sovereign territories, through an uplifting story about the 'world' that I have characterized as the *historial*. In fact, in order to understand what is at work in our modern history of the State, it is important to grasp how the thematic of a universal history, inaugurated by Jacques-Bénigne Bossuet, accompanies and gives meaning to the project (if not a programme, whether providential or otherwise) and is an integral part of the fable of sovereignty. This develops deep within a spirit that is the bearer of meaning, the meaning of a 'world'. The fable in question does not perceive events and things that happen in time as the simple succession of the historical, that is to say, as materialities, but as the occurrence of meanings, that is, signification. If the historial, then, is part of the fable of sovereignty, it is because the work of sovereignty is a work of meaning and the spirit—it delivers a message that political discourse elaborates and philosophy thinks. It is also necessary to grasp the historial where the narrative of a universal history is centrally deployed, the history of human beings and their State, as the spiritual element, however profane, of sovereignty. If sovereignty is not content, so to speak, to give place to a history of materialities but to the deployment of a historial meaning, the spiritual sublimation of the historical, the edifying credo of a profane State, it is because the bearer of meaning is the 'sovereign people' whose spirit and will elaborate those codes. In sovereignty, it is 'the people' that thinks—it thinks the historial, without which there would be no meaning to political life, so profane is its foundation.

The present inquiry thus takes on the elucidation of the historial as the guiding thread which allows the politics of sovereignty to give way to *cosmopolitics*. It is not a question, however, of simply following in the footsteps of the Kantian heritage[1] of 'perpetual peace', without any further elaboration. It is perhaps the novelty

---

1. I have tried to do this in my book, *Le Dieu mortel. Essai de non philosophie de l'État* (Paris: PUF, 1987), where, taking into account the culmination of sovereignty in Europe, I take up the Kantian thematic of peace again. See especially, pp. 130–62.

of our era by comparison with Immanuel Kant's that we cannot talk about the 'world' without referring its definition to the workbench of philosophy.[2] In fact, the world of cosmopolitics is the European world. It is Europe as world that forms the substance of the cosmopolitan law. Or at least that is the proposition asserted here, because it is a newly constituted Europe that makes possible the reality of a freedom of a higher kind than that inherited from the historic States. This is also true by virtue of the culmination of sovereignty, in the sense we have outlined. From this point of view, cosmopolitics must itself be redefined only after the general context of morality, that established by sovereignty—the particular morality of a particular people—has been elucidated. So the philosophical task today, as we stated at the outset, consists of the obligation to rethink how freedom has been thought. Philosophy in this sense cannot avoid restaging—within the context of the new world of Europe and the worlds that surround it—a new conception of the *question of freedom*.

This reinterrogation would not be an engagement with the 'examples of things past' as Montesquieu described them in his definition of the *general spirit*. The sovereign order of the world is a European one and the requirement of a renewal of morality finds its source in the exhaustion of this order. We remarked above that Europe was not content merely to unfold a history, but that it also told the world a story about the *orbis*, a historial fable, which was edifying because it was emancipating. If, as we demonstrate here, that fable is over, then the question of freedom is effectively once more on the agenda, and can be dealt with adequately only if we take the European experience of the world seriously. 'Seriously' means recognizing that the 'examples of things past' show us that the sovereign order of the world was established by war, so much so that it was twice necessary

2. On this, see section entitled 'On the Constitution of the Free Life' in the Conclusion in this volume, and the discussion of Habermas' theses on cosmopolitan right.

for Europe to globalize war for that very order to be thrown definitively into question. And this led Europe to a new obligation: to think a future morality, the ethics of its freedom, not in terms of the mechanisms of a new age of war but in peace.[3]

The Question of the 'World'

To be sure, freedom is first and foremost a metaphysical notion. However, this book does not endeavour to examine the metaphysical question of my freedom but, rather, the political and moral question of my freedom. If from the outset I deploy a certain facility, I do not think that it involves a betrayal of philosophical wonder and its habits since I do not imagine that a discourse that presents itself as a *philosophical* discourse claims to be altogether free of metaphysics. At root, when an historical State engraves *liberté, égalité, fraternité* on its system, it cannot escape metaphysics on the pretext that it intends to inscribe freedom in historical arrangements and institutions. The illusion (even *naivety*) would lie in thinking that one could expatiate on political freedom, equality or fraternity and escape any trace of metaphysics. In most respects, human beings are nothing but metaphysicians—they question themselves (whatever their culture, wealth or poverty) about the nature of their freedom and about whether they know they are free. That is why revolutions happen in the world, and these are great metaphysical events. If, then, I use the term 'morality' to name *the form of the free life*, the way it is philosophically stated, is because my intention is not to produce a metaphysical treatise outside time but a moral and political treatise for our time.

The book, then, is a philosophical inquiry into the subject of this form: how it is defined, what it produces and how it has reached its culmination in the world—not the world in general, but this world, in particular the European world. It is a

3. This is the aim of the Conclusion, in this volume.

philosophical account of sovereignty from its invention in part of Europe between 1576 (Jean Bodin) and 1651 (Thomas Hobbes) up to the present day. However, even though these dates might be incontestable, they are idealized—*Les Six Livres de la République* (Six Books of the Republic, 1608) and *Leviathan* (1651) are only *books* after all. Books, even philosophical ones, are not beginnings. History does not begin with books, and the *word* is not the first building block. The history that is the backdrop of this inquiry (or account) must be dated not from the appearance of a book but, rather, from the appearance of a world—1492. That is the date of the birth of Modern Times. We should believe Michel de Montaigne: 'Our world has just discovered another one', he notes with some astonishment. And this sober account comes close to filling him with anxiety, since this new world is not just unknown but already the sign and annunciation of the decline of the old:

> Our world has just discovered another one, and who will answer for its being the last of its brothers, since up to now its existence was unknown to the daemons, to the Sibyls, and to ourselves? It is no less big and full and solid as our own, its limbs are as well developed, yet it is so new, such a child, that we are still teaching it its ABCs: a mere 50 years ago it knew nothing of writing, weights and measures, clothing, any sort of corn or vine. It was till naked at the breast, living by only what its nursing Mother provided. If we are right to conclude that our end is nigh, and that poet is right that his world is young, then that other world would only be emerging into light when ours is leaving it. The world will be struck with the palsy, one of its limbs will be paralysed, while the other is fully vigorous . . .[4]

So, let us follow Montaigne in dating the birth of our world, which is the birth of the *world*, from 1492. This is the point from which we must appraise the moral-

4. Michel de Montaigne, *The Complete Essays* (M.A. Screech trans.) (Harmondsworth: Penguin, 1987), III, 6, p. 1029.

ity that made a *world* (ours, in truth) from what was just the *orbis*. In any case, this is what the present book intends to examine with all the means that philosophical inquiry has at its disposal. The morality in question belongs to the historical States of Europe, its peoples and nations, and it is against the backdrop of the birth of this *world* that particular and private moral codes themselves have been developed. It is this sort of *world* that this inquiry investigates, seeking to discern its principles, its most general theoretical structures, and even its metaphysics of morality. That is why we have to start with sovereignty, a notion that was alien to political discourse prior to its colossal and systematic appearance in Bodin's *Six Livres de la République*, but which finds its full philosophical determinations with Hobbes. We must then examine its different developments, reprises and rectifications in the corpus of moral and political philosophy from then on, and in the concrete history that philosophy expresses as the form of its concept. Because sovereignty is the concept that underlies both war and peace in modernity, it is, for that very reason, the concept of modern freedom. There is no other concept that is so central or so determinant.

But just like anything else in this finite world, a concept or idea can never transcend finitude but only express it. Which is to say that this inquiry, having followed the paths of the concept and recognized its historical works—born in Europe, sovereignty returns there finally after constructing a world—will have to reveal its end, albeit not its death, since sovereignty is still very much alive. On the contrary, the inquiry will just reveal its culmination, because its world is over, and with it, its *morality*. So this work announces a closure—*for us Europeans, the sphere of sovereignty is closed, the fable of the sovereign is finished*. This reflection takes seriously Charles Loyseau's precise formulation in *Traité des Seigneuries*: 'Sovereignty is altogether inseparable from the State . . . it is the form in which the being of the State is given'.[5] I have often subsequently used this limpid formulation, and do so again in the present work—sovereignty is the key to the thinking of the State as form. To think the State as *form* is to think its concept and the principle from which its concrete historical institutions can be clarified. This is why *political philosophy* is something other than a theory of government (however necessary this might be elsewhere). It should not be confused, as it has been in recent decades, with a theory of the 'rights of Man', because its object is precisely to *think the thought of freedom*, which, as I said above in the context of sovereignty, is to think freedom as the foundation of morality. It is useless to try to think politics within a philosophical order without thinking it as form. To think (philosophically) is to think a form. In addition, the thesis or philosophical claim of this inquiry is that this *form* has exhausted the prodigious capacity to produce freedom that it introduced into the world—sovereignty has arrived at its *culmination*. This means that it can no longer inform our own historical world, namely the European world to come. This assertion obviously cannot be demonstrated here in an introduction. There are good reasons for this: even less than ordinary language, philosophy offers nothing coherent before discussion is undertaken. The theory formulated here was prepared and sketched out elsewhere[6] but it is now pressed into internal coherence, so to speak: as we say, there is nothing new under the sun, and the reader should not expect to find revolutionary novelties here. And even if the theory I advance seems to have a certain novelty, this is because of its novelty of presentation rather than the new things it has to say or because the world that philosophy endeavours to understand conceptually is new. In this sense, *Fable of the World* is a good title for the work: it retells an already well-known history—the fable of freedom. It tells how human beings endeavour to live well, that is, to live *freely*, without ever definitively becoming so. In the contemporary world, this requires from them a revolutionary supersession of the present.

5. Charles Loyseau, *Traité des Seigneuries* (Paris, 1608).
6. See, in particular, my *Le Dieu mortel*; *Discours d'Europe* (Paris: La Découverte, 1989); *Le Principe de souveraineté* (Paris: Gallimard, Folio essais, 1996).

The World: the Fable and History

To know this world, it is necessary to leave it—the derealization of the world is the condition of its explanation. Look at René Descartes resorting to *making up* or *inventing* in order to explain something real and not invented. In doing so he founds a physics of the world which is at the same time a metaphysics. In any case, the reality of the world can be apprehended only if it is reconstructed by the spirit in a simulation that takes the form of a fable. Descartes had himself painted by Jan Weenix with the famous motto in clear view in the open book of the world: *Mundus est fabula*, 'the world is a fable'. There we have the trajectory of epistemic reason—it recounts the fable of the world, elaborates the fiction of a new world, and takes the path of a derealization of the world as given. It is necessary to step back from this world, to take one's distance, as they say—it is by rising above the world through thought that the world's active principle can be grasped. Hence the advice that Descartes gives his reader:

> Allow your thought to leave this World for a while to arrive at an altogether new one which I will bring to birth within imaginary spaces . . . my intention is not to explain how things are in the real world, but only to make one up at my pleasure, in which there would be nothing that the cruder spirits could not conceive . . .[7]

Descartes announces that he will make up a world through the fable, so that the world itself becomes a fable. Even so, this making up is not a free play of the imagination—it is not a question of arbitrarily imagining a new world in relation to the old one, or even a world that is different to the real one. The fable states a proposition about a possible world such that this could be represented as more real than

---

7. René Descartes, 'Chapter 6' in *The World and Other Writings* (Stephen Gaukroger trans. and ed.) (Cambridge: Cambridge University Press, 1998), p. 21f.; translation modified.

the real world, precisely because it delivers the truth of the latter. Because the truth of this world—ours, like that of Descartes' vortices—is that it has come to its end.

Making up, invention, is thus not a fabulation but a construction that allows me, through leaving the world, to reconstruct it in a way that is truer than nature, so to speak. Inventing a *made-up world* thus has the effect of verifying the world as it is, interrogating it and eliminating the false appearances and true illusions that claim to explain it. The procedure of the fable contains a critique of the world as it is, without recourse to the ought-to-be, that is, to imagining an ideal world. By contrast, it allows access to the *true idea* of the world as it is, to its truth, even to its founding principle. The detour through the fable, and the invention this involves, thus places me in the presence of the order of things, by putting me in the presence of the *form* without which there would be nothing but material without law. Invention leads to the following—it is possible that the made-up world is truer than the world I take for real. To put it another way, the fable leads me to a possible world, a new world that is superior to the old one or deprives the actual world of its future. The fable reverses the order of the actual and the possible by bringing the latter over from the side of truth. The other world, the one I take for the true one, thus takes on the form of the past, so that what opens up in front of me is the real possibility of the new world as *true world*. Descartes declares that he loves his world too much to renounce it, which is to say, he seems to prefer the possible to the actual.[8] This stems from the fact that in searching for 'the laws of nature of this new world', he is definitively diverted and distanced from the recognized unrealities of the old: 'Know then . . . that by Nature I understand nought of Goddess or any other imaginary power'.[9] The specification is necessary here, no

8. René Descartes, Letter to Mersenne, 25 November 1630: 'The fable of My World pleases me too much to let go of it'. See C. Adam and P. Tannery (eds), *Oeuvres de Descartes* (Cerf, 1896–1913), i, 182.
9. Descartes, 'Chapter 7', in *The World*, p. 25; translation modified.

doubt, because in imagining a world we might think that this world is imaginary. On the contrary, if it has more reality than the other world, it is because the made-up world really places me in the presence of its truth such that what I took for the true world now appears to me to be nothing more than a tissue of illusions. We can thus see that thinking the new world through making up has nothing to do with the abstract imagining of a world more desirable than the given one but, rather, with the philosophical constitution of the world. To constitute the world philosophically is thus to de-realize it in the sense in which the fable reconstructs the world, refashions it: to make up is to reconstruct the world by designing, in detail, a possible world within the folds of the actual world. It thus appears that the *true idea* is nothing other than the idea of the *possible*.

That is why the present inquiry follows in the wake of the Cartesian proce-dure of a 'made-up world'. The philosophical constitution of the world is the grasping of the possible within the given, the recommencement of the world in the culmination and supersession of a world. And just as Descartes removed the archaic figure of the goddess 'Nature' from his world, now the constitution of the world of morality calls for the destitution of the old world, that is, the understand-ing of the given world as *past*, or tradition. The question then is to know what it means to comprehend morality under the category of 'world'. Put another way, why should the fable be the constitutive narrative of a *world*? It is the same in morality as in science—nothing is given for ever. The system of modern freedom is finished because the thinking of the thought of freedom is itself historical. The first characteristic of the world is *finitude*, so that the form of its freedom is itself finite—to think its form is to conceive it as finite. Moreover, an essay in under-standing morality is an attempt to grasp what it is within the existing system that brings the world that proceeds from it to its culmination. The second characteris-tic of the world is that it forms an organized and coherent totality that contains within itself its own principle of order. Finitude and totality are the metaphysical coordinates of the world of morality—they form the axes of the definition of the distinction between the just and unjust.

In this sense, we might set up three models or schemata of the world of morality, distinguished according to three different foundations of the system of thought of freedom: a natural world, a divine world and an historical world. The first (that of the ancients) is formally dependent on a harmonious *cosmos* such that the order of morality consists in founding the crucial distinction between just and unjust on the structure of nature understood as *physis*. The necessary frontier between the just and the unjust is traced by observing the constituted order of *physis*. This observation reveals a (natural) law—some are masters and others slaves. The same law, the law of things, dictates that the stone falls and the flame rises. The second model for the foundation of freedom sees its principle in the injunctions of the divine law. A god, who is just by definition, orders the material aspects of life and existence according to his own law and irresistible will. God is the foundation, something indisputable, since men are his creations. How could the created creature question his creator? It is certainly possible that God has also willed that everything is for the best for human beings, just as nature itself had ordered things so that every being had its necessary place and carried out its pre-destined task. God's hierarchical distinction between elect and reprobate must be regarded as just—the distinctions he makes are for the common good of humankind, with every man seeing himself rewarded in proportion to his faith and obedience. Finally, the world of morality can be founded on the historical, that is, against the divine, from which it is ruptured just as it is from the natural world. Here there is no god, or nature, just will and action—the relations of force form the norm of justice. Human beings have taken the place of both gods and nature. The world of morality is a profane world. Not that the sacred has been removed—it is perhaps, on the contrary, more present here than elsewhere (in other worlds). In the natural and divine worlds—ancient and mediaeval respectively—Nature and God are self-evident. Human beings find them formidable entities, and it is spiritually difficult to revolt against them, despite the few who defy the gods or who introduce novelty into the civic order. The sacred is anchored in bodies and souls, for all it transcends the human order. Philosophical revolt and the slave's rebellion are forms of sacrilege; in the same way, the doctrinal difference of the heretic is a sacrilege. But in both cases the sacred as distinct from the order of mankind is not annulled by revolt—it is merely displaced or redefined. The line that distinguishes just and unjust is simply displaced—the god says something else and nature arranges things otherwise. The profane world contains no such idea of the sacred, because here the sacred is the *profane* essence of the foundation and this foundation is the will. That is to say, the *will*, in its very nature, is what changes. If I am what wills, then it is the nature of my will to change what it wants. By definition, I am not submitted to my will. The Moderns in the modern world of morality made the following discovery—if the world is the disposition of my will, then there is no norm that is necessary and that can be uttered once and for all. The element of the will is finitude and the rule that it states is itself finite. The traditional separation of the sacred, situated beyond men (in nature or in the gods), renders the just as beyond dispute, inaccessible. It is merely a matter of applying it without question. What the will introduces into the world, by contrast, is the sovereignty of the human over what is just. Which is to say that there is no way of knowing how to definitively establish what is just—freedom seemingly hangs from the will and its whims. A fiction of eternity might gravely soar over the worlds of tradition; by contrast, it is no longer possible to compel belief in something being eternally right. The Moderns decided to *dispute among themselves* over the nature of the just and the good, or, in other words, about the nature of their freedom. But they did not do so in the light of Reason's contradictory readings of the observed world, nor in terms of what the god had communicated to them through his prophets. The Moderns no longer discussed the ultimate significance of the divine *logos* or the natural *logos* in order to define their freedom. Freedom emerges from the human *logos*, which alone is competent. The morality of modern humankind is altogether constituted in the grammar and idiom of the human *logos* of the will.

It is thus the human *logos* that is systematically recounted and elaborated in the modern fable. Just as there exists a *logos* of the natural world and one of the divine, the human *logos* encloses a world within itself or, rather, it generates one. If one can in general assign each of the three schemes of morality to a different historical epoch, this does not mean that the passage from one scheme to another takes the form of an absolute rupture. The world of the Moderns is haunted by the Greek *logos* of the world and the God of monotheism still resides in modern souls. But their foundations are radically incompatible. You cannot have recourse at the same time *both* to (an eternal) God *and* to the (historical) will as foundations. You have to choose. Choices of this sort are always revolutionary and bring with them many of the disasters and troubles that human beings have experienced, especially in Europe. If a history of freedom is possible, it has to avoid two pitfalls: first, that of making the ruptures between schemes too abrupt, as if the *logos* of monotheism owed nothing to the *logos* of the ancients, or the modern *logos* nothing to the other two. Such a history would be absurd. The other pitfall would be to see the continuous genesis of each by the others in a sort of germinal fresco, in which the present figure would mark the completion of the former. The modern tradition of the history of morality must be found between the two extremes, borrowing from both with the aim of producing an understanding of the modern idea as referring back to the perfection of the old, which was always present but transfigured. At root, this account of history retraces the modalities of the presence of the origin in the present with the aim of rendering it intelligible. Rather than being simply past, the old continues to be the norm of the present, its principle of evaluation. This is not because the ancients offered a truth that could be used to evaluate what was to come afterwards, thanks to some calibration of the new by the old, but because the meaning of the new can only be given by the action of the old which precipitates it like a reaction in a test tube.

It is this alchemy (whose effects we shall see presently) that finds an exemplary instance in Jean Barbeyrac's vast and erudite *Préface* to the 1732 French edition of Samuel von Pufendorf's *De officio hominis et civis juxta legem naturalem* (The Law of Nature and of Peoples). He thus discovers a foundation for the morality that the Moderns were in the process of establishing, giving an excellent résumé of it in the presentation he offers of Hobbes' *Leviathan*. It is the principle of *self-preservation* that is the foundation of modern morality, and that can be seen and elucidated in the distance established between the Moderns and the Ancients and Christians. This provides a foundation for modern natural law as opposed to classical natural law. The 'science of morals', Barbeyrac says, is revived by the Moderns after the 'dark' scholastics. He then produces an account of the formation of modern natural law. The translations of the works of Aristotle by Boethius

> created the foundations of this prodigious and truly despotic authority, which Peripatetic Philosophy subsequently acquired, and which is still upheld in various places. The *Arabs* held on to it during the eleventh century and introduced it into *Spain*. Thence was born Scholastic Philosophy which spread throughout *Europe*, and which leads barbarism to be more prejudiced towards Religion and Morality than towards the Speculative Sciences. The Morality of the *Scholastics* is a Work of bits and pieces, a confused body, without order or fixed principles, a *mélange* of the thoughts of Aristotle, Civil Law, Canon Law, maxims from Holy Scripture and the Fathers of the Church. The *Casuists* of the last centuries have only

produced vain subtleties, and worse, abominable and monstrous errors, as everyone knows. Let us pass over these unfortunate times and come finally to where the Science of Morals has, so to speak, been revived.[10]

A history of what determines morality (which is more a history of political, moral and juridical philosophy) is being constructed here, and this is also a chapter of morality itself—the history of an object is an element of the object to the extent that this history is the means by which the object is determined. Its determinations are three in number: first, the science of morals in general is inaugurated by the Greeks, which the 'Sacred Writers' and the Romans enriched; it was eclipsed until the rediscovery of Aristotle, and we should note that Barbeyrac does not fail to tell us (something of a novelty in our times) that it was the Arabs who brought Aristotelianism to the West. But the appropriation of Aristotle by Scholasticism gave rise to nothing but a tissue of abominable errors. Then the Moderns arrived. And the science of morals is 'revived' as a beautiful equilibrium between the scepticism of those pure disciples of Enlightenment reason *and* those pure disciples of submission to Revelation without natural enlightenment. Second, there is a type of progress in the discovery of 'the true foundations of Natural Law and the right method of explaining this Science'. This is what Hugo Grotius inaugurates, for example, and what will be fully achieved by Pufendorf. This is not to force Barbeyrac into saying that progress in morality, whose bearers would be the Moderns, only has value in the theoretical history of the morality of morals but, rather, it is in the historical *freedom* that slowly, but irresistibly, accompanies it in mankind. This progress in doctrines is in Barbeyrac's eyes the sign of a progress of morals themselves, to the extent that what reveals the evolution of doctrine is the abandonment of the excesses of what he calls 'Historical

10. Jean Barbeyrac, Preface to the fourth edition of his translation of Samuel von Pufendorf's *Le Droit de la nature et des gens* (Caen: Université de Caen, 1987), p. cxv.

Pyrrhonism'—that scepticism of Reason with regard to Revelation and vice versa. The luminaries of Faith cannot do without Reason and Reason cannot be opposed to the Scriptures. Thus, progress in thought, that is to say, the fact that it leads towards the establishment of 'true foundations', expresses in theory what modernity establishes in fact. Modernity has the advantage over what it is not: an Antiquity that is too pagan and a rationalism that is too sure of itself and marked by atheism—witness Hobbes.[11] Modern morality is what transcends 'Historical Pyrrhonism'. Just as the 'Sacred Writers' were content to supplement what was missing in certain ideas—ideas, which, however imperfect, were no less true—the Moderns illuminated the moral precepts of religion by the light of Reason. This shows

> what depths it is necessary to go to . . . those who having worked with all their might to demolish the certainty of the light of Reason, call us back to the light of Faith to fix our doubts: as if the light of Faith did not require that of Reason and as if the proofs one has of the truth of facts on which Revelation is founded or of the sense of a great number of passages of Scripture were more evident than the maxims of right Reason on the subject of our Duties and of their true foundations; not to say that these Gentlemen carry *historical Pyrrhonism* just that little bit further.[12]

11. Barbeyrac's presentation of Hobbes has great relevance: 'He [Hobbes] published in Paris in 1642 his *De cive* where, among other errors, he tries to establish, through Geometrical order, Epicurus' hypothesis which proposes as principles of Society the preservation of the self and private utility. He builds on this supposition that all men have the will, as well as the forces and power, to do evil to one another; and that the state of nature is a state of war of all against all. He gives to Kings a limitless authority not only in the affairs of state, but also in matters of religion [. . .] He reveals himself better in this Work [i.e. *Leviathan*] and there advances the straightforward proposition that the will of the Sovereign creates not only what is Just and what is Unjust, but Religion itself, and no Divine Revelation can impose obligations on the Conscience, since the authority or better the whim of his *Leviathan*, that is to say of the Arbitrary and Sovereign Power, to which he attributes the Government of every Civil Society, grants to it the force of Law [. . .] He passed though Atheism, and one does not make too much of an error in passing this judgement. He believed that all is corporeal' (ibid., p. cvii).

Finally, the third determination, perfectly consonant with the previous two, is that Europe is the historical sphere of this progress. Paradoxically, Barbeyrac mentions Europe only at the moment when he condemns the 'barbarism' of the Scholastic who spreads his abominations throughout Europe. However, this turn towards the geography and history of morality is of capital importance, since it refers to something that will be essential in the future. The future will reveal what Barbeyrac's contemporaries themselves knew—that Europe is the sphere of mankind's moral progress. The error of scholasticism will be corrected and the thinkers of the Enlightenment will spread through Europe, resurrecting the concepts of natural law and Revelation. Europe is thus incorporated into the history of morality—it is the very body of morality, its *res extensa*.

The matter of *morals* is the object of a theoretical elaboration which, at the very period when its concepts are being formed and its definitions asserted, contributes to the philosophical creation of a *moral world* which is the world of Europe. Like physical science, the science of the moral world develops within the geopolitical world of the European world. This is the unconscious foundation of Barbeyrac's historical discourse—morality extends properly speaking over the space of Europe from Greece to the West. And this world will be determined by morality, that is to say morality possesses an extension which it informs: Greece, Rome, Christianity, Reason, the Republic, will all form part of the *mise en scène* of progress, albeit not without obstacles, chaos or revolutions. A spirit will unfold over the theatre of Europe. While *spirit* is not a category that Barbeyrac makes use of, it is made part of the Enlightenment arsenal by one of his contemporaries, the brilliant archaeologist and art historian Johann Joachim Winckelmann.[13] Morality, like art, is a chapter in the unfolding of spirit, and *what* then unfolds is

12. Ibid., p. cxxv.
13. See Chapter 2 in this volume.

Europe. Morality as a chapter of spirit takes form as the European body—(modern) States are philosophically conceived and are established by the historical actions of sovereigns. Modern freedom is thought in the same way that Europe thinks about and identifies itself, as Montaigne had already begun to do—it is the land of civilization, and for that reason will establish its *reason* as a principle of its expansion within the extension of the *orbis*. Making the *orbis* moral, civilizing it, will be the means by which Europe will generate its own identity. Europe is the backdrop of morality, its system and its history. The philosophical conception of modern freedom will be the conception of the extension of a part of the *orbis* as the European world, as the world of reason and freedom, the form of world *tout court*. The major and most important effect of this is the appearance of *Atlantic freedom* which will take shape with the revolutions in America and France.

Europe, not the goddess but the territorial extension, is thus the true object of the fable of a world (its own), not the history of ideas. Better, where the history of philosophy (of which political philosophy would be a region) illuminates the assembly and disassembly of the world of ideas, the fable by contrast reconstructs the true idea of the world. In this sense there is no history of moral and political philosophy; if such a history exists, it is as a function of pedagogy rather than as a genre within philosophy. Such a history would involve what I have termed historial affabulation—the historical taken as the story of meaning, and, properly speaking, as a fable of meaning. As we will see,[14] the symptom of the history of morality as the creation of the true foundations through a progress that filters truth and error is fully at work in the constitution of Europe as world of spirit. The idea that we have of Europe is that of a history of reason of which morality is the attestation that reason is republic, so that *natural law* (something Barbeyrac perceived) is nourished by the common reason of human beings. In this sense the

14. See Chapter 2 in this volume.

historial constitution of Europe is consubstantial with the political philosophy of the *European world* as the spirit of the world. The inverted teleology of the historial—whether conscious or not—which makes us think that we are the descendants of Pericles, the virtuous citizens of Rome and the apostles of the Holy Spirit is present in the reassuring illusion that Europe has a universal destiny. An illusion to which Edmund Husserl clings furiously:

> We pose the question: how can the spiritual shape of Europe be characterized? Thus we refer to Europe not as it is understood geographically, as on a map, as if thereby the group of people who live together in this territory would European humanity in this. In the spiritual sense, the English Dominions, the United States etc clearly belong to Europe, but not the Eskimos, or the Indians presented as curiosities in fairs, or the Gypsies who constantly roam about Europe. Here the title 'Europe' clearly refers to the unity of a spiritual life, activity, creation, with all its ends, interests, cares and endeavours, with its products of purposeful activity, institutions, organizations.[15]

This passage is altogether remarkable and it shows the sombre clarity of spirit as it orders the sense of the historical. When the historical materials (theoretical and practical) of Europe are ordered by virtue of the meaning that their historial *mise en scène* envisions for them, Europe becomes the ancient goddess, transfiguring the dark world of the *orbis*. For *spirit*, and Europe as spirit, to be born and develop, some Greek thinkers had to create a thought that would throw a universalizing gaze on the particular. Hence philosophy's rectifying function, which was to discover between the two world wars which had originated in Europe that European humanity in its truth directs humanity *tout court*. The uni-

15. Edmund Husserl, 'Part 1' in *The Crisis of European Sciences and Transcendental Phenomenology* (David Carr trans.) (Evanston: Northwestern University Press, 1970), p. 273.

versalization of the European spirit, a project shared with the Americans, is what is articulated by history, and its ultimate meaning is the advent of a 'supranationality of an entirely new kind'. 'I am thinking' says Husserl, 'about the spiritual form of Europe.' Kant had already noted in *The Idea of a Universal History from a Cosmopolitan Point of View* (1784) that Europe had no choice but to take charge of the education and civilization of the other continents.

These precise directions and orientations of history will provide the context in which the fate of Europe will be played out during Modern Times up until our own conjuncture. In the movement of ideas, we have lived through the naive and dangerous Husserlian certainties of a European spiritual mission, which the very narrative of this European history of ideas and affairs bears witness to. It would be a mistake for us to withdraw from the attractions of the historial just because they are the product of a translucent spirit. History is more an object of faith than an historical science, and fuels our imagination without giving us knowledge. As we have already said, we imagine ourselves to be Greeks when we are nothing more than prosaic wage-earners in a profane world, preoccupied with satisfying the needs that self-preservation requires. We have lost Apollo's isle—it was forbidden for anyone to be born or to die on Delos, Apollo's sanctuary, a prohibition that lasted from the third period of rule of the tyrant Pisistratus to the end of Antiquity. Our world is not the sanctuary for some god from Olympus or anywhere else. This world of polychrome gods is no longer ours, in the sense that our own history cannot be rendered intelligible to our thought if it sees in Greece and Rome a radical *alterity* to our own profane world. On the contrary, to invest what is historical with the 'spirit' born in a mythified Graeco-Roman past whose origin is always present is to misrecognize the modern *logos* of the world. It is far more important to relate (political) philosophy to its object—the thought of freedom as thought in the world as it is. This means separating the historial illusion from the work done in Husserl's ideological jumble of spirit: 'Within European civilisation,' he writes, 'philosophy has constantly to exercise its function *one which is archontic for the whole of humanity*.'[16] So there is a place for rethinking European humanity, which only the fable can do by exercising a constant and salutary 'historical Pyrrhonism'.

Thinking Freedom

Particularism is what defines modern freedom—the peoples and nations of our era have been formed by constituting their own freedom. It is this particularism of freedom that leads irresistibly to reposing the question of morality in its determinate and precise historical context. Hence the hypothesis that this fable examines, which can be posed as follows: *the culmination of sovereignty understood as the principle and foundation of the particularism of modern States, creates in Europe a political and moral void at the heart of historical nations. If they do not constitute their freedom in a new way, Europeans run the risk of being dispossessed of their historical being.*

It seems to me that this hypothesis can be justified in the light of the experience of the past which illuminates our present by virtue of three essential historical determining features, which are, so to speak, the backdrop of our inquiry. The first of these is the absolutely unprecedented nature of the Second World War, its unprecedented character lying in the fact that a modern, highly cultured people could give rise to a criminal State, the Nazi State, which founded its existence on carrying out (not merely projecting or envisaging) the extermination of a part of European humanity in the camps. And this was done following the procedures of the technical, administrative and legal rationality of the modern State. This single fact in itself signifies an absolute transgression of a fundamental principle of political modernity, that is to say, respect for the human person as such, the protection of the rights of the individual and his goods. In place of that, the Nazi State in transgressing the

16. Ibid., p. 289; emphasis added.

foundations of modernity—posited by the principle of sovereignty which asserts the absolute equality of individuals—opens up the sphere of a politics of death and violence by asserting the radical identity of politics and war. This aspect of the immediate past of our current historical European world would in itself suffice to plunge it into a moral nakedness, and which requires its principles to be radically questioned. In the era of the Nazi death camps, the moral configuration of Europe has been irredeemably overturned and this ruin is the ruin of Europe itself. We know that *Europe's suicide* was traced out in the camps. That is why, since the end of the War, Europeans have undertaken not merely their mutual reconciliation but also a literal resurrection of and re-engagement with the enormous project of their political and moral union. But this is precisely what is at issue in our time—the ability to live in peace which we Europeans have acquired through the War, or better, the many wars. In the course of the half a millennium of Modern Times, Europeans have rarely—perhaps never—been able to live in peace. It is just the circumstances of this peace that should make us designate it 'a phoney peace'. Because it is a *de facto* peace, which has, so to speak, befallen us, in a state of exhaustion after the innumerable wars through which we were constituted as autonomous and free nations. Which brings me to the second determining feature: Europeans live now in the context of the end of empires. This means that the Europe that conquered the world, and in so doing built the great modern empires, has now come home. That is to say, the vast universal process of decolonization liberated the colonized peoples, who have regained a lost sovereignty, or have instituted a new sovereignty for themselves. Subsequently, this process has forced Europe, having come home—that is, returned to its own *extension*—to live from its own capabilities, or, at any rate, no longer from those that its conquests and colonial imperialism generated.[17]

17. We should observe in passing that this colonial imperialism nourished the expansion of 'spirit' until very recently. A civilizing activity visible in two sorts of work: *conversion to Christianity* and

We must not lose sight of the fact that European decolonization redefined Europe itself and its States—a redefinition that continues today but which finds its expression in the process of European unification. It is essential to have in mind that the birth and development of modern States unfolded in the context of the discovery of the New World and the colonial appropriation of the world *tout court*. The institution and consolidation of the metropolitan States was achieved in the conflict between the European powers (principally Spain, Great Britain and France) for the conquest of the world. The conflicts linked to the colonial development of empires are the principal historical source of the formation of the States of modern Europe and its nations. Colonization was an essential, if not the only, motor for the division of Europe, our Europe, which we can date symbolically from 1492. Be that as it may, this foundation of historical States has been achieved, sovereignties have been established and Europeans now live out a 'phoney peace' between themselves.

The third determining feature of our Europe and its present exceptional situation is the fact that on the European continent itself, from Ireland to the Urals, empire itself has collapsed. With the end of the Soviet Empire, Europeans are no longer globally opposed to one another, along the lines of the East–West cold war.

the opening up of the *market*. We can see an illustration of the first in a book used for teaching reading, where we read: 'Togo is a little pagan. Father Martin took him to the mission school. Togo saw his little friends, who were just like him, black as ebony, frizzy-haired, and happy to live in the mission. He learned to love the good Fathers. He knew Jesus. One day he went to find Father Martin. "I want to be baptised", he said. They gave him instruction, and then one feast day, the little black boy Togo was baptised. Now he is the little Christian Henri. He is happy. He loves the missionaries' house' (F. Auget and J. Dedieu, *Du vocabulaire à la phrase. Cours élémentaire*, 11th edition [Paris: Les Editions de l'École, 1951], p. 81). As for the second type of work, we can find a statement of it in a manual of philosophy for high-school students, in a chapter entitled 'Duties of the Colonising Nations': 'When it is absolutely necessary to use force, for example against a rebellious town, always think about the role that this town could and ought to play in the organisation of the country. The officer who, before taking a village, considers the market that he will establish there afterwards, will not take it in the same fashion' (André Bridoux, *Morale* [Paris: Hachette, 1945], p. 223). See section entitled 'The Aborigine' in Chapter 3 in this volume.

The most decisive effect of this recent novel reality is that the peoples of Central Europe have recovered the principle of their sovereignty and which they now exercise within the European Union.

It follows that the contemporary European problem can be stated as follows: the principle of sovereignty opened a particular sphere of morality, the morality of Modernity or Modern Times. The foundation of modern morality—the system of freedom which each nation effects for itself and in relation to the others—was implanted in Europe largely by war—either civil war, war against other states or colonial conquest. It is through war that the peoples and nations of Europe were formed in their particularisms, and were constituted as states, that is to say, by sovereignty. It is precisely such a process—*the individuation of historical peoples*—that subsequently reached its culmination in Europe. Culmination in the sense that in their general formal tendencies, the nations of Europe can no longer wage war.[18] If the nations themselves were constituted through wars, they are now being lived and experienced and no longer need to oppose each other in order to exist. The consequence of the process that has now come to a head is the sort of *problematic peace* that Europeans are experiencing for the first time: a *non-constituted peace*. In effect, this peace is not the result of a moral and political choice but of a *de facto* situation inherited from the three determining features that I have just outlined. There is no political peace, because for such a peace to exist it must be the peace of a political space, the peace of a republic or of a community conscious of itself, that is to say willed by the multitude. This question is the theme of the last chapter of this inquiry.

18. I have in mind the general trend of European history since the end of the Soviet Empire. In other words, I do not ignore the wars of sovereignty in its wake, in the Balkans for example, or Chechnya. However, if war in Sarajevo did not launch the European powers into a generalized conflict, this was because Sarajevo today is not the Sarajevo of the nineteenth century. And if that is the case, then generalized conflict is tendentially excluded from the Europe of our times.

Let us recall that sovereignty is understood here as the historical form of the State. This means that it is the mechanism by which Europe has become what it is today—the sphere of division and historical particularism. Far from attesting to a unitary spirit, *one* born in Greece or somewhere else, the basis of what we nowadays refer to as Europe is division. In fact, the result of our modern history is prosaically that *there is* a Europe, constituted by a multiplicity of nations, each experiencing for itself what I have called profane freedom. The term 'Europe' refers to the world of divided European humanity, and that is the fundamental result of modern history—to have manufactured Europe and the Europeans where once there were empires, kingdoms and principalities. If sovereignty is the historical form of the State (and not some figure of 'decision' as I will show in Chapter 1), that means, among other things, that those we term 'Europeans' are henceforth the multiplicity of peoples and nations living together, coexisting peacefully within a geographical space known traditionally by the name 'Europe'. Put another way, there is no foundational unity properly speaking, that is to say, no universal common foundation for morality. There is no *archè* such that today the peoples and nations of Europe would finally form a historically constituted and homogeneous moral community that would be the very foundation and concrete space of peace. Europeans have the confused feeling that the peace that emerged from the war lacks a solid guarantee, and that this peace must be constituted. What is important then is *to constitute the peace*—it is not enough to receive it as a negative gift, so to speak. That is why this fable has undertaken the task of examining the novel question of morality within Europe's own historical context, without which such an examination would be simply a speculative fiction, abstracted from life and merely academic.

Because the essence of sovereignty was the principle of individuation of historical peoples, it has produced a divided Europe of national egoisms. It produced the multitudes opposed to one another, whose only common tie is the market (this is the theme of Chapter 4). In producing the historical peoples that we are acquainted with, sovereignty produced the citizens at the very heart of the nations but has been and remains incapable of producing a citizenship of nation to nation. There are no citizens of Europe in the sense that there are, for example, citizens of Greece or France—there are only consumers. It is effectively—and only—the tie of the market that establishes a relationship between the French and the Greeks, for example, not a two- or three-thousand-year continuity of spirit. And from the point of view of morality—that is from the point of view of the freedom enjoyed in France or Greece—a Greek citizen and a French citizen are two *foreigners* in relation to each other. If there is no European citizenship—save in the cant of politicians—then Europeans have the status of *foreigner* for each other. Frenchman and Greek are as foreign to each other as Frenchman and Chinese are, for example. This comes because they have no common public law. If Europeans are foreign to each other, they form what the political philosophy of the seventeenth and eighteenth centuries called a multitude living in a state of nature. As foreign to each other, they are outside civil life—they have no civic status in common. They have only interests, for which reason, in considering their relation to each other, nation to nation, they are not citizens but consumers in a state of nature. The market functions as a trap for morality. It is this apolitical and a-civic situation that in keeping them 'in a state of nature', as philosophy would say, renders the peace they enjoy problematic since this is nothing but the peace of the market. This is what the Conclusion demonstrates, and where we will see that the political constitution of peace in principle has the effect of producing a schism within the Atlantic realm of freedom.

What the culmination of sovereignty in Europe renders manifest in concept and what subsequent history will express in fact is that the European constitution of freedom—in the form of the European body of the republic—splits Atlantic freedom into two pathways: the American and the European. Escaping from a state of nature that America still finds itself in (that of the conquest of the extension of the *orbis*), Europe discovers another state of nature (that of historical particularisms at peace) where 'modern' freedom reduced to the market exhausts itself, so that it can no longer face up to the tasks of the future: to provide the foundation of the morality of the new world.

To sum up: what we call European history—and thus 'Europe'—is the division and partition of European humanity that in our time has surrendered to the peace of the market. This is a process that gave birth to nations; it is the vast process of the individuation of historical peoples each with its particular will, mostly brought about in foreign and civil wars. It is a process that is succeeding before our very eyes in transforming the former citizen-soldier into a depoliticized citizen-consumer. It remains true that it is in and through wars that peoples gain a *consciousness of self*—they gain a sense of their particularism, that they are a particular people, and that they are this *common moral self* about which Jean-Jacques Rousseau speaks. This is the moral significance of war in Europe, its moral paradox—war in Europe has brought Europeans to a degree of morality such that, faced with their own particularisms, they can no longer engage in war and are suddenly left to the mercies of the market—hence the forgetting of morality. And, more generally, Europe's political renunciation of an effective engagement in the world. That is why the modern cycle of morality (that is, sovereignty) has reached its culmination. If, from the point of view of its metaphysics, sovereignty is the profane and historical concept of morality, then from the point of view of history, sovereignty is the advent of the particularism of freedom. It is this process—the advent of the moral particularism of historical peoples—that culminates before our eyes. Before our eyes, sovereignty has accomplished its task of providing the foundation of nations and peoples and now retreats from its role as support of modern morality to yield its place to the market. This means that the state model of sovereignty is no longer appropriate to the future of a Europe divided into particular nations which it has nevertheless produced. So, in its present form, as the simple *result* of modern history and which begins beyond the Atlantic, Europe has no future, although there is no going back to the worlds of the divine or of nature. All of a sudden, Europe contemplates its own modern history and seeks once more to identify itself with its ancient past—it is fixated on its history, which it henceforth relives in the mode and time of tradition. In other words, the political time of our contemporary Europe, for some twenty or thirty years now, has been that of the imitation of self: Europe, it seems, has renounced the new and the future in the absolute fear that she will try to commit suicide again, and this time accomplish what she failed to achieve in the world wars of the last century.

Sovereignty having done its work, the Atlantic system of freedom disappears, and, since real history is still too marked by the illusions of the historial, it is necessary to have recourse to the *fable* which announces the freedom of the *new world*.

Chapter 1

Common Being or the Discourse of Sovereignty

Human art consists of the production and government of a world, and the manufacture of the world is what we call politics. The modern art of politics posits freedom as the only goal of politics, its perennial object. In consequence. the free life consists of obeying the rules and precepts that the philosophy of morality establishes on the unique foundation of sovereignty. What is modern here is not to be found in the links between politics and philosophy (an ancient linkage) but in the philosophical definition of freedom as the stake of politics. Hence, the question of morality becomes that of the political constitution of the free and organized life, whose principles are defined by philosophy. What we call 'world' is thus the coherent system of philosophemes of morality that politics makes concrete. Politics in this sense is the practice of morality in the midst of a world— it manufactures a world as the moral space in which human beings are drilled into obedience to the laws without which there would be no commonly accepted distinction between what is just and what is unjust. If morality is tied to freedom—it is the latter's grammar, so to speak—the body of rules, the element within which free action unfolds, where the free life is effectively lived, is a *world*, and this world is moral.

At first glance, this might seem overly abstract—because we are used to saying that politics is the general government of the affairs of the world, that is to say, the ensemble of things taken materially in their totality, not the government of moral matters. Politics is generally represented as the activity practised by those who wish to apply concrete solutions to the concrete problems of the world. That is why the assertion we have just made about the subject of politics—*the fabrication of the world of morality*—can seem abstract (even marred by idealism) in the face of the real life of human beings and our lived experience of political life. However, we must hold on to our proposition since the doubts that it raises rest on a misunderstanding about what is concrete and what is supposedly abstract. If real politics consists in finding concrete solutions to problems posed concretely to human beings in some civic space, in the end it consists of choosing one solution out of the many possible ones (solutions that we cannot always claim to be just or effective) to a problem that is unique. For example, in particular circumstances a State might decide to go to war against another, even though other courses (not all of which are just or effective) that would permit the outstanding dispute to be resolved are possible. In the best of cases, the governors of a (democratic) State will call on the people to concur or simply to give their opinion. The example of war is probably the best one we could have chosen to illustrate the morality of politics because war is the highest and most serious affair that can confront a government and a people. What is at issue here is not deciding whether war is moral or immoral—this type of questioning being close to meaningless if it is posed (abstractly) in these terms. Let us suppose that, for reasons of their own, those in government are inclined to go to war while the majority of the people reject this policy. This difference of judgement might stem from a difference of information: those in government perhaps know something that those outside do not. Their decision to go to war might be founded on information that in their eyes justifies war. For their part, the people generally possess knowledge (by definition not secret, unlike that of those in government) which informs them about how affairs proceed in the world—public opinion thus forms, openly declaring itself against the recourse to force. Let us note that it might turn out that in such circumstances the government is right to decide for war; while in other circumstances, the people in opposition to government are right to oppose the move to war. It is not a question here about the essence of things but a matter of concrete situations. To put it another way, the people are not by nature peaceful and the government by nature warlike. When the question of war is posed, the answer that is required is absolutely concrete—the actors (governors and governed) will be determined by their respective passions and reasons. And, even though concrete, the choice is no less moral—it is a choice within morality because it engages with common freedom. To desire war or reject it are determinate decisions, that is decisions taken in the knowledge of cause and effect. It is thus a founding political act, as is the correlative act of establishing peace—what is at issue is a moral act because it engages with the freedom of a human totality during an extreme political experience. Only the act that constitutes a nation can be compared with it, an act which is itself eminently concrete. The foundational politics par excellence, war (like the Constitution) engages the *freedom* of a people, a nation, who themselves are formed or are in the course of formation.

We are right to say, then, that politics is the totality of actions that aim to resolve the problems that are concretely posed to men wherever they might be, so long as we specify that what is at stake in the game of politics is the freedom of men. Politics in this relationship is the practice of morality, the fabrication of the world of morality. That is why the reproach of abstraction amounts to making freedom itself an abstraction, when in fact it is what is most concrete in men's lives. Political action is not moral by nature (the moral tendency of real politicians is, rather, immorality); rather, it is moral because it is the only means by which human beings have any chance of leading a free and organized life. There is no moral politics in itself, but it is through politics that there exists the *possibility* of freedom among men. And just as the ultimate decision about extreme action (war) is neither moral nor immoral, the fact that those in government, *ex hypothesi*, opt for war while the majority of the governed reject that option, in the circumstances we are considering, means that the actors have a different understanding of freedom and assess the risks of winning or losing according to different criteria. Hence the existence of a political problem—individuals and groups confront each other because a priori they have no common morality.

The Common World as World of Finitude

In connecting modern politics to the fabrication of the world of morality, I am merely reflecting its own founding principle—sovereignty. Sovereignty has constructed the modern world through its project of constructing a *common being* for human beings (which is, as we will see, the being of common justice) in which they participate. Moreover, it is this participation in 'what is common'[1] that is the primary source of citizenship in our democratic republics. The citizen is the per-

---

1. The expression is Bodin's: 'A Republic is the rightly ordered government of a number of families, and of those things that are their common concern by a sovereign power.' See Jean Bodin, 'Introduction' in *Les Six Livres de la République*, VOL. 1 (Gérard Mairét ed.) (Paris: Livre de poche, 'Classiques de la philosophie', 1993).

son who takes part in the world of sovereignty and its morality. Correlatively, citizenship is not universal in the sense that it would make a citizen out of any individual subject to its law. If I am travelling, or even resident, outside the State of which I was originally a citizen, and am subject to the sovereignty of the country in which I find myself, I do not have citizenship there. This situation might be entirely satisfactory but it could also be unfortunate—being subject to the sovereignty of the country where I happen to be, there is an unequal balance between the duties that are incumbent on me and the rights I enjoy. This shows that the (democratic) sovereignty that structures a space of freedom where rights and duties are tendentially in equilibrium only guarantees this equilibrium in a single case—when the individuals who depend on it participate in the same world. The common being of sovereignty is that of a common *world*. It is neither the nature nor the essence of this common world to be the indeterminate world of the universal multitude. As a singular individual, I am not part of the world of morality in general but of a particular world, this one, which is the country of which I am a citizen. The world in which I participate has its limits and these are the frontiers of sovereignty. I can no doubt claim to be part of the world of humanity in general, and present myself as a citizen of the world, but I am no less a citizen of a particular State, and I do not participate in the (absolutely abstract) universal sphere of rights and duties but in the determinate particularity of the country where I am a 'member of the sovereign', as Rousseau nicely puts it. It could be that I was a member of the sovereign in another world than this, and my situation would be the same—I would be tied to the particularity of the laws and justice, even if the laws and justice elsewhere had common abstract bases and practical dispositions. In the best of cases, this would not substantially change my position as a citizen of a determinate and particular sovereignty such that what is permitted here is not allowed there (or might not be).

Sovereignty creates its own worlds that are at the same time common worlds—a particular nation forms its own world for itself, a world proper to it. And this is a common world in which the individuals of the multitude participate—they have this world of their own in common, which is practically their norm of justice which determines the extent of their liberty.

At the heart of the question of politics lies the question of the world. The condition of existence of the modern *res publica* is the extension of its sphere of action (freedom) to the limits beyond which the extension of its world becomes impossible. And action becomes impossible at the precise moment where another *res publica* begins, itself limited by the first. Politics is what defines the *extension,* the *space*, in which the modern State—sovereignty—constructs its world, one that is different from its neighbour's yet agreeing with its neighbour on the delimitation of its extension. By definition, this extension is not infinite, and the task of the sovereign is to increase its extent because it is a question of increasing freedom. The world of morality is the world of freedom and it is in the nature of liberty to reach out or better to tend to reach out to infinity. If this is the essence of pure freedom—movement without hindrance, like water that flows, cascading over barriers to continue on its way—political freedom is limited by another freedom. Politics does not know pure freedom, so that it only flows in a closed and limited world. Like the world itself, freedom is marked by finitude. Like the extension of which it is only a modulation, the world of morality has its existence held by the limits that restrict it. If on the other hand we were to deny the finitude of the world created by politics, we could not explain the major moral fact of Modern Times[2]— the material and immaterial (territorial and moral) division of its space into sovereign States.

2. Well illustrated by modern Europe after 1492, the date of the discovery of another continent, a discovery that would be an important driving force (if not the only one) behind the modern genesis of historical States.

One cannot represent the possibility of a State that is infinite in a spatio-temporal extent. That is why limit and, hence, negation belong to the essence of sovereignty. When the latter is defined as that which orders the common being of some multitude, of some nation, that means that this common being is, by nature, limited and finite. Its limitation follows from its very nature, for what would be the substance of an infinitely extended being, and, *a fortiori*, what would be the common being of this being? To participate in what is common in this being, it is necessary that the being of this community is limited in extent, in other words it is logically and not just politically necessary that some have the right to participate in this community and that others do not. Sovereignty selects those who have the right to citizenship. This reveals what is at the root of citizenship—for my citizenship, my being the citizen of some *res publica,* to have both logical and political meaning, the status of citizen must be reserved for some, of whom I am one, and not for all. If everybody participates in the common being in which I participate, then this participation no longer has a proper meaning. If my citizenship is also the universal citizenship of those individuals of the multitude who people the *orbis*, then it is obvious that the very notion of citizenship is deprived of meaning. It is not a question of refusing citizenship to this or that person—it is a question of logic. Given the world as it is, if a State (as in its own world) granted citizenship to any person who asked for it, *ex hypothesi* this State would enjoy a reputation for perfect happiness and everybody would be a citizen of it. But there would no longer be any interest in being or not being a citizen of that State. In reality, if the human beings of the *orbis* universally became citizens of this State, the notion of citizenship would dissolve and all individuals would be either free or slaves. Homogeneity in servitude as in freedom would be absolute and we would stand before the *infinite* State. But this is an absurd logic with no purchase on the world as it is; in this real world, States are finite beings, limited to a finite extension, and practising the morality of finitude in which what is regarded as just within a particular sovereignty ceases to be so outside it.

The essence of the world of morality which sovereignty creates is that it is a world of finitude, whose common being exists and subsists only on the crucial condition that it acts to preserve itself as this world, the world that is proper to a nation, that is, the common world of the citizens. This, then, is the fundamental category of *extension* which allows us to elucidate the nature of politics in Modern Times. And as sovereignty is the principle of modern politics, this leads us to think the *res publica* (the State) as founded on the immanent morality of the world of finitude.

Freedom and Salvation

The men of modernity slowly acquired the idea that what appeared to be the question of their salvation actually referred to their *freedom*. Since in the religious tradition of sin, the condition of men's salvation involved another world, beyond this one, transcending the givens of material life (that is space and time), the Moderns made time and space into conditions of freedom here below. The passage from salvation to freedom is the acceptance of a finite human world and the abandonment of the infinite world of the divine.[3] It was a question of the Moderns appropriating the finitude of the extension of the world, that is its imperfection, for, they discovered, there is no world beyond this one; or, if such a world exists, its existence has no effect on this imperfect one. Let us look at the opposite hypothesis, the hypothesis of the perfect world.

3. This passage, it must be stressed, did not take place either categorically or instantly but is in embryo from the fourteenth century onwards, in the conflict that opposes the French king to the Pope; it grows through the Reformation and the Machiavellian revolution and becomes consolidated in the seventeenth century in rationalism. That is how we saw (see the Introduction) the invention of what nowadays we call Europe.

What would a perfect world be like? At first, we might define the perfect world as being a world whose inhabitants have no desire, inclination or need to escape from it. Such a world would be fully satisfying because hope for another world would be non-existent or useless. To all appearances, this would be a world where, by definition, the very word 'perfectibility' would be unknown in any language, living or dead. In the same way, this world would lack the word 'progress' or any other term referring to the idea of improvement. In this world there would be no time, that is no consciousness of the present, or, more correctly, the immediate. In effect, the notion of the future must be absent from the perfect world, since the idea that the state of this world could be different from what it is today might give rise to the idea that it could be better than today. Doubt about the perfection of the present world would be the worm in the bud. Once doubt is installed, we have the possible ruin of the republic and its world, the ruin of the order of the world. However, looked at more closely, this way of envisioning the perfect world is inadequate because the perfect world is understood in an entirely negative form. It lacks everything that exists in the real world that leads us to characterize it as imperfect—it lacks desire, the passion for the future and regret for the past. Suddenly, we witness an unexpected reversal of things: the so-called perfect world is in fact imperfect, while what we have called the imperfect world turn out to be perfect. In this respect, it is the best of all worlds, precisely because another world would be impossible, if by another world we understand an altogether other world which would not suffer the evils of this one, its imperfections. This perfect world is in fact impossible, since, according to my definition, I am brought back to that reversal that I mentioned above—it is the perfect that is imperfect and the imperfect perfect. The perfect world has to be defined in a different fashion, such that that world would be possible and not caught up in the imperfections of this world of which it would, so to be speak, be merely the negative.

The thought of a world which is not only possible but real, whose imperfection is its very perfection, is to be found in the eschatology of the world of the Fall, the world of finitude whose salvation is guaranteed by the divine world at the minor cost of obedience to the worldly requirement of faith in the final coming (or previous advent) of a saviour. The authentic thought of a perfect world is linked to the eschatological morality of salvation. It is *because* of its very imperfection that this world is a perfect one, or at least one incapable of improvement. Its reform is thus possible and engages the partisans of faith to act so as to bring about the advent of a better world, beyond the present one. This better world would be situated beyond the given world of works and pains, in a world of tomorrow that sings and promises, outside human time. If this world is the best one possible, and if one could in all conscience call it perfect, it is not because it is entirely without pain or unhappiness but because its imperfection leads to the idea of a possible perfection as *recompense* and reward for its pains. It is thus cleansed of all imperfections because it leads to the perfect. It is the vestibule, the terrestrial conduit to heaven—the sufferings of time prepare for the blessedness of eternity. In this sense, our finite world is more than simply finite—it is a propaedeutic to the infinite, a trial and an initiation.

It is this eschatological model of salvation that the Moderns have progressively abandoned in favour of the model of historical freedom. They do not place their salvation in a hoped-for coming of another world but accept this world as the only one they have and conceive their freedom according to the needs of life and the procedures of a rational calculus—the needs of the body and the constraints of their existence and not the articles of faith. And if the latter persist within the modern world, they are no longer at the base of the morality of the world; there is, instead, the autonomy of the (human) historical world which orders the sphere of finitude. What distinguishes traditional salvation from modern freedom is that the former conceives freedom against the backdrop of the infinite which would be its rule and measure, whereas the latter relates men's actions to finitude without the infinite, a human world without a divine world. Hence, modern freedom is founded on the autonomy of the given world, which human beings understand as their world, a world they dispose of, at times to the point of imagining they have mastery over it. Dispensing with the infinite, now become the contingent figure of the singular religious consciousness, but in full awareness of the universal finitude of things and of their own being, the Moderns thought their world outside the universal, discovering within it, by contrast, the marks of the particular and the contingent. They see that the solution to the question of imperfection is human, that is to say, historical—it is to be found in rational calculation, in a geometrization of the just and unjust. The just does not flow from a configuration of law and salvation, whether divine or natural, but from an appreciation of the finitude experienced by living and suffering human beings. Suddenly, the world—the given *extension*—ceases to be the universal testimony to a superhuman (or extra-human) order and becomes the particular series of particular worlds, each seeking with the means at its disposal to constitute itself as an empire in the face of finitude. It is such an *empire* that the sovereignty of modernity passes on to the modern world of finite worlds. Sovereignty is the *imperium* of finitude.

On Sovereignty, I: the Position of Sovereignty

The autonomy of the human world, emancipated from the divine, leads the Moderns to define their place, their position relative to spatio-temporal extension. The appearance of the discourse of sovereignty[4] in the period of the birth of modern Europe must be related to *power* and *necessity*. Such a discourse should not be

---

4. As is well known, it is Bodin who is the origin of this discourse, and those authors who follow him draw inspiration from this work.

taken *in abstracto*, as if it were simply a question of an academic exposition to which equally academic glosses need to be added.[5] When Bodin produces this concept—the concept of the modern *res publica* (the State) before being the concept of the power of the State—we have the definitive uncontestable demonstration of the defeat of the *Christian res publica*, of its impossibility even. The dream of the Middle Ages (the dream of salvation) is only barely realized from the middle of the eleventh century to the middle of the fourteenth. There was the idea that God governed men through the Roman Church, and the West, it was believed, was the entire world. The space that would become Europe but then comprised Western Christianity had, for nearly three centuries, known a unity of faith during which the temporal and spiritual magistracy of the Church of Rome knew its period of greatness. In the sixteenth century it would become a divided space. The various forms of Protestantism put an end to Western Christian universalism, so that faith became largely the particularist affair of States, or better, nations, in the formation of which religion became irresistibly the servant of politics. Religion ceased to be the *koiné* which nourished the civil association of men. Rather than uniting men, the discourse of God tended to divide them radically and irremediably. On the cusp of Modern Times, the force that had founded kingdoms and empires and which, during the period of the dominant Church, was no more than the armed extension of Catholicism, became the medium of nationality, that particularism of faith and morals carved out of the universal, so to speak. The embryonic nations are pieces cut out of the tatters of the universal and the particularisms of faith (the different interpretations of revelation) are seen by power as the means of ensuring authority within a determinate territory. This territory will soon be defined as the *territory of sovereignty*, that is, the profane authority over all who live there. The fundamental characteristic of this definition is that it is established

5. Or simply worldly because political.

by philosophy, by the arguments of profane reason. As for theology, the arguments of revealed reason, it is at best the stimulant of a foundational discourse of the *res publica*. Such a (philosophical) discourse finds in itself only in the non-contradiction of its own discursive logic, the principles of common being, in whose first ranks we find the systematic principles of justice that will institute the republic of the Moderns. Theologies give way to philosophies, as the Church gives way to the State. This passage is the passage of sovereignty.

The stakes of such a revolution are the constitution of the common being of a people as nation. It is only from the perspective of such stakes—the notion of the proper freedom of a people—that sovereignty can be understood. In a register that was more metaphysical than political, Gottfried Wilhelm Leibniz seems to reveal, albeit unintentionally,[6] the irrelevance of the question of God to the new question of freedom. According to Leibniz, the inventor of the term *theodicy*, there is no contradiction between the existence of evil and the infinite goodness of God. He explains this by the geometrical metaphor of incommensurables—God cannot bring it about that his creation of the (perfect) square does not necessarily entail the freedom (if I can put it like that) that would allow the hypotenuse not to be commensurable with the side of the square. This would be seen as being *ex hypothesi* an inevitable 'imperfection' given the very nature of the square, which God cannot justly avoid. To put it another way, *evil* flows from God's creation of a world ('the best of all possible worlds' which prompted Voltaire's sarcastic attacks), but not because God made an error in creating evil or in omitting to prevent its emergence (all contrary to His perfection). Rather, evil is the result of men's *freedom* in the world, in short, a freedom badly used. So, sin, evil in general and the

---

6. See Gottfried Wilhelm Leibniz, *Dialogue effectif sur la liberté de l'homme et sur l'origine du mal* [1695] in *Système nouveau de la nature et de la communication des substances* (C. Frémont ed.) (Paris: Garnier Flammarion, 1994), pp. 47–60.

calamities of the world flow *necessarily* from the effects of things otherwise harmoniously created (like geometric beings and their properties). Evil cannot be imputed to God; He is thus exonerated of all responsibility in the matter.

What is interesting for us in Leibniz's spiritual demonstration is that God is here a figure who is rhetorically necessary to the argument about perfection but radically neutral, if not merely decorative, with respect to the existence of evil. He is doubly so, because, first (which is what Leibniz wanted to show), He does not intervene in the existence of evil, and so for this reason He is not responsible; and, second (which is what counts here), if God did not exist (that is, if He were not the Creator) the incommensurability of the diagonal of the square would not be in the least affected, and the imperfection of the thing, like the evil of which it is the metaphor, remains outside divine jurisdiction. So that man's freedom (to do evil or not) is in effect independent of the existence or non-existence of God. This point has a direct concern for us, since this Leibnizian model of a God *de facto* indifferent and irrelevant to human freedom furnishes one of the two possible models for the metaphysics of modern freedom—the second being outright atheism. Whether I believe or not, the divine (however understood) is no longer a recourse, since it is not even a cause. I can believe or not, but this does not alter one jot the nature of my freedom, something purely and simply within my own competence—whatever other illusions I might have about its extent. I can think and believe that an infinite and good God created the world, but I can also believe that there is no god or that there are many, some of them good, others bad; this has no effect on my freedom. The ultimate proof of that freedom is that it allows me to believe or not (I *can* think it).

The freedom of the Moderns is metaphysically of a Leibnizian nature. It is the freedom of finitude, and fits perfectly with a finite world. From the moral and political point of view, it is like extension, limited by my power. If I *can* do evil (or good), because I am free to do so (God being absent or in any case contingent), it is in effect because what I call freedom refers prosaically to the actions that I am capable of accomplishing by reason of my force and my power. Freedom has to do with a philosophically defined proportion, not a (divine) transcendental determination or a (natural) exterior one. Neither God nor nature can be invoked to limit my power to act.[7] It is my own nature that places limits on my freedom (since these limits are the limits of my own nature) and my nature is understood metaphysically and politically through philosophy. The idea of my freedom being finite (because it is linked to a world of finitude) expresses the essence of modern freedom which is the autonomy of action of a subject (individual or collective) such that the subject in question is limited by its own nature, as by the spatio-temporal field in which its power is deployed. What expresses sovereignty is nothing other than the system of autonomy of power, and that in response to the violence of the finite world.

The problem that the discourse of sovereignty seeks to resolve is that of the violence of the finite world, knowing that the solution must consist of a guarantee of freedom, but that this guarantee cannot be found in God. While there are solid reasons for thinking that the philosophical project undertaken by the Moderns (where sovereignty is the (political) solution to the question of freedom) has come to grief in the world as it is, this is not altogether the fault of philosophy, though the latter cannot plead complete innocence. If the finite world knows violence (or what the theologians call evil), that would not be a philosophical fact but one that

---

7. If I say that God created me weak, which is the reason for my weakness and my lack of power, I have said nothing about the nature of what I am, or in any case nothing more than if I were to give up the belief that God created me—this is the thesis of the indifference or contingency of God. For such not to be the case, it would be necessary to demonstrate that my creation as I am is contained within the definition of divine power, a demonstration that it is necessary to the being of God that I be created as I am.

belongs to the world and its finitude. As we have seen, no perfect world can be thought without contradiction on the basis of the recognition of the imperfections of the real world. Therefore we must take this world as perfect, an untenable position if we are in good faith, or as having nothing to do with the category of perfection. The latter is the better point of view—the world involves scarcity and necessity, as we will see, from which all violence flows. To guarantee freedom is to control scarcity, to master necessity, and sovereignty is the system of guarantee and control—it is the system of the mastery of necessity.

From the point of view of its metaphysics, sovereignty appears as a response to the modern recognition of finitude, linked to the contingency of the divine as recourse and (founding) principle, and must be understood accordingly. But it would be a misunderstanding of nature to conclude from this that the sacred has been eliminated altogether from profane politics. It would be truly an absurdity because what defines politics (the moral production of the common being as *world*) is precisely the common relation of men to what is, for them, sacred. Through this relationship, politics is the definition of what is sacred and the common organization of the defence of the sacred. Common being (a determinate order of common justice) is the element in which what is sacred for the multitude resides. What is held in common as sacred crystallizes the proper world of a multitude organized into a nation, under the authority of the State which administers and watches over it. As to *what* is sacred for a people, for a nation, by which this people or nation is constituted, this is no different from what is sacred for an individual—*their life*. Concrete politics in producing the system of practical morality is the totality of material and immaterial procedures by which the life of this people or nation is preserved. Subsistence is the very substance of common being, and it is in the power to subsist that the freedom of a people or nation resides. It is in the power of a people, the power of a nation, that the reality of their being as people, the actuality of their being as nation, resides. To preserve themselves in being, to maintain themselves in existence, is what forms the sacred for a multitude already constituted or in process of constitution. Considering the matter closely, we see that the sacred, for an individual as for a people, is what gives rise to sacrifice. What I am prepared to risk my life for, to sacrifice it for, to lose it for—that is what is sacred for me. Nothing is more sacred for me than my own life, and the same is true for a collective individual. If I accept the sacrifice—give up my own life—it is because my life does not consist of the physiological substance of my organism: to live is not just breathing here and now, but desiring the future. If I accept the sacrifice, it is because my life is more than my immediate body, it is also my power, or properly speaking, my *freedom*. It is in the light of the preservation of my freedom—a free spirit in a free body—that the sacrifice becomes acceptable. I wish to lose my life if the price of keeping it is slavery—I am prepared to *risk my life* if that is the price of the free life. It is the same for a people—a people accepts the sacrifice of its life because it cannot accept the sacrifice of its freedom. Life itself is the free life. A suppressed people always struggles for its life—it fights for its freedom, for the just life. And if the combatants are prepared to make the supreme sacrifice, it is because they are fighting for their singular freedom and for that of the people or the nation.[8] It is in the identity of life and freedom that what is sacred for a people or nation resides. It is in the evaluation of this nature that we can measure the passions of a people and the heroism and resistance of a nation up to the point where it is negated by a hostile nation, the enemy of its freedom. Therefore the Moderns have not lost the sacred, yet their politics is *profane*, since

8. If the material cause of extermination of the American Indians by the European colonists between the fifteenth and nineteenth centuries is the military superiority (firearms) of the conquerors over the conquered peoples, its *moral* reason is that the Indians were exterminated because they resisted—because they preferred death to servitude. Just as today landless peoples will fight to the death in order to be free.

the freedom they preserve as their common good is a good which, in being sacred for them, is no less profane since it is *alien to salvation*, given that God is simply a possibility, a matter of contingency. Life, for us Moderns, is the freedom of the finite world. It can be appreciated relatively in the spatio-temporal extension that I hold sway over, and measured absolutely in the power that is mine, the power by which I alone can appropriate for myself the goods that are necessary for body and spirit in the goal of achieving a free life. If grace is necessary for my salvation, it is not necessary for my freedom. Having accepted the finitude of the world (having accepted that I live in a world which I know to be finite for me) does not mean that I have given up desire nor the free life. This might appear to me otherwise, if I am a believer, as a sort of salvation which finitude would allow me to hope for. But where faith guaranteed my salvation, it is subsequently reason (calculation) that organizes my freedom. Put another way, the sacred, for us Moderns, is the profane foundation of our freedom.

Considered thus, sovereignty expresses the autonomy (or the solitude) of man in the world in struggle with the latter for his liberty. In declaring sovereignty over extension, modern humanity manifested the sovereignty of his omnipotence over the definition of present tasks as well as over the conception of the material and moral ends that it would allow him to attain. In this matter, philosophy, because it mobilizes the 'light of nature', is the means of calculation and the rule of evaluation. This is why sovereignty is first a philosophical discourse about the world and also produces a world, only then becoming an ensemble of technico-juridical procedures and dispositions. It is a *thought* of the *res publica*—the profane thought of a finite freedom—before being a description of the power-authority it exercises there.[9] Juridical dispositions certainly exist, but as differentiated

---

9. A distinction that misleading commentators (Carl Schmitt) overlook but that is essential to the understanding of the principle of sovereignty, as we will see.

translations of interested positions on what the men of modernity call 'world' and which they incorporate in their republic. If sovereignty is manifested differently (within institutional systems), it is not because there are different principles of sovereignty but because the world is not identical for the totality of human beings populating the *orbis*. The world is not single but multiple as humanity is multiple. So conceptions of freedom are not the same, just as the means of achieving it are also different in different places—one is not free in the same way in Spain or France, Great Britain or Germany, not to speak of China or some Inuit republic. The conceptions of the world are different, even where they proceed from the same foundations. This explains the slow unfolding in Modern Times of different juridical and moral traditions, the slow constitution of national philosophical traditions that developed as nations confronted one another as allies or enemies.

Whatever the case, sovereignty expresses in philosophical language what the morality of nations lives out politically: the quest for particular liberty within humanity in the *orbis*. Because it is the *imperium* of finitude, it philosophically defines *the form of profane freedom of men confronted with extension.*

On Sovereignty, II: the Description of Sovereignty

It is because the finite world is the world of scarcity that its specific category is necessity. Niccolo Machiavelli's major discovery, *necessity* is the modern category par excellence—it circumscribes the field of human action and elucidates nature as the ensemble of materialities that human beings are concerned with and which in turn result from their action. Necessity is the concrete setting of freedom that the common being of a republic makes possible; it is the material of founding political action; it is *what* the multitude transforms in its quest for freedom. It is the profane transformation of materialities which the free action of human beings comes to appropriate in the course of their survival. If necessity has to do with the

primary material to which human action is applied—the *what* that is given outside them—it is also the *what* that they become. Human beings become what they
are by working materials, and in so doing constitute the world of necessity, as well
as being constituted by it; it is the milieu of their existence, their action and their
thought. Humanity in the *orbis* is not outside the world, separated from an external 'nature', purely nature on which they act from the outside. If the field of human
freedom is necessity itself, this is in the sense that I am not altogether free to imagine a world and bend it to my will.[10] Or, which amounts to the same thing, I can
imagine a world, but this world is just an imaginary world and for that reason I
have no grasp on it. Being unable to imagine a world with the intention, for example of changing it, arises from the fact that the 'world' as primary material for my
activity is given: it presents itself to me as a given. If I sow wheat before winter and
reap it the following summer, at the moment of harvest the wheat field extends in
front of me like a given, like the material of my labour. It is external to me, even if
through my labour it becomes part of myself. Without my actions, without my
having sown it, it would not be there, within the extended world, waiting for me
to harvest it. The world of necessity is like a wheat field—I have made it and it
remains to be made. It is not just a question here of the world in general (*orbis*)
but also of common being as a particularism of the world. The world is not only
an immediate and external material world but also a world mediated by action
(intellectual or manual labour) carried out in the past and given to me in the pres-

10. However, there is a widespread opinion here which is at the root of spontaneous reflections
on the world and its government. In most cases, this opinion also underlies the thought of ordinary people in government who have the naive philosophy (ruled by ambition) that the world is
at the disposal of their will—and they make *decisions* about it. But this is something about *politicians*, not *statesmen*. The latter are those who rightly do not subordinate their vision of the world
to the illusion that they have to master it through their will but, rather, seek to organize it practically through *thought* and with *prudence*—and these are scarce. There have only been two in
Europe since the last great European war: Winston Churchill and Mikhail Gorbachev.

ent. So the world of action in general is the world of becoming, and for the common being of a republic, it is *history*, the becoming human of materiality.

It is to Machiavelli that we owe the insight that political action can be understood as *historical* action—as action which founds an autonomous human order in which force and even violence are the primary (originary) ingredients of that foundation. If politics ranks highly in human affairs, it is because it is engaged with the given which it endeavours to appropriate to serve the necessities of life and the constraints of subsistence, and taking into account the scarcity of goods (their limitation) and external distribution. In a word politics, which is the fabrication of the world of morality and the application of rational calculation to necessity. Politics is the profane seizure of a profane world with the aim of a life of sufficiency. In electing necessity as the principle of their actions, which are responses to it, men of Modern Times have not thought the determinations of the *res publica* in terms of a platonic model of the Idea where common justice would be the paradigm of foundation, but on the basis of material in the becoming of which they themselves are an element. For them, nothing essential and completely given exists—there is no given that is outside time on which the foundations themselves could be built. The order of necessity, by contrast, is uninterrupted, becoming where each thing lasts only for a time. Universal finitude is not measurable by the eternity of the idea, for *ideas* are themselves things in the world—not archetypes outside it The moral world is, so to speak, at the disposition of the amorality of finite worlds; it flows from and depends upon them, and is immanent within them. The common justice of human beings in different place is the aim of action, in the very history of materiality, and not the (imaginary) model of what they ought to imitate. Practically, the world of morality is the political world of conquest, and justice in the republics of the *orbis* is reduced to the demands of their extended territories. Itself materiality, justice is historical and cannot be thought in terms of the beautiful universality of

the worlds of antiquity or the divine. That is why modern politics (the State) introduces time, historical temporality, into the conception of common being and its
concrete realization. The politics of finitude, because it seeks to overcome necessity, must thus be described as profane politics or historical politics. Sovereignty is
the concept of this politics: it is the concept (or 'definition')[11] of the modern *res
publica*: it is, properly speaking *the form that gives being to the State*.[12]

Sovereignty must thus be understood not as a juridical apparatus of the
power of State (a simple technology of command) but as the *form* in which the
modern *res publica* is constituted historically. If we had to write a history of sovereignty (I mean the genesis of the concept), we would see various conceptions of
the State unfold, according to the needs of the time (for example, more or less
democratic, constitutional or tyrannical). What we would not see is conceptions
of power or Power—in relation to their foundation. We would precisely see the
differentiation of the practices of the institution of the State and its preservation,
all of which practices have an eminent characteristic of sovereignty in common—

11. Bodin's treatise opens as follows: 'A republic may be defined as the rightly ordered government of a number of families and those things which are their common concern by a sovereign
power. We must start this way with a definition because the final end of any subject must first be
understood before the means of attaining it can profitably be considered' ('Introduction' in *Six
Livres*, VOL. 1). The whole of the *Six Livres* consists of methodically defining each of the elements
of this 'definition' of the State by sovereignty.

12. From one of my works which has already been around for some time, I have chosen a quo-
tation from Loyseau (who inherited Bodin's theory of sovereignty) as the title of the Introduction
to the present volume; Loyseau managed to find the best and most succinct definition of sovereignty as Bodin had constructed and bequeathed it. See my 'Introduction', *Doctrines de pouvoir*
(Paris: Gallimard, Idées, 1978), as well as my *Dieu mortel*, pp. 60–1. 'But sovereignty', says
Loyseau, 'cannot be separated from the State: without sovereignty, the State would not be the
State . . . For in the end, sovereignty is the form that gives being to the State, and State and its
sovereignty taken *in concreto* are synonyms, and the State is so called because Sovereignty is the
summit and period of power at which the State must stop and establish itself' (*Traité de
Seigneuries*, Chapter 2, Sections 1–2, in *Cinq Livres de Droit des Offices avec le Livre des
Seigneuries et celui des Ordres* [Paris, 1613]).

the distinction of Power and power. This is one of the keys to sovereignty as the form of the State, and it is no surprise to see it clearly established in Bodin.

To grasp its nature (all that concerns us here) we need to recall that the question of sovereignty is itself a question of the origin of power. In other words, to the extent that power (*potestas*) is received from God ('all power comes from God' proclaims Paul, and all subsequent Christian politics), the question of its origin need not be posed, or, rather, the solution is already given in the question. Its origin is given—in God—and so is utterly unproblematic and need not be questioned at all.[13] In this context, there is no *theoretical* problem about sovereignty. The exercise of power in the earthly realm devolves on Peter's successor. There are only *practical* problems—true, it is God who makes kings and emperors, and the practical political problem is to discern who will be king or emperor according to Peter (his descendants), who is the undisputed and indisputable guarantee. There is thus no theoretical problem about sovereignty within Christian politics because God is the *foundation* of all authority. But there is a theoretical problem when such a foundation disappears or is no longer recognized. Discussion can and *must* then take place about the following question: what *founds* authority? Who is *founded* to hold and exercise power? Is there a Grandee, a Lord, a Master, *someone* who solely by their existence or presence is indisputably the holder of power? The reply is in the negative. This is because the answer is not given in the question; there is a political problem, and this is the very problem of sovereignty. If *no one* in the multitude can straightforwardly and by *their nature* be king, this is because sovereignty lies else-

13. We still find in Kant himself the legacy of this prohibition on the questioning of origins, *Doctrine du droit*: 'It is *futile* to seek out the *historical origins* of this mechanism [the unification of a people in the State], that is to say, we cannot return to the point of departure of civil society (because savages plan no act of submission to the law, and the nature of these uncivilized men already leads us to believe that they were initially subdued by violence). But if such an investigation were undertaken with the intention subsequently of changing the current Constitution by violence, this would constitute a punishable offence' (Paris: Vrin, 1971), p. 223.

where. The foundation of power is somewhere other than this or that person or this or that dynasty, which could be said to incarnate it. If God is absent, there are only human beings left, and the matter of sovereignty—its *foundation*—can only be elucidated among them. Sovereignty is a human not a divine matter.

This expresses the fundamental position of the concept that defines power by perpetuity, not eternity. The theory of the *perpetuity of power* signals a revolution in the European conception of the *res publica*. Here we finally arrive at the topic of the durability of common being, not as a simple strategy of government (a more or less relevant series of technical measures) but as the constitutive essence of the State. If the *res publica*—the *polity* in general—is always directed towards the goal of its perdurance, only the modern State inscribes durability and time within its definition, as its very foundational substance. The idea that in sovereignty power is perpetual means that the State—its concrete institutional structure—is ordered in the long term; that, because its being is finite, it is conceived so as to thwart finitude itself and create a sort of artificial version of eternity. It is not the tactics and strategies of Power but the very substance of the *res publica* which allows the continuance of common being. The modern State does not exist in the present—its being is in the future. The notion of perpetual power—which is the essence of the State—puts politics onto the terrain of the overcoming of the present.

The *political time* of modernity is the time of the historical—neither past nor present but the future. By contrast with (perpetual) power, Power is temporary, limited and finite. It is a warrant received from power for a determinate time and purpose. Sovereignty appears as a reappropriation of eternity, a pure artifice which Hobbes' term 'mortal god' defines with admirable precision. The unity of the political and the historical, their symbiotic system, is the very theoretical substance of the modern response to necessity. The latter is inscribed in time and is the hallmark of universal finitude and that absence of a foundation outside the human of which it signals the condition. If the human condition is finitude, necessity is its content. Sovereignty is thus constructed in response to the newly posed problem of foundation. And it is constructed through philosophy ('the light of nature' as the Moderns call it) which effects a revolution in passing in *thinking* it, from the investigation of the speculative Idea to the elaboration of the concrete idea determined by the world of necessity. The philosophers will take over the new world and turn sovereignty into a *philosophical idea* which will become that of profane politics. The revolutionary act of profane politics is to move the foundations from heaven to earth—from God to the people. The *people* is the new figure that sovereignty introduces into the world and which will be subsequently the basis of the world of morality. If a history of sovereignty had to be written, it would be that of the modern people. It is the people—sovereign and foundational—who impose their perpetual reign on Modern Times, from the absolute monarchies themselves, passing through the tyrannies and the despotisms, to the democracies, whether real or adulterated. The people is the *body* of the State, and its soul is sovereignty. The modern sovereign State is the mystique of the people, the mystical body of the people, we could say. The people are the enigma of politics, its mask and its pretext; it cannot be defined once and for all because it lies at the origin of definitions. The people are declared by the Moderns to be sovereign, hence the foundation—they are the central character in the fable. But in Europe, it is the precisely the people who are in process of disappearing as the foundation of morality. The people are retreating from the scene and with their retreat, a period of morality is coming to an end.[14]

But for the moment it is important to examine the *time of sovereignty*. Here Bodin should speak, as he thematizes sovereign power as perpetual power. There

14. On the understanding of the philosophical idea of the people, see Chapter 3 in this volume.

is a sort of eternity in this word,[15] of the order of infinite duration, which human beings might appropriate. Hobbes' *mortal god* is perhaps already located between the lines of Bodin's text. Bodin is the first to think the political time of the Moderns as an artificial infinity, so to speak: 'For just as this sovereign and powerful God cannot create a God like himself, seeing that he is infinite, and that there cannot be two infinite things,[16] by necessary demonstration, so we can say that the Prince whom we have posed as the image of God cannot create a subject equal to himself, and his power cannot be annihilated.'[17] In his way, the sovereign is a mortal god—his power lasts for as long as he lives, which is as long as a mortal being lives. As for absoluteness, it is, properly speaking, *solitude*—there can be no equal (no 'companion' says Bodin) in sovereign majesty, which would annul the solitude of power. Sovereignty is essentially solitary—the king is alone. We are thus in the presence of a conception that we could call, paradoxically, a finite infinity, a mortal infinity—the infinity of mortals. The perpetuity of power allows the question of Power to be thought in an entirely new way. Power—which is *not* power—is a warrant, a commission, which power gives for a time; it is the authorization to command and govern accorded by the sovereign. In this sense, Power, in the modern State, is substantially a modality of power. The sovereign grants power, or, to put it another way, gives a warrant (Power) to act in its name, for a determinate purpose and for a determinate period of time. There is no thinking of sovereignty which is not founded on a thought of finite infinity (the perpetuity of power) and simultaneously on the finite duration of Power as warrant. Power and power are distinct, but necessarily linked. They are one and the same thing, like the two faces of a coin, the recto and verso of the mortal god. We cannot talk about Power in

15. 'It is necessary to understand this word "perpetual"', writes Bodin, 'through the life of someone who has power' (*Six Livres*, p. 116).
16. Here Bodin is referring to Book V of Aristotle's *Metaphysics*.
17. Bodin, *Six Livres*, p. 155.

general and power in general without conceptualizing the link which unites them—a link which is the metaphysical relationship of the modern politics of time.

It is in effect through the conception of a conscious and rule-governed appropriation of finitude that the Moderns have philosophically elaborated the system of morality of their world. The perpetuity of power refers necessarily to the temporality of Power, so that all thought of the State is of its order, all representation of the common being of men is marked subsequently by the project of the appropriation of the future. Sovereignty is a politics aiming at durability, not as a simple programme of government but as the profane spiritualization of life.

Because the world of morality, constituted by sovereignty, takes charge of finitude, the latter ceases to be an absolute fatality. At the same time as sovereignty structures a duration that can be apprehended (we can represent it concretely in the form of an electoral warrant), it opens the field of the *possible* where all that exists is the immediate given. Free action is what projects the subject into the future. The possible must thus be radically distinguished from promise. Sovereignty promises nothing; it does not create an eschatological temporality, or a future in some other world. Rather, the possible is the time of this world. There is nothing beyond this finite world that I can be promised in exchange for my accepting present subjection. Nevertheless, my subjection is real under sovereignty (as we will see) but it is not justified by the promise of the heavenly city, the perfect world. The possible is defined by power itself—it is what is *in potentia* in the present. It is the sovereign State that produces the determinations of my freedom, of my power to act—at least this is how the State understands it. When the State thinks, it thinks the conditions of my moral action and establishes the limits within which my freedom is exercised. If then the field of the possible opens up to me, that is, if I have a *future*, this flows from what the State inscribes for me, or at least makes possible. The apparatus of power is an apparatus of freedom, a freedom that can be concretely apprehended in the fact that *Power* is a warrant that I receive from power. It is the *authorization* that I receive to act with a view to the final satisfaction of my needs.

Power is in effect a pyramid of Powers, a pyramid of warrants, commissions, authorizations. There is an order of sovereignties in this pyramid where Power is what makes possible—not what forbids. It is the law that forbids, not Power. Whatever it might be, sovereignty must be understood as the modern political metaphysics of time. It is the construction of common being according to the extension and necessity attached to it. The distinction of the two durations—perpetual and finite—allows Power to be understood only as the possible. However, if Power is what I can do, what I am allowed to do, if it is what is possible for me to do, it should be clear that I cannot do everything. Not only because I do not have the energy or the capacity (*puissance*) but also because the field of my action (as we have said) is necessarily limited and finite. Where I forget my finitude, which is a modality of universal finitude, the *police* and the *courts* of the sovereign bring me back to concrete reality. That flows from the fact that, as Bodin points out in the passage referred to above, *there cannot be two infinities*. There is thus a single infinity—the solitary sovereignty of the mortal god—and facing it is the multitudinous citizenry or subject. The republic has *two* parts. Common being has two parties: the governing party and the governed. There are the subjects or citizens (these are the same thing) on the one hand and the sovereign (the recto-verso of power and Power) on the other.[18] In sovereignty, some command and others obey. There is nothing new here. The novelty lies elsewhere, in the fact that obedience in the present breaches the possible: the subjects (the citizens) are not tied to the narrow horizon of the here and now.

18. Bodin, who is very insistent on this constitutive partition of the republic, calls the 'division' prince-subjects. This division is so essential to the republic that to the extent that it does not exist in the 'popular state' (where governors and governed are the *same*), says Bodin, then the regime

Obedience is the only guarantee of the future—it is the means of this guarantee because it flows not from a promise but from a Power that authorizes action. Promise cannot be active because it engenders waiting and authorizes passivity. Most importantly, it assumes that, to be effective, the thing that is promised—here the perfect *polity*—becomes the object of a belief and faith in the life hereafter. It has nothing to do with Power; Power promises nothing, it only makes possible. More importantly, Power speaks of this world because what can be gained through action can be obtained here. If in promise, the eternity promised is not of this world, by contrast, through Power, the possible is actual because it has the same status as the world as it is; in this world, sovereignty allows the human condition to think its finitude in the modality of a certain eternity. Nothing is impossible a priori for man, and if this world is imperfect, as appears to be the case, it is in the nature of the finite human condition to work toward its improvement. Within this framework (work) there is no limit—freedom is total. The human passions are not sins, even though they must be channelled and even civilized— and this is precisely the task of Leviathan, the mortal god. It renders the possible possible—the sovereign produces the future. In this sense, subjection here is historical, it is marked by time, and is in no way passive, pure obedience submitted to a transcendent will or external order. The obedience of sovereignty is altogether human, because the power that organizes it is altogether profane—which means that absolute obedience is compatible with the freedom of the subject[19]—or at any rate this is what Leviathan itself thinks. Producer of the possible, it is the author of modern freedom.

is the worst type. Bodin writes: 'The Monarch is devised by the people and in the Aristocratic State the lords are also devised by the people, so that in both forms of republic there are two parties, that is the one or those that have sovereignty in the one part and the people in the other' (*Six Livres*, pp. 125–6). On this question, see my *Le Maître et la multitude* (Paris: Editions du Félin, 1991).

19. Thomas Hobbes, *Leviathan*, Chapter 21 (C. B. Macpherson ed.) (Harmondsworth: Penguin, 1968), pp. 264–5.

This allusion to Hobbes is relevant because, as a good disciple of Bodin, he distinguishes power from Power in defining the latter as warrant.[20] But, above all, he relates the foundation of sovereignty to the advent of time, that is to say, to the genesis of the human as the animal (body) open to time. Through this opening to time—which is *spirit*—it ceases to be pure *res extensa*. As the inverse of the natural animal, the (human) political animal escapes from the pure immediate nature of the given extended thing. It escapes from the now of need and its satisfaction. Hobbes thinks sovereignty as being what for us is the historical. It is the becoming of materiality and the consciousness of becoming, a consciousness that manifests itself in the rational and articulate project of bringing into being a possible world from which sudden death is removed and where the natural violence of finitude is transmuted into contractual political freedom. Thus we cannot have a full understanding of sovereignty as foundation if we neglect the metaphysics of time, and hence of finitude, which alone justifies Bodin's and Hobbes' distinctions on the subject of time.[21]

The question of obedience is also intelligible by reference to the metaphysics of profane power, as we have seen. Let us ask: *who* obeys in sovereignty? The

20. Hobbes' understanding of Power as the authorization to act or (*Power = authority*), that is to say, *warrant* or *commission,* can be given a different interpretation as Jean Terrel does, cf. his *Théories du contrat social* (Paris: Editions du Seuil, 2001), notably p. 388. It would appear that Hobbes often uses *power* and *authority* indiscriminately—in both cases it signifies an authorization given with the aim of accomplishing an action. See my edition of *Leviathan* (Paris: Gallimard, 1st edition 2000, 2nd edition 2004), particularly NOTE 1, pp. 272–3.

21. In this regard, Chapter 3 of Hobbes' *Leviathan* is a required reference: examining 'prudence' (which Hobbes points out does not distinguish men from animals), he nevertheless discerns what is proper to the human in its capacity to represent the future as a deduction from the past—the human art of conjecture within finitude: 'As Prudence is a Presumtion of the Future contracted from the Experience of time Past: So there is a Presumtion of things Past taken from other things (not future) but past also. For he that hath seen by what courses and degrees a flourishing State hath first come into civil warre, and then to ruine: upon the sights of the ruines of any other State will guesse, the like warre, and the like courses will have been there also. But this same conjecture has the same incertainty almost with the conjecture of the Future, both being

question is extremely complex because it touches on the origin of sovereignty—it touches on the people. If it is the people who are the principal figure of sovereignty, as we have said, it is because the people are at once the origin and end of obedience—master and subject, governor and governed. We will have to come back to the question of the people,[22] but it is important here to underline how the schema of time is properly speaking constitutive of sovereignty. It is the schema by which the concept of sovereign power is thought philosophically and by which the original holder of sovereignty is designated. It is hardly surprising to find unanimity on this between Bodin and Hobbes, those two thinkers of finitude engaged in the systematization of the common being of the Moderns on the basis of what founds it: profane power and its foundation in the people.

When Bodin undertakes to set out his definition of the republic,[23] he does so by referring to 'the people' as the originary foundation of sovereignty. We should understand that Bodin always evokes the people in the chapter entirely devoted to the definition of sovereignty as 'perpetual power.'[24] He makes a distinction (now familiar to us) between perpetual absolute power and absolute power 'for a certain time' which is the distinction between power and Power. Bodin develops the theory of sovereignty as 'the principal foundation of every Republic' and bases his

grounded only upon Experience. There is no other act of man's mind that I can remember, naturally planned in him, so, as to need no other thing to the exercise of it but to be born a man and live with the use of and his five Senses [. . .] For besides Sense and Thought and the Trayne of thoughts, the mind of man has no other motion, though by the help of Speech and Method the same Facultyes may be improved to such a height, so as to distinguish men from other living Creatures. Whatever we imagine is Finite. Therefore there is no idea or conception of anything we call *Infinite*' (*Leviathan*, pp. 98–9). Note that in the passage *finitude* is precisely the reason why 'the Name of God is used, not to make us conceive him (for he is *Incomprehensible* and his greatnesse and his power are unconceivable) but that we may honour him' (ibid., p. 99).

22. See NOTE 18.

23. See NOTE 1.

24. Sovereignty, Bodin says, is '*the foundation of every Republic*. And in as much as we have said that Republic is the rightly ordered government of a number of families and those things they

argument on the idea that it is the people (or the 'Prince') who give Power for a certain time. Power (*puissance*) is precisely what all limited Power flows from, *and* what the people (or the 'Prince') are originally endowed with. There is, then, in the very idea of sovereignty, the revolutionary idea that the people are sovereign and, in consequence, have power at their disposal. That the 'Prince' is sovereign is an idea that goes without saying. The idea that the Prince might be the people is revolutionary—and highly problematic, because, as we have seen, the people in this figure (which is the figure of sovereignty) have to be *at the same time* both sovereign and subject. It remains for us to discover how the understanding of the essence of sovereignty passes through the people. This is what is revolutionary, and all the more so in that the other possible holder of sovereignty—the 'Prince'—presents no structural or conceptual difference as to his sovereign capacity; he is a possible sovereign on a par with the people. The people can give Power to anyone (magistrates, officials and others), but power always returns to them after the mission has been accomplished, the warrant or 'deposit' finished. Sovereignty is the place from which all Power flows and to which all Power returns. Such is the nature of its perpetuity considered in its functional and practical modalities. Temporality consists in determining the subject of sovereignty. This could be any subject within the finite world—but first of all the *people*. Save by simply denying sovereignty or falsifying its concept, the people have to be a possible sovereign, since nothing a priori can take sovereignty from them. This is a revolution of major proportions,

have in common by sovereign power, it is necessary to clarify what is the meaning of sovereign power. I said that this power is perpetual because it is possible to give absolute power to one or many for a certain time, and once this time has expired, they are nothing but subjects; whilst they are in power they cannot call themselves sovereign Princes since they are nothing but agents and lieutenants of this power, until it please the people or the Prince to revoke it. The true sovereign always remains seized of his power. Just as a feudal lord who grants lands to another retains his eminent domain over them, so those who delegate authority to judge and command, whether for a short period, or during pleasure, remain seized of those rights of jurisdiction actually exercised by another in the form of a revocable grant, or precarious tenancy' (*Six Livres*, pp. 111–12).

since the fate of common being—and hence of common justice—is determined by the people. Modern freedom is enacted by the slow and inexorable rise of the people as the holder of sovereignty. This is the very history of the modern republic as it is punctuated by the revolutions that aim to establish the people in sovereignty and replace the 'Prince'—without necessarily deciding *who* the people are.

On Sovereignty, III: the Falsification of Sovereignty

Whatever the identity of the 'people' (the eminent political problem of modernity), Bodin's discovery—the archaeological exhumation of the *people*[25]—refutes a common misconception—the idea that the (Roman) dictator is sovereign. He is not sovereign, says Bodin, because he 'has nothing but a simple commission to wage war, or repress sedition, or reform the state, or create new officials. For, sovereignty is not limited in power and responsibility, nor to a certain time',[26] and Bodin concludes:

> I say nevertheless that those do not have sovereignty, given that they are merely depositaries of power which is granted to them for a certain time. Also the people relinquish no sovereignty at all when they create one or several lieutenants, with absolute power for a limited time, and more the case if power can be revoked at the pleasure of the people without specifying that time.[27]

If the question of the dictator is important (and Bodin deals with it immediately after his definition of perpetual power), it is because it allows Bodin to mark the relation of sovereignty to *war*, and thus clarify the status of the sovereign, that is to say, of the status of the *exercise* of sovereignty. These questions cannot be

---

25. In effect Bodin looks for his examples in Greek and Roman antiquity (by way of Malta and Florence); the exhumation begins before him with Niccolo Machiavelli in his *Discorsi sopra la prima deca di Tito Livio* [*Discourses on Livy*], *ca*.1513.

26. *Six Livres*, p. 113.

27. Ibid., pp. 114–15.

elucidated if they are not related to their metaphysical condition of possibility—time. The act of sovereignty is not an act that is deployed outside time; on the contrary, it is time that grants it reason. That is why Bodin, who structures the concept of sovereignty through the relation of power to time, takes care to state that the (Roman) dictator does not enjoy sovereignty. Basing himself on Cicero's writings, he rejects any understanding of the dictatorship in Rome that involves sovereignty because dictatorship is precisely what Bodin, Hobbes and their successors construct the concept of sovereignty against, as we shall see. Bodin writes:

> If we say that Sulla obtained the dictatorship for four years by means of the Valerian law, I would reply as Cicero did, that this involved neither law nor dictatorship [but] a cruel tyranny, which he nonetheless gave up four years afterwards, once the civil wars were over . . . and however much Caesar desired perpetual dictatorship, he did not withdraw the right of opposition from the Tribunes, but in as much as the Dictatorship was expressly abolished by law, and that nevertheless he had invaded the state under its guise, he was killed.[28]

Bodin's position is perfectly clear: all Power exercised by warrant and commission—in other words for a limited time—is not sovereign power. The only power (*potestas*) that is sovereign is that which has authority to grant Power for 'a certain time'. This distinction (argued at length below) leaves no doubt about Bodin's intentions in regard to the definition of sovereignty as perpetual power. The perpetual power it is concerned with is not the power of some individual or assembly—these are only its material and physical embodiment or personification. Hobbes established this once and for all.[29] The perpetuity of power is the essence of sovereignty because sovereignty is the essence of the modern *res publica*—the State. It is thus the State that

28. Ibid., p. 114.
29. In the rich and complex Chapters 16 and 17 of his *Leviathan*.

is thought philosophically as perpetual being, substance, *causa sui*, by the human act of foundation which is both voluntary and rational (calculative). The invention of the State operates through the distinction of power and Power, the second proceeding from the first, and their difference being of the order of time.

We need to underline the fact that these clarifications of the concept of the modern republic are not done in a simply academic spirit. The question of sovereignty is not a purely academic one, since an adulterated version of its concept has been developed in the course of the twentieth century. A quasi-Roman and warlike version was used to justify counter-revolutionary struggles seeking to re-establish a former regime (the France of the counter-revolution) and it develops in Weimar Germany in the interwar period and gives rise to a politics of violence that identifies politics with acts of war and the *goal* of politics with the acquisition of territory and the conquest of peoples. The falsification of the principle of sovereignty was the work of Carl Schmitt,[30] an important Nazi in his time and a militant in the *ecclesia militans*. His definition of sovereignty[31] is not only misleading but it also proceeds from a conception of politics that is pre-Bodin and pre-Hobbes (although Schmitt relies on both Bodin and Hobbes to establish it).[32] It is not important for

30. And we find it today in Europe, across the spectrum of political morality, in the disciples of Schmitt, who, either through *conviction* or *fashion*, prosper in the world trade in ideas.

31. In 1922: 'Sovereign is he who decides in the state of exception' (Carl Schmitt, *Political Theology: Four Chapters on the Concept of Sovereignty* [George Schwab trans. and introd.] [Chicago: University of Chicago Press, 2003], p. 4); as well as this other proposition of the militant Catholic: 'All fecund concepts of the modern theory of the State are secularized theological concepts' (ibid., p. 48). We will see how his theory of 'sovereignty' attempts precisely to de-secularize its concepts, that is to re-theologize them along the model of the ancient assertion of *plenitudo potestas*.

32. See the following works by Carl Schmitt: *Die Diktatur* (*Dictatorship*, 1921), *Politische Theologie* (*Political Theology*, 1922), *Verfassungslehre* (*Constitutional Theory*, 1928), *Begriff des Politischen* (*The Concept of the Political*, 1932), *Der Nomos der Erde im Völkerrecht des Jus Publicum Europaeum* (*The Nomos of the Earth*, 1950). These works have to be read against the background of modern European history in the first half of the twentieth century: the Treaty of Versailles, Weimar, the Russian Revolution, the German Revolution, 1933.

us to comment on Schmitt himself, but we need to recognize him for what he is—the best theorist of anti-sovereignty. In the historical context of the exhaustion of sovereignty, or better, its culmination, Schmitt does not attempt to transcend the world that it engendered and try to discern the figures of the new world. Rather, he tries to return to the ancient world of warlords who are enlightened and guided by a revelation that has vanished from modernity and vanished because of it. Schmitt holds no interest in terms of his conceptual clarification, but because his *falsification* of the concept shows how much his thought is the symptom of a time which is founded on the reactionary negation of sovereignty. What sovereignty wanted to eliminate from the world, its negation brings to criminal realization—the politics of death and servitude, the abasement of humanity and the tyranny of the all-powerful. Schmitt is relevant then only because his dedicated falsification of the most important concept of modern morality theoretically anticipates the world that practically culminates in the Nazi extermination camps. It is as if sovereignty, come to the end of its historical production in the fundamental constitution of the nations of Europe, must be reduced to nothing, lacking a future for humanity (in Europe or elsewhere), and must therefore founder in the nothingness of the history that produced it. It is as if the modern rights and freedoms that sovereignty brought with it must count for *nothing*, because they are *nothing* in the eyes of those who in the time of tyranny defended politics as the Power of life and death; the reduction pure and simple of the human to *res extensa*. There is thus no intrinsic interest in Schmitt's writings. These do not clarify the concept, but do throw light on the time in which the concept is corrupted. Schmitt makes possible the elucidation of a discourse that is self-consciously organized and aimed not at understanding the meaning of the discourse of sovereignty as the modern discourse of morality, in its categorical and historical closure, but at destroying the very morality of modernity. It is in this sense that Schmitt has to be read and understood—at the catastrophic point of no return of European historical sovereignty.

Let us briefly examine Schmitt's thesis. He declares that he is in full agreement with Bodin—the dictatorship of the commissioned officer does not involve sovereignty. But since he wants to justify recourse to the dictator of the state of exception, he sets out to forge the notion of 'sovereign dictatorship' through the juridical technology of public law. This rests on the substitution of 'constituent Power' for the concept of sovereign power, or Pope Gregory's *plenitudo potestas*[33] for Bodin's perpetual power.

The Substitution of Constituent Power for Sovereign Power

To pose the question of the nature of sovereignty, Schmitt first poses the question of *Dictatorship*: why? Because on the one hand he reasons like a jurist and on the other like a Catholic fundamentalist. As a jurist, Schmitt follows Bodin and examines the question of the Roman dictatorship; he does not therefore pose the question of its foundation, but asks how—that is by what positive law in force in a constituted State—could a 'sovereign dictatorship' be defined, to the extent that the foundation of sovereignty consists (as Bodin and especially Hobbes had shown) in defining an absolutely non-dictatorial political form, legitimate because of its foundation in the people. If dictatorship is a commission, that is a mandated or warranted Power, temporary in duration and purpose, Schmitt's question is to determine the conditions of a sovereign dictatorship—which originally is a contradiction in terms. To put it another way, Schmitt tries to eliminate Bodin's problematic of foundation (the modern problematic), replacing it with a problematic of the *exception*. Through the state of exception, he seeks to replace the question

---

33. Gregory VII founds on the plenitude of power the principle of the universal superiority of the Pope over the temporal and spiritual. It was to combat this thesis that Marsilio of Padua wrote his great work *Defensor Pacis* (*The Defence of Peace*, 1324). On Marsilio as a political theorist of the secular State and as anticipating what would become the profane State, see my *Le Maître et la multitude*, pp. 62–70 and 135–72.

of (popular) perpetual foundation by the question of the juridical justification of the Power of exception, understood by him as the exercise of dictatorship. The concept involved in this substitution is that of 'constituent Power' which specifically ignores the constitutive distinction of sovereignty (since Bodin) between power and Power, that is to say, between *potestas* considered as principle (properly speaking 'perpetual' power) and *potestas* considered in its exercise (temporary Power or commission). Schmitt's substitution of 'constituent Power' for 'sovereign power', an operation that is made possible only by forgetting the articulation of the two times of sovereignty, aims at the promotion of the theme of exception. That is why Schmitt throws out Bodin's theme of perpetual power, which he judges as irrelevant, because to keep it would obviously ruin any attempt to redefine sovereignty. To the metaphysics of time, Schmitt opposes the juridicization of the moment. The exception is by definition outside ordinary political time;[34] so that the moment of exception is the (revolutionary) constituent moment, in the two senses of the word 'constituent', both ontological and juridical at the same time. If the situation is exceptional (something the would-be dictator decides), it puts political action into an a-temporal and radically a-constitutional frame. The framework of the exception is a-juridical for the reason that the action deployed there becomes itself a-juridical, outside the norm, since it precisely aims at founding the new norm. The a-temporal action of the exception thus escapes every rule by its very nature, because it *is* the rule, its foundation and justification. The State is constituted through it, and constituent political action is that of a constituent Power in action. We see then that sovereign power is eliminated to the benefit of

34. Which makes Schmitt say: 'In such a situation it is clear that the State remains where the law recedes. Because the exception is different from anarchy or chaos order in the juristic sense is still prevalent, even if it is not of the ordinary kind. The existence of the State is undoubted proof of its superiority over the validity of the legal norm. The decision frees itself from all normative ties of obligation and becomes in the true sense absolute' (*Political Theology*, p. 12). A State entirely *outside the law* is a de facto State where only violence rules.

dictatorial action, which, as its name suggests, absolutely *dictates* the rule that installs the new order that replaces the old—it eliminates the enemy and this elimination is foundation.

Identification of Sovereignty with the Decision for War

According to the author of *The Concept of the Political*, then, it is in this sense that politics is specifically action that unfolds according to the rhythms of the dialectic between friend and enemy. Politics is essentially warlike—it is the seizure of land and the conquest of peoples. Not only does it discard the values of representative democracy, of parliamentarianism and the separation of powers but it is also against the State of liberal law and its formal norms. There is an undisguised relationship here[35] with the themes of the Bolshevik Revolution and, in general, with the fundamentalist Marxism of the 'dictatorship of the proletariat'. Bourgeois liberal dictatorship is legitimately opposed to the dictatorship of the projected new order. In effect, it is a question of 'legitimate defence' itself identified with sovereign dictatorship. The problematic of war in a revolutionary situation, the problematic of revolutionary war founds the notion of sovereign dictatorship. Schmitt offers two major illustrations—Cromwell and Robespierre. The latter emerges from the revolution in France, and specifically from the Convention,[36] as a sort of formal ideal type of dictator, disposing constituent Power in the name of a representative assembly but superior to it in conferring on the assembly itself the legitimacy which the latter procures for him. He is the heroic figure of the great

---

35. See the 1921 preface to *Die Diktator* (Munich and Leipzig: Duncker and Humblot).

36. The model of the Convention is topical. From 1792 to 1795, says Schmitt, the Convention saw the Committee of Public Safety govern *de facto* and *de jure*, and at the heart of the Convention, Robespierre had effective sovereign Power. In other words, representation (the Convention) is only decoration in Robespierre's system of *constituent Power* (ibid., pp. 148–54).

man, this Napoleon of the revolutionary spirit, master of the moment of exception, dominating in his vision and *decision* the refoundation of the State in the crucial period of revolutionary war. True, Schmitt would not have approved of the cult of the Supreme Being. No, he preferred Providence, but Robespierre and Cromwell are both superior providential men because they are the saviours of the State. The sovereign dictator is *sovereign*, that is, he *decides in favour of the State* in times of exception, not in favour of his private aims.

Behind Schmitt's scholarly falsification of sovereignty—the theorization of the *leader* in terms of the 'sovereign dictator' whose politics is defined as the exercise of 'constituent Power'—lies a nostalgia for a dominant Church. This nostalgia is based on the scandal that the foundation of power has moved from heaven to earth, from God to the people. This is an extraordinary fall that throws Schmitt into modern counter-revolution. But if Schmitt is anti-modern, it is because he is pre-modern. He militates in favour of a republic which, even though it must be created by the action of a providential dictator, would take the form of a revived Church. This is why he rejects the Weimar model of the (Roman) dictator instituted by Article 48 of the Weimar Constitution. This would be too secular a republic, based too much on the people. The fundamental crisis of Weimar through the Twenties is also for Schmitt the model (one might dare say ideal) of a situation of exception requiring a solution that only a dictator of exception, exercising *plenitudo potestas*, could bring about. For Schmitt, the maladapted character of Article 48[37] does not just proceed from its technical dispositions. He rejects not so much the principle retained by the Constitution, which in times of State emergency might call on the model of the Roman dictator, but the principle of

---

37. The text of Article 48, Paragraph 2 states: 'The President of the Reich can if security and public order are gravely threatened or compromised in the German Reich take the necessary measures for their re-establishment: in case of need, he can resort to armed force. To this end, he can suspend, totally or partially the exercise of fundamental rights guaranteed in Articles 114

every existent Constitution in a period of revolutionary disorder or war. This is in fact the key to all of Schmitt's arguments about sovereignty: sovereignty in action—the pure moment of foundation, free from any positive juridical determination—stands outside any Constitution. According to him,

> In spite of formulas like 'unlimited Power' or 'full Power' used to designate the powers of the President of the Reich conferred on him by Article 48, paragraph 2, he cannot, by virtue of this constitutional disposition, ever exercise a sovereign dictatorship, even in collaboration with the government of the Reich which countersigns. Either sovereign dictatorship or Constitution: one excludes the other.[38]

It follows from this that only the leader *is* the Constitution. The Third Reich would realize this proposition, but without reviving the Church. Schmitt would nevertheless give it his blessing.[39]

The thought of sovereignty is the thought of the people as originary foundation of the juridical order of the *res publica*. It is thought on the basis of what *is*

(freedom of the person), 115 *(inviolability of domicile)*, 117 *(privacy of correspondence)*, 123 *(right of assembly)*, 124 *(right of association)* and 153 *(guarantee of property)*.' We can see that Article 48 must have in fact inspired the framers of Article 16 of the 1958 French Constitution, which in effect envisions a Roman dictator were there a danger at home.

38. Commentary on Article 48, in Schmitt, *Die Diktator*, p. 234.

39. Schmitt's thought is structured by a providentialist conception of history, recalled in pertinent fashion by Olivier Beaud in the introduction he writes to *Theory of the Constitution* (1928): '[The] militant vision of the State as guardian of natural law is founded on a providentialist philosophy of history, or more exactly on a theology directly borrowed from St Augustine. The Christian conception of linear time allows a meaning and destination for history to be glimpsed and an eschatology to be formulated. History can thus only be understood from the point of view of God and salvation. The specificity of this historicism lies in the place occupied by the providential enemy, the Antichrist, and the defender of Christianity against this enemy, the *katechon*, who takes on the eminently "moral" decision—which Schmitt talks about in *The Concept of the Political*—to decide between Good and Evil, between Christ and Antichrist. The apologia for this decision is thus a "*metaphysics of the decision*" which rests on a providential theology of

common. In this sense, sovereignty is constructed and developed, as the form that gives being to the State. It is not politics as war; it aims, by contrast, at the installation of politics as peace. This does not mean that the thought of the common does not require the determination of those who do not take part in what is common. War is an instrument of the politics of finitude, not its essence. And if common being presupposes those who are outside the common (for being to be, there must be non-being), it remains the case that in its constitutive essence, the common being of the Moderns posits the common a priori, and peace as its aim. In common being, what is posited first of all is that which includes, not that which excludes. And if the foundation of common being passes through war—we will see why this is so later—this nevertheless does not provide the definition of sovereignty. If we stick to the word, sovereignty begins by positing a principle of friendship as the condition of possibility of the *res publica*, a principle of friendship without which there would be neither democratic people nor free citizen. The 'friend' is the person who has the same norm of the *just* in common. The 'friend' is the person who recognizes my freedom as my own good. It is on such a foundation that the common justice of a republic is unfolded, in a particular framework of historic nations—as *the thought of recognized freedom*. Such a thought is constituted in the course of a history (Chapter 2) as the thought of a people (Chapter 3) and as the life of the citizen (Chapter 4). It is this history, this thought and this life which have been subsequently brought to culmination in Europe, because they have been achieved.

history. Schmitt gives the impression here of being a man of the Christian Middle Ages, a zealous partisan of the *ecclesia militans*, closer to the Popes of the triumphalist Gregorian Church than to his twentieth-century contemporaries' (Introduction to *Théorie de la Constitution*—the French translation of Schmitt's *Theory of the Constitution* [Paris: PUF, 1993], pp. 54–5). We could not put it better.

CHAPTER 2

The Historial or the Spirit of the World

The world of finitude is an historical world in the sense in which the word 'history' is the name given by the Moderns to the very acceptance of that world. This acceptance does not mean submission to an originary and primordial order, emanating either from God or nature, which is imposed on human beings who thus have no other option but to submit. On the contrary, the acceptance of finitude means managing necessity, that is, evaluating the needs and measuring the obligations that necessity requires us to observe and satisfy. At first glance, then, what we call history is the totality of practices, so that history becomes the frame of the moral world. This is the way that we normally understand history, even if we do not usually think of it as the world of morality, because the spectacle of the world is the spectacle of its immorality. But this is a difference of words—we understand morality to be the ensemble of practices (which common sense judges to be moral or immoral) constitutive of the free and organized life, or, as we said in the previous chapter, existing within the *political* system of common being. If politics in general is the highest form of the fabrication of the world of morality, then politics and the historical are one and the same thing—the acceptance of finitude as the horizon of the profane life. The historical world is thus the world of morality, not because this world is good but because it just as good as it is evil. If such is the case (which would be difficult to deny), then there is in sum an equal amount of good and evil, so that history is precisely what finally brings the two into equilibrium. In this case we can only understand what we call history by *judging* the practices that are woven together, so that history would be that very judgement by which the universal becomes the norm of the particular.

Moral History

What *properly* distinguishes the political from the historical? We must pose this question if we want to understand what history consists of, since at the outset we do not connect it to the moral judgement of good and evil. Politics being in itself the fabrication of the world of morality, 'history' must then be understood as the *element* of this fabrication. History is the medium, the milieu within which the finite world of men unfolds, and in which human beings act so as to lead a free and organized life in spite of (or thanks to) necessity. History is the sphere of expectation. It is not about hope or dreams or waiting for the Messiah. On the contrary, it is the milieu of effective action, that is, of practices through which the hostile and abstract given of nature is turned into the concrete goods of existence. History is the totality of practices through which human beings transcend the immediate given of the world—pure *nature*—to make it into *their* world, a common world (which is also a world of their own). From this point of view, history is part of what is common to men—they have history in common, or, better, they have *a* history in common, that part of history which constitutes their own world. Men here have a history in common which they think of as being *theirs*, just as, elsewhere, other men have another history which they also think of as theirs. This shows that history is predicated on possession. This is because we understand history to be the appropriation of the given which variously appears as the object of effective human action, an appropriation accomplished collectively. The human beings who are engaged in this collective enterprise reflect on it the history of a people, or, better, a nation, of that particular nation which is *theirs*. History, then, seems at first glance to offer the solution to the modern enigma of finitude (the acceptance of finitude) in forming the spiritual frame for the profane life.

Being the totality of practices by which freedom is realized, history is equally and at the same time the *thought* of these practices, their writing, or, more broadly, their narrative. By history, then, we generally understand both the fact *and* the statement, either oral or written, of the fact. We are concerned with the chronicle of what is done (realized and made the object of a narrative) within the human order of the foundation of common being or the world of morality. But the fact that we also understand history to be the *narrative* of the practices does not change the meaning of this term. To say that history is the element in which unfolds the totality of practices that contribute to the (political) fabrication of the world of morality is to say that the narrative of practices is itself a practice. In this sense, history is very much fact and its statement, because to say is to do. If the narration of practices in an account of history is of the order of the philosophical, then it is simply absurd to say that the philosophy in question does not refer to historical practice. The philosophy (of this history) is itself of history, and therefore it runs in parallel to the history of the historian, or history-science.

As for the substance to which the term 'history' refers, there is no difference between writing history and making it. To write history books, whether for children or scholars, is to bring about an action which the Moderns designate as historical, that is, an action inscribed within a series of causes and effects that stitch the fabric of morality together. So the difference that we occasionally draw between history-action and history-science is irrelevant to what interests us here because the second is itself one of the practices that it undertakes to know—and which is there to know. To write history is therefore to make history and in no less a sense, so that writing the history of the revolution in France (or anywhere else) is to construct spiritually the common being that this revolution has constructed materially. If the event were not just as much a fable as an act, it would not exist historically.[1]

The meaning of this statement is not that historical fabulation is itself historical in the sense that, as we have just said, the narrative of history is an historical practice. It is, rather, to assert that practices, that is the totality of meaningful human acts, require fabulations about what happens in what we usually call 'history'. If we consider the matter from the point of view of *morality*, as we are doing here, history can be understood as nothing but the totality of events that enter into the constitution of the common being of a nation, or, more precisely, of nations. This is the process of morality to which we Moderns have given the name history. What is accomplished in and through this process is the modern (moral) project of emancipation from necessity and liberation from finitude—it is this *project* that is historical. Hence, history refers to the appropriation of a good by which human beings achieve their very humanity. From this point of view, the modern fable is the advent of what—for us—is *human*, which is the reason why the element of history (history as the setting for action) is a moral element—history is itself morality.

1. Of course, there is a difference between history as a science and history as act—the procedures of the former are not those of the latter, but I am not directly concerned here with procedures. See my *Le Discours et l'historique. Essai sur la représentation historienne du temps* (Tours: Mame, 1974).

This is firstly because, according to the fable, the human is not given in nature—it is originally pure and simple nature, pure and simple *res extensa*. In the primordial order of the *res extensa* there is nothing human—there is only the animal. So it is necessary to see the (modern) fable of morality in what we call history, because in and through history the human animal constructs itself as a moral being, that is to say, appropriates its own humanity. Morality hides, so to speak, in the state of nature in extension as humanity hides in animality, as the statue still sleeps within the block of marble from Mount Pentelicos. It requires no more than that Phidias should approach the mountain and chip away a small piece for the body of a god to be born from the block—the advent of spirit and history. However, that *it is enough* is not a simple *fiat*—it is not a creature but a work, and it is this work that men achieve in what they call history. This work is their very humanity. A moral work, then, always thought as such, the element of a spiritual history. What is at work in the work is the advent of a world, and this (moral) world is historical because it is spiritual. For the Moderns, there is spirit in history, and this is why what is 'historical' is human, that history is spirit. We understand that the world is not moral by nature, so to speak, it is not so in and by itself—it is only moral through the human decision to make and think it so under the category of the historical. Which amounts to saying that there is no morality without there being a world, that is, something that human beings think of as 'world', moreover, as *their* world. This is because history is where something is accomplished: it is becoming in the given which originally lacks meaning. The historical thus belongs to the order of foundation; in history, humanity is founded as the moral being of natural human animals. History is the process of moralization of natural human animals—it makes thought penetrate into extension. As a consequence, such a foundation can be articulated only in the discourse that states it, in the account that narrates events and in the fable that articulates the moral of history.

The question of the meaning of history can arise only in relation to a possible *moral of history*. We can deny such a question—the question of *meaning*—only if we deny the basis of the Moderns' humanity. If what the Moderns call history is the passage from animality to humanity, then this passage is meaning. The choice is the following—either meaning, that is, history, or nothing at all, that is the *res extensa*. We cannot deny the relevance of the question of meaning without denying the existence—for us Moderns—of history. History is meaning in operation: a history that had no meaning would be a contradiction in terms, like 'square circle'. This does not mean that a history that is meaningful has the same meaning for everyone. On the contrary, history is in essence contradictory and history has many meanings because there are *many histories*. *History*, like humanity, is multiple. That is why there is no universal history in nature or by nature, neither inside nor outside the world. The question of the meaning of history has sense only in relation to the human actions that occur in history and (historical) human action is always action in relation to what is better. What is better is not the same for everyone. So that the question of meaning only arises in relation to a history understood as the project of a possible *future*, one that is better. In effect, history has meaning for me only in relation to the act that I carry out to bring about a better world. The passage from a bad (arbitrary) world to a good (meaningful) one is what makes me undertake the action that will be regarded as meaningful. Meaningful action, that is action aimed at introducing sense or meaning into a violent world where it is absent, is reasonable action. And it is this totality of reasonable actions (thought as such) that we commonly call history. It will be said that there are thousands of actions that are not reasonable. But that is to forget that an action that I might call reasonable is one that my neighbour might and legitimately call violent and arbitrary. Just as meaning is not universal, so also action is not meaningful for everyone. In the world there are many worlds, and in history many histories—the meaning of one history is lacking in another, and the violence of one world is not violence for another. The example of war is helpful. War is always regarded as just by each of the enemy camps; this, however, does not remove the enigma of the nature of justice. In a period of civil war or war against outsiders, there is no *common justice*—if there were, there would be no war. So one must accept the idea that justice is the spirit of history, since all historical actions are characterized by the project of establishing a common norm of justice. An action is reasonable (meaningful) if it confers on history the sign of the meaningful and the reasonable. But this meaningful history of reasonable actions is not singular. What is designated as history is not what is given immediately here and now, but, on the contrary, the transcendence of the given, its radical annihilation. But the project of a better world always collides with those other better worlds of those who do not agree with this project or who oppose it.

We come back to the question of meaning, to pose it in its own terms. It has a background of radical doubt that has led to argument and conflict: *Is there a good history?* and again: *Is a rational world possible?* What these preliminary formulations of the question of meaning have in common is an anxiety that is connected to the nature of human action. Does my action (or, more precisely, the totality of my actions) allow me access to a good history, which would replace a bad history? Can I attain a rational world, which would replace a world that I judge to be arbitrary and violent? This is the general context of the question of meaning within a world thought (of) as a historical world, that is, as the next world, the world to come, a possible world.

What comes out of these considerations is that the question of meaning is tied to the acts that transform the given, whether this given is the pure and simple *res extensa* or the result of the action of thought on extension. To put it another way—regardless of whether the given is the human world or the natural world, meaning appears as soon as human beings represent the given in question as being apprehensible, that is to say, at their disposition, capable of being an object of appropriation for them, of *digestion* by them. Among the Moderns, meaning is what justifies assimilation and produces the milieu of the free and organized life. It gives rise to a discourse (the discourse of *philosophy*) whose task is to set out definitions or revise them, and give their grammar, with a view to stating the meaning of history. Meaning lies in the interpretation of the historical world as a *human* world, and we cannot understand such meaning without relating it to the historical tale of its achievement by action and its unmasking by philosophy. Meaning is the *necessary* link between actions that liberate a better world that springs forth from the entrails of a world that has been judged and condemned, and the statement of the significance of those actions in the philosophical appropriation of meaning. A philosophy of history as the hermeneutic of action and the totality of practices reveals a meaning without which modern man would lose both his foundational autonomy and his reasons for action.

So we must ask under what auspices the modern theme of the historicity of human action (and passions) is constituted so as to give rise to the modern representation of history as a meaningful history, that is, a history that is truly moral and hence worthy of being lived in a human fashion. This moralization of practice is the presence of the historial in the historical. By 'historial', as we will see shortly, I understand the meaning of meaning, that is to say, the procedure by which historical material acquires a meaning on the basis of an agency external to it, a non-historical agency, some sort of revelation, so that the historical does not possess its own intelligibility within it. Church and State concur on an interpretation of the world as the *sign* of a truth of which they are the guardians and which they are empowered to state—they dispute the monopoly of the interpretation of the world. In the context of the modern recourse to history, the historical is like a book whose text is said to be unintelligible by itself. Its meaning is to be found in interpretation, that is, in decoding its cipher with the help of keys that are not to be found in the book but in tradition, and preserved by those (Church or State) who are authorized to read and interpret the signs.

So what the Moderns designate as 'history' is properly the tension between the historical and what I call here the historial, between the becoming of what they are and the interpretation of this becoming. It is this tension that writes the fable; and from the conflict that pits the historial against the historical is born our history as violence and the deployment of grand collective passions in these Modern Times that for this reason we call 'historic(al)'.[2]

The Historial and the Historical: the Interpretation of the World

History, as the Moderns think it in thinking what they are as 'modern', is influenced by the Tridentine complex of *interpretation*. The Council of Trent offers the model of the historial interpretation of the world, which haunts, so to speak, the history of Modern Times, which are inhabited by the spirit of the world. It defines the procedures by which meaning is elucidated—the agency that enunciates meaning in a sovereign manner, and the orthodox tradition of meaning. By this I understand that the thought of the Moderns about the meaning of their action and their becoming must have had to be related to the double structure of the universal and the canonical interpretation of a meaning. The first structure goes back

2. It might be useful to clarify that the use I make of this adjective 'historial' owes nothing to the French translation of *geschichtlich[keit]* by '*historial[ité]*'. See Martin Heidegger, *Être et temps* (E. Martineau trans.) (Paris: Authentica, 1986), p. [375 German edition] 259; in English: *historical(ity)*. See Heidegger, *Being and Time* (J. Macquarrie & E. Robinson trans.) (Oxford: Basil Blackwell, 1987), p. [375] 427. Heidegger's project revealed in 1927 in *Being and Time* of a fundamental ontology elucidating the 'historicality' of *Dasein* is the most elaborate and most developed metaphysical illustration of what I characterize here as the *interpretation* of the historical by the historial (meaning of meaning). See section in this chapter, 'The *Spirit* is Dead'.

to the unification of a world reflected as a univocal *continuum* of the revelation of the truth, the second to the semiotic bifurcation by which the Moderns have redirected the paradigm of sacred history towards profane history. Through the first structure the world is identified as a world, that is, as a homogeneous totality intelligible on the basis of a single principle that emerges from a centre; this is the world of tradition, that is, of the repetition and preservation of originary meaning. There is thus nothing new under the sun, and the world constantly bears witness to the becoming of the same and the identical. Through the second, the Moderns have understood finitude as the temporal framework of a becoming that can be mastered, and have understood as a corollary that external nature is the material framework of the work of transformation of their own human nature. This is properly historical time, the time of the future and the project. Human time and labour thus become the two constitutive elements of moral life, the two pillars of modern humanity. The freedom of the Moderns takes meaning from them, and meaning is precisely understanding them together as defining the course of modern freedom. Indeed, the universal (of the world) and the (canonical) interpretation of meaning are one: they are an indissoluble unity that only analysis is obliged to distinguish. In life (or, to put it another way, in the lived *world*), the world and its meaningful interpretation are one. It is just that—their *unity*—which is the unique condition of free action. Modern life is *human* precisely through the humanization of time and labour, those two pillars of the meaningful life—this is the way that we think of ourselves as 'modern'. If history is spiritual because we can discover meaning there, then it is the unfolding of the human as the subject of a *single* meaning, as the creation of a *single* world which, in the last analysis, the profane State institutes and guards because it is the personification of reality.

The presence of the historial in the historical—the becoming of the totality as the constitution of meaning given by a hidden meaning—is perfectly illustrated by the Tridentine doctrine of interpretation. The norms that produce the canonical meaning of Scripture as the Council of Trent defined them tacitly work within our philosophical discourses on profane human becoming and its meaning. The Tridentine purveyors of doctrine carefully defined several formal principles so as to establish and guarantee an orthodox meaning: purity of meaning, originary publication, transmission, preservation and reception—and anathema.[3] These criteria of interpretation go back to the principle of magisterial authority whose permanent seat is the Church. This means that what is at stake in the question of meaning (and its interpretation) is, properly understood, the durability of a certain orthodoxy in 'truth' and 'discipline', but, especially and essentially, in the understanding of the nature of historical time as the temporality of sacred history. As for profane history, it will be up to the sovereign to state its principle and spirit.

The canonical interpretation of meaning implicitly presupposes a canonical conception of temporality. The ecclesiastical time of *true* meaning is the time of

3. The Council of Trent properly began with the fourth session (April 1546) where the Council's *Doctrinal Declaration* was finished, of which the following is the most important section: 'the holy Council of Trent, ecumenical and general [. . .] always having before its eyes the desire to destroy error and preserve in the Church the very purity of the Gospel, which, after having been formerly promised by the Prophets in the Holy Scriptures, was first broadcast through the mouth of Our Lord Jesus Christ, Son and God, then by his apostles to whom He gave the mission of announcing it to every creature as being the source of all truth about salvation and of all discipline of mores; and considering that this truth and this moral rule are contained within the written books and non-written traditions, that, received from the very mouth of Christ by the Apostles, to whom the Holy Spirit had dictated them, transmitted from hand to hand, have come down to us; the Council, following the example of the orthodox Fathers, receives all the books of both the Old and New Testaments [. . .] as well as the traditions concerning both faith and morals as coming from the mouth of Christ himself or dictated by the Holy Spirit and conserved in the Catholic Church by a continuous succession; it receives them and venerates them with an equal respect and an equal piety. If anyone does not receive [as canonical] all these books [. . .] and if he misunderstands with deliberate intention and aim the mentioned traditions, let anathema be upon him' (A. Vacant and E. Mangenot, *Dictionnaire de théologie catholique*, VOL. 15 [Paris: Librairie Letouzey et ane, 1946], pp. 1311–12).

tradition, that is, the *past*. It is through the question of meaning (its interpretation) that the notion of becoming—in the course of which meaning will arrive—takes shape. When we interpret the course of the world in terms of a revealed truth, that is to say, a truth proclaimed and disseminated in an originary way, written down (or not) and transmitted, the time of this becoming is the past which the interpretative present merely revives. The key to meaning lies in the link between past and present that must be respected. Meaning does not have a future as far as orthodox content is concerned. It does not belong to the order of the project because its very condition is to refuse the new. The truth of today is legible and comprehensible because it is *identical* to the truth revealed at the origins. There can be no novelty in the world without rendering the latter obscure; cancelling out revelation will deprive it of meaning. From the point of view of revealed meaning, the future is not of this world. The problem of revelation (of all revelation), if one can put it this way, is that it can only live in the relation of the past to the present—not of the present to the future. By definition the future is unknown, or, put another way, its truth is precisely what is *lacking*; but for tradition, a world without truth has no meaning. For meaning is already known and it is stated by past tradition. The identity of the past and the present, that is, the co-presence of the origin and the current, is the time of revelation, the time of tradition. It is true that in this context (the Tridentine context) it is important for the survival of the first truth that it should not be disfigured or ill-treated by present truths and heresies—in a word, *error* threatens the truth. In the nature of things, there can be no reformation of truth, which can only be understood in terms of tradition. The world of tradition is nevertheless a *historical* world, because here the historical is the repetition and reprise of the same.[4] Beyond the torments of the secular (of the world)

4. The Tridentine *Profession of Faith* (November 1564) is the explicit source of the astonishing *Sermon Against Modernism* of September 1910 (Pius X's decision against a 'modernist' Christian current that tried to make revelation and scientific positivism compatible), whose fourth clause

there is something permanent and stable, meaning in person and personified, so that the becoming of the world becomes intelligible through it. Meaning is thus the meaning of meaning—the permanent is the key to what is becoming, received truth the arbiter of error, spirit the judge of the thing. Originary meaning is the key to given meaning. What happens in the world is explicable by what is beyond the world, just as what is given in the present is illuminated by the time before the present, its past. This is the time of political theology—the time of a 'continuous succession' according to doctrine, of the immutability of a primary meaning, a succession in which the present is a modality of the past. The absence of the future—the future as non-being—is the ontological character of the present. What is not pregnant with the future is the result of the past. To be pregnant with the future, a truth must be prepared that can be accomplished in the future. But the time of political theology forbids it, and this prohibition is ontological and political. Ontologically, the being of the present is signified by the past from which it takes its status as the receptacle of tradition. Politically, orthodoxy must be preserved (on pain of anathema), or, in other words the difference between received truth and established and transmitted truth is the very name of what is called *novelty*, that other name for error. It falls under meaning, that meaning just cannot be renovated without being altered, betraying the truth of which it is the sign. There is thus no novelty possible in the present, which forbids any politics that seeks to order the given world in the light of a new one.

is: 'I sincerely receive the doctrine of faith transmitted to us by the Apostles ever in the same sense and interpretation by the orthodox Fathers; for this reason, I absolutely reject the heretical invention that dogmas evolve and pass from one meaning to another, which is different from what the Church first professed. I equally condemn every error that substitutes for the divinely revealed truth entrusted to the Bride of Christ for faithful safe-keeping, a philosophical invention, or creation of human consciousness, little by little formed by the effort of men, and which an indefinite progress would perfect in the future' (*Les Textes doctrinaux du magistère de l'Eglise* [Gervais Dumeige trans.] [Paris: Ed. de l'Orante, 1996] p. 56). This sermon was obligatory until 1967.

The Origin

The essence of the historial thus lies in a *certain relation to the origin* in which men find themselves when they think about the world and about the meaning that is needed to make this world *their* world. For their part, the Moderns cannot escape this relation to the origin in which they think their history as sensible history or as possible history. But what characterizes them as modern is that they think their present, which is the political present of action, as origin, which makes the time of their history the future. This is the *philosophical* time they call history. And this time is the meaningful relation between the present and the future, the latter being in potential in the former. Meaning is that very relationship. It is this potential, this power, of which the *people* (whatever modernity has put under this heading) is the actor which incarnates the humanity which meaning creates.

However, the passage to philosophical modernity, which creates a rupture with theological expectations, does not allow a radical emancipation of interpretation. It is not only the Moderns who interpret their life as a meaningful 'history' according to the Tridentine procedure of orthodox interpretation, but subsequently *meaning* proceeds not from some revelation but from the imagination of a world. The history of the Moderns is the site of the imagination with which philosophy replaces tradition in conceiving a new vector of time (and meaning) that does not flow from the past to the present but from the present towards the future. Imagination invents a duration that creates order (a moral and political order) through which animality undergoes mutation in the slow production of an animal of a certain kind, *humankind*. As to what *humankind* is, philosophy replies by imagining a process which engenders and brings into being a substance, *thought*, which emerges from a distinction in and an emancipation of pure extension, and finally its mastery. From Descartes to Voltaire and beyond, the philosophical process of the modern engendering of meaning is elaborated, a process on which the prophetic genius of Georg Wilhelm Friedrich Hegel (up to the Heideggerian ambiguity of *Sein und Zeit* [*Being and Time*, 1927])[5] will bestow final clarification.

Descartes establishes how being is thought and extension. The domination or appropriation of the *res extensa* by the *res cogitans* is the source of meaning. It is the enigma of the human condition and its final resolution, henceforth reflected and conceptualized as the passage of a nature without duration and lacking sense to a meaningful history understood as profane human becoming, that is, as the future of the human. This evolution from nature to history is the evolution from animality to humanity (even if Descartes did not envisage thus). At once, there is also a resolution to the enigma of the present which is no longer the substantial result of the past, but the promise of a future. In contrast to the theological time of tradition, the philosophical time of history interprets the past in the light of the present, of which it is no longer the prefiguration but the very negation—it is the present's imperfect. Yesterday, it *was* not today. To become what it is today, humankind must cease to be what it was yesterday. The work of negation is the work of the advent of meaning. Yet if this discovery of the significance of the past in terms of the present does not make the present a simple result of the past—it is rather an origin—it is because the movement that runs from the present to the past has its ultimate meaning in the understanding of the present as the bearer of the future. The present is not the end, but the origin of the history that is in play. The conquest of extension is never achieved and thought remains the substance of the infinite process of thinking. What modern philosophy thinks is the meaning of a history which happens in the future whose origin is the present (as result). It is what remains to be made what is possible to make (and think) so that what is done/made (in the past) is not lost, and, more importantly, so that the imperfections of that past will be corrected in the future. This is because the result—the

---

5. See section in this chapter, 'The *Spirit* is Dead'.

present—is imperfect (unsatisfying), because the imagination of a perfect world begins anew at every moment of the present. The conquest of extension can never be imagined as coming to an end. This would be to refuse finitude, that is, to renounce *work*. But such a renunciation is impossible, since the modern acceptance of finitude consists precisely in facing up to it, that is, occupying time (by labour which is the conquest of extension) so as to face up to necessity and the satisfaction of needs. It is thus by the anticipation of the future—the imagination of what must be—that the present is historical, or, in other words, has meaning. If the present is worthy of being lived in a human fashion, it is because the work and practices deployed there are not in vain—they are a promise of the future. If history is intelligible for the Moderns, it is not because it bears witness to an originary meaning, the deployment of a primary truth made public, but because the present is the origin of the future and for that reason the key to the past as well.

It is why (meaningful) human history is thought by the Moderns as universal history. There is no reason, in fact, why meaning should not unfold universally: the universal *is* meaning. Meaning has to spread over the surface of the *orbis* and in this expansion universalize humankind, effecting the passage from animality to humanity, and much as good news or an oil slick spreads, ensuring the universal reign of the *res cogitans* over the *res extensa*.

In his enormous *Essai sur les moeurs et l'esprit des nations* (*Essay on the Morals and Spirit of Nations*, 1756), which is something like a secularized version of Bossuet's *Discours sur l'histoire universelle* (*Discourse on Universal History*, 1679) brought up to date (it had originally broken off with Charlemagne), Voltaire explicitly works the philosophical field of the modern historial. His point of view is historical, by which I understand that he outlines the events of a universal history.[6]

6. It is Bodin, however, who in his *Méthode de l'histoire* (*Method for Studying History*, 1566) is at the origin of a conception of universal history, as G. Huppert points out. 'To my knowledge,' he

But the account is *philosophical* because this sequence of practices, events and 'facts' is in itself significant; what is particular to events is that they bear witness to the universal, the cunning of spirit that Hegel will stress *ad nauseam*, until the concept finally becomes arid. In any case, the series of statements and acts that irrupt into the world indicate the human essence of humankind, which is separated from the essence of the animal. Universal history is constructive, it produces the human, or, put another way, a meaning that can be perceived whose visible external sign is precisely the historical[7] as the advent of the human meaning of the world. No narrative of the historical (practices) without resort to the historial (the meaning of meaning). Voltaire's meaning of history exemplifies the modern historial meaning: a philosophy of culture according to which *time* is the element in

writes, 'Bodin's *Méthode* is the first publication to propose independent of any religious consideration a theory of universal history founded on the study of the development of civilisation. Such a vision of history is certainly not uncommon among the humanists and jurists who dominated the intellectual world of Bodin's Paris. But Bodin is the first to publish on the subject. Furthermore, he outlined his theory in a much more systematic way than any of his contemporaries—even if some of them were inclined to criticise his excessive spirit of systematisation, his tendency to be a "contemplative doctor" as La Popelinière put it. Nevertheless in spite of its weaknesses, the *Méthode* was always read with respect by those in the sixteenth century who were interested in historical thought. And it was even because his attempts at generalisation were so ambitious that Bodin evoked agreement and criticism from the best historians. He was something like the Max Weber of his times' (*L'Idée d'histoire parfaite* [Paris, Flammarion, 1970], p. 110).

7. In fact, Voltaire takes care to stay close to the 'historical' to attest to meaning, which for him is the progressive penetration of civilisation among peoples and nations. The clarification that he makes when he prepares to narrate the beginning of the history of the Jews consists of clearly separating the 'historical' from the 'divine'—a distinction that moves the historial from the theological to the philosophical. 'We will touch as little as possible on what is divine in the history of the Jews' he writes, 'or if we are forced to talk about it, it is only because their miracles have an essential relationship with the sequence of events. We have the appropriate respect that is due to the prodigies that continually mark the steps of this nation: we believe them with the reasonable faith which is demanded by that Church which replaces the synagogue; we do not examine them; we keep a close connection to the historical. We will talk about the Jews as we would talk about Scythians and Greeks, weighing probabilities and discussing the facts' (*Essai sur les moeurs et l'esprit des nations*, VOL. 1 [Paris: Garnier, 1963], pp. 135–6).

which the *universal* reveals itself in the form of the (European) humanization of the nations of the *orbis*: 'It is only too true,' he writes,

> that human nature has for long centuries been plunged into a state approaching that of brutes, and inferior to them in many respects. The reason for this [. . .] is that it is not in the nature of man to *desire what he does not know*. It has everywhere required not only a prodigious space of time but fortunate circumstances for man to raise himself above the life of animals.[8]

An uncivilized nation becomes cultured only through the action of another nation, that is to say, 'fortunate circumstances' or the action of time—which amount to the same thing. We thus have the cunning of history whose proper essence is that the future accounts for the past. That is why the work of history, which is history as work, always consists of imagining the future as the perfection of the present; cunning consists of acting today so that in the future we might live according to the rules of the free and satisfied life which we do not fully enjoy in the present. This comes down to turning the human animal from the natural state of uncivilized brute to the cultural state of humankind. We cannot object that Voltaire's historial vision belongs to an enlightened Europe that was still primitive by comparison with what we Europeans have become more than two centuries after Voltaire wrote his *Essay*. Adducing such a primitive character would just be the proof of a historial meaning of history by which we would become emancipated from that primitive character of thought. What is more, we would be doing so under the illusion that we are outside the transition that we are still involved in today, just as we were such a short time ago, which is moreover a matter of philosophical nobility.[9]

---

8. Ibid., p. 201. This text echoes the remark in the Introduction: 'For a nation to be assembled in the body of a people, for it to be powerful, hardened and clever takes a prodigious time' (ibid., p. 9).
9. Husserl, following Kant: 'To my mind, and it is a feeling that we have (which in the absence of

From Hegel to Voltaire and Bossuet, the Moderns have elaborated a meaning for history as the accomplishment of a *work* which is spirit itself which can be discerned as the meaning of the human, or the achievement of its freedom. The terrain of history here (apart from in Bossuet) is that of profane becoming where in consequence the divine is no longer articulated as the engine of history (the spirit of a people or nation) because history no longer fulfils a preordained design. Above all, it is Hegel who brings the historial to its philosophical climax.[10] He expresses the historial of history at the level of the highest philosophical generality, so that the Moderns invariably refer to him when they reflect on their acceptance of finitude as 'history':

any clear notion is well justified), our European humanity conceals an inborn entelechy which dominates every change that affects Europe's form and which confers on them a meaning, that of a development orientated towards an eternal pole' (Edmund Husserl, *The Crisis of European Humanity and Philosophy* [1935], in Y. Hersant and F. Durand-Bogeret, *Europe de l'Antiquité au XX siècle. Anthologie critique* [Paris: Robert Laffont Bouquins, 2000], p. 448). See Introduction to this volume.

10. The case of Karl Marx is singular: from *Thesis XI on Feuerbach* ('The philosophers have only interpreted the world, the point now is to change it') to *Volume 1* of *Capital* there is a fundamental critique of what I call the historial. In effect, in these works, Marx sketches out a theory of *forms*, their production and disappearance, which will allow for a *thought of the historical*. However, Marx does not give up thinking history as an element of the emancipatory work whose subject is the working class—that authentic *people*—so that the latter is the bearer of a meaning of history that had once been held by the bourgeoisie. No doubt this comes from the fact that historical discourse is political in the sense that political action, as we have already noted, aims at the construction of the world of morality—which Marx expresses by thematizing the future of the working class as the advent of a superior stage of morality. This is the Marxist idea of the working class as the 'universal' emancipatory class, that is the subject that will produce a new form of freedom. For a science of history as the science of forms to be *really* possible, it is probably necessary for it to eliminate the *passions* of the historical; such a project would not be just absurd (which would only be a misfortune for philosophy) but criminal, because only total tyrannies could undertake to bring it about—which would be a misfortune for what the Moderns call the 'human species', and certainly its *end*. In any case, history as discourse (science) is not like cosmology, since though the stars are (apparently) impassive, human life is made up of nothing but pure passion(s).

The general point of view of philosophical history is not abstractly general but concrete and eminently actual because it is Spirit which dwells eternally by itself and ignores the past. Like Mercury, the conductor of souls, the Idea is in truth what leads the peoples and the world, and it is Spirit, its rational and necessary will which has guided and continues to guide the way the world unfolds.[11]

History, as science that is to say as philosophy,[12] cannot escape the Tridentine complex. It is in effect Trent which teaches both the necessity of a canonical meaning of becoming (in this case the fables of sacred history) and the continuity of meaning, piously preserving it intact. Like the Church but in opposition to it, the State can put itself forward as the administrating agency of meaning. But while theology became the key to revealed meaning, it is now philosophy that possesses the keys to profane meaning: it would be the thought of the State that thinks. No other established agency than the State (unless a philosophical sect were to constitute itself as and like a Church) can subsequently order the meaning of history—only *good sense* can enunciate the meaning of profane human becoming and the axioms of the fable.

Philosophical Fabulation

Let us enumerate the three axioms of the modern historial:

a) *History is the name given to the difference between the given and becoming*

For the Moderns, there is a foundational and originary difference between what is given, pure nature, and what is constructed: the world. Moreover, we would have to

11. Friedrich Hegel, *La Raison dans l'histoire* (K. Papaioannou trans.) (Paris: 10-18, 1979), p. 39.
12. If a historical science is possible, it presupposes a philosophy of *history* where the possibility of a historical science that is not philosophically determined would rest on a highly problematic dialectical theory of the *forms of the historical*. See my *Discours et l'historique*, especially pp. 161–217.

say that the *world* is what human beings oppose to the given of pure nature, pure and simple *res extensa*. Such an opposition cannot be understood as a spatial arrangement where two things are pitted against each other in a static conflict, so to speak. Rather, the opposition of the given and the constructed must be understood in the sense that the modern historial—this is its very essence—opposes what is to what is becoming, so that being produces being *as* becoming. If there is a difference between the given and becoming, it is because the being of the world proceeds from the negation of the given—the world is not what is put there in front of me as something inert and, for that reason, other than me. The world is not my other—it is, rather, the dwelling place of what I am. This is what the current expression *to come (in)to the world* means. For the Moderns, this just means making *the world come to pass*. For there to be a world in which I have my place when I arrive, it is unnecessary for the world to be there, because what is there is nothing at all if I am not there to make it be there. For me to arrive in the world, it is apparently necessary for there to be a world; but that is in fact nothing but an illusion, an appearance, because the *ontical* condition of the world is that there must a subject that states the being of the world. And this subject is myself when I arrive in the world. If no 'consciousness' is conscious of the world, there is no world at all. Put another way, to come into the world is to make the world come about as world.

We will not go into the question of whether there is a world that exists independently of the 'consciousness' of a subject. If a subject falls into the world, that is, comes into the world, that does not mean that there is a subject that exists without the world into which it falls. For, just as there is manifestly no world without a subject, there is no subject without the world. We have to think that with these two particulars—world and subject—we are dealing with one and the same unit, not because it would be possible to conflate them but because the being of one of them is inconceivable without the other. To speak like the philosophers—there is no 'subject' substance and no 'world' substance, if by substance we mean something that exists for itself, needing nothing but itself to exist. But we can discard this venerable vocabulary and note that the first axiom of the historial is the assertion that the being of the world is the process by which the human animal comes into the world by transforming the given into *world*. The world is thus the name of what *is* when, as in the current expression, someone comes into the world. We can ask *what* arrives when someone comes into the world—what arrives is meaning. And we understand by *meaning* not some revealed mystery that transcends the world and sheds light on its primordial darkness but the significance of 'coming into the world' is precisely to make a world come to pass just where there had been nothing at all. If to come into the world is to make a world come to pass, then what is called 'meaning' is what allows there to be a world and not nothing at all. It is meaning that opposes becoming to the given, the world to nature, and I call this meaning historial because it is effected concretely within history (what the Moderns call 'history'). In other words, the historial refers to the subject of this history (the subject of what becomes world from what is simply given as extension) and this subject is, at first sight, the human animal.

However, looking at it more closely, the Moderns developed the idea that with human beings it is not the animal that comes into the world with the world. What makes the world come to pass is man *tout court*, that is, that animal that slowly unmakes his very animality in making just his humanity appear. Looked at from this angle, the difference that exists between the world and the pure given is the difference between humanity and animality. The world *is* man—or it is nothing. The modern historial meaning is to think the difference between the given and the world as man's becoming man. Better put, the human is not a being given in nature, but in history. The difference between the world (becoming) and the given (the inert) is the difference at the heart of the human animal. The being of the human animal is a sort of non-difference (an originary mélange, a primary con-fusion) between what is animal (bestial) and what is human. The being of man is pure becoming. When we speak about someone coming into the world, what are we saying? We are saying that the fall into the world is the fall into the human. We are saying that the process of coming into the world is the process by which the human animal, in unmaking his animality, at the same time brings about a world, brings about a meaningful totality. The birth of man, since this is what is at issue in the fable, is thus not instantaneous. Humanity is not given by coming into the world, because the world is yet to be made, and, in making it, humanity makes itself—and can unmake itself as well. Such a process does not turn humans into the subject altogether created from a world which would already be there, because this world is yet to be made, and coming into the world, we have said, is to bring about this world.

The first axiom of the historial is the first axiom of modern philosophical anthropology—men make history, albeit in given conditions. If men make history, their own history, it is because the knowledge they have of their own freedom is compatible with the knowledge they have of their own finitude. The Moderns know that the historical freedom that they enjoy is determined by both the fini-tude of extension and the finitude of time. The knowledge of the spatio-temporal conditions of their freedom is the mechanism of the freedom by which they act on the given to bring about a world, or better *their* world. And their world is the finitude of space-time. The Moderns have renounced the infinite and it is in this very renunciation that they come into the world in the sense we have been using. To renounce does not mean to resign oneself, it means *to know* (what is the case) and this means to *know how* (to act). It is in this knowledge of the finite condition of things (and of themselves among things) and in the knowledge of what deter-mines things to be what they are (and not otherwise than they are) that the

Moderns have understood human animals not merely as animals but as humans. This is the regulative idea that the Moderns have used to reflect on their own becoming in the world, not as simple 'beings' but as 'living beings'. For the Moderns, to live is to produce for oneself the means of free and organized existence. This is the modern postulate par excellence—it is the postulate of profane life by which the human constitution of the free life proceeds from human beings themselves. This presupposes a rupture with the world of received divine–natural tradition through which the given world is always already ordered and meaningful for the human beings who fall into it. There is nothing like this for the Moderns. In the grip of finitude, they have only their own finite condition as their means of life or, so to speak, as the exit from the game—there is no god in heaven and no natural law that has the value of human law. The human is not natural but the negation of the natural. If the common order of nature is an inert infinity, a sort of immobile eternity where the repetition of the same and the reproduction of the identical reign, season upon season, that is, if the cosmos is infinite (because the idea that it could have a limit implies that there could be necessarily and by definition something beyond the limit, just as one field always adjoins another field) then the world is a finite totality for me and a finite totality for the human species. To the extent that the world is something brought about by finite human action we cannot represent it as infinite. The finitude of the world consists precisely in these—spatio-temporally—'determinate conditions' which human action is concerned with in thinking itself as free action. Freedom then consists in living in the light of finitude, and it is through this relationship that human beings create a radical rupture with divine or natural solutions to the question of finitude. The first axiom of the historial is thus the axiom of profane life—meaning flows from human beings, from human action, in other words from history. History is meaning. This means, fundamentally, that for us Moderns what is human is historical, in the sense that the being of man is the being of the historical itself. *Time* (the category of finitude) is the category of freedom. If the notion of history has any meaning, it is precisely this—in and through history, the human animal produces itself freely as human, and in the midst of animal species it constitutes a kind, humankind as an historical kind. Hence, man *is* time. This is the essential discovery of the Moderns, that which characterizes them as *modern* with respect to the conceptions of tradition.

At the heart of the historial, then, we have time as the element and milieu where human freedom unfolds and where human action—*labour*—can be thought as history and the becoming world of the given as historical becoming. Time—finite duration—is the Archimedean lever of the world—the world comes about through time. If we habitually say that it takes time to make a world, that is because the world is not given. But this proposition—the world is not given—essentially signifies the following: the humanity of the human animal is not given, but acquired or conquered. This conquest can be described without paradox as infinite. This is true to the extent that we cannot assert (without bad faith) that the animality of human beings has been vanquished in our present world. That is a historical given against which no god or nature (human or non-human) can be invoked. When we say that it takes time to make a world, this seemingly anodyne remark, in fact, implies that the world is unfinished. In other words, *there remains work to be done* for humanity to be truly *human*, that is, for humanity to lead a truly human existence. Which could be formulated in the following way—there is still work to be done so that humans are not just 'beings' but '*living* beings'. To live is not to be there, to exist, but to enjoy freedom. At the root of the historial—the meaningful narrative of the profane world—there is thus the modern conviction that time is the fabric of a truth which unfolds in human-historical duration. Time is the bearer of another revelation—not what comes to us from the past but a revelation that the present prepares and the future will render visible. Modern faith is that the future is the beneficiary of the present. But this is not the conviction of a consciousness captive to a received truth to which it submits. Rather, modern consciousness wills the future as the reality and perfection of the present. While the religious consciousness takes its being from *being* as the conservation of what has been given, the modern—profane—consciousness achieves its present being in the anticipation of the future. *Modern* time is the midwife of meaning and becoming, the element in which labour takes place—what is to come must be included as part of accomplishing that work. The reason why tomorrow will be better than today—humanity further away from animality than it is today. This is the modern conviction born from finitude—the conviction that history is progress.

b) History is the name given to the process of moralization of humankind—history as the fable of sovereignty

The historial thought of the world, or the thought of the historicity of the world not as a simple process but as the revelation of the human meaning of the world, is the elaboration of the world of morality. This thinks of the human animal as a political animal. The axiom of sovereignty without which modern morality would be properly illegible consists of reflecting on what is political in the human, that is, establishing the conditions by which political life is fully human life. Hence the second axiom of the historial, which organizes the idea of profane human becoming (history) on the political assumption of the human meaning of the world. If there were only becoming, if there were only the process of formation and transformation of materiality, there would be no human meaning of the world. Quite the contrary, the human meaning of the world proceeds from the politicization or moralization of humankind. The human animal must not only be separated from extension by the labour of becoming properly human, but this separation must also operate through the passage to the political state and to the State *tout court*. To abandon nature is to enter history *and* politics, a process by which humanity turns from natural to political, which means at the same time moral. Humanity is not a zoological concept but a moral one. The formation of morality is not a natural process but a process against nature. In nature, there is neither history nor morality; there is no politics either. Or rather, the political animal is indeed in nature but only in potential—it has only to be extracted. The modern emancipation of nature is the beginning of morality itself, the *beginning* is that of history itself. The passage to history is the political passage to morality. This is the key to sovereignty: this is the concept that begins the modern. Sovereignty is what inaugurates the historicity of Modern Times and the historiality of the world, its meaning and order.

Considered from the point of view of morality, sovereignty is a myth. That is to say, like all myths, it is an account of origins, a fable of foundation. This narrative—or this fable—reduces to a sequence of simple events which, tied together, produce an ordered and meaningful world where human beings, free from finitude and servitude, no longer lead an immediate natural existence but a free life, that is, one turned towards the future. The fable of sovereignty allows us to concretely think human history as project and process and not as the simple becoming of materiality. It allows us to think the effective conditions of the free life, a wholly free life because it is lived absolutely, that is, truly liberated, if not from death then from the fear of death. The metaphysical truth of modern sovereignty lies in the fact that it is the thought of a moral world thoroughly made by man. The humanity of the human animal comes about through the sole action of his free and autonomous will, as he acts rationally to defeat finitude. In affirming his humanity, the human animal asserts his sovereignty over nature, an assertion which is the declaration of his sovereignty to the world and over the world, because the world is his own fabrication. The fabrication of the world—the pure act of human sovereignty—is the production of the world as meaning. And this world is historical because it is in becoming, but this becoming is itself historial because it is the foundation and assumption of meaning.

Hobbes is the greatest teller of the modern fable. It is he who inaugurates the thought of history as a metaphysical cosmology of the State, thinking the coming of morality as the ontological difference at the heart of the human, between the *being animal* of the human, the body as the prisoner of the moment, and the *being human* of the human animal, thought as open to time. If Hobbes offers an essential key to the modern historial, it is because he thinks the coming of a moral and political order simultaneously as human action and as historical action, in the sense that we must enter the historical for morality to come to be. The identification of the historical and the human, of becoming and meaning, is absolutely necessary because it announces a rupture with the given and immobile order of the *res extensa* (a rupture equivalent to a liquidation of tradition) and this is the germ from which the modern fable of sovereignty unfolds. Such an identification can be read in the care with which Hobbes shows how *human* life, that is, life within the *res publica*, is determined by the human appropriation of time. In Hobbes' thought, the passage to the State (the passage to sovereignty) is the passage to the future, the abandonment of the present or better its transcendence (*dépassement*). Hobbes' idea that the transcendence of the present is the coming of the historical world as a politico-moral world, which turns the present into the very origin of a world or republic (where a common power and a common law rule), will be subsequently commented on and developed by the Moderns. It signifies the link between politics and the historical. Philosophy will make use of this link to establish the elements of a moral cosmology organized through a series of major oppositions: *human* versus *animal*, *res publica* versus *res extensa*. What opposes the first terms to the second is time. Just as a human being is an animal that discovers time, the republic is nature open to the future, a sort of denatured artificial nature.

However, it is the first opposition—that between the human and the animal, the 'beast'—which is determinant, the one from which the rest flow: this is the opposition that grounds the possibility of the republic. For there is no republic among animals. What is a human being then? To answer this, Hobbes defines the specificity of human *thought*. In *Leviathan* we read:

> The Trayn of Thoughts is of two kinds; One, which of an effect imagined we seek the causes or means that produce it, and this common to Man and Beast. The other is when imagining anything whatsoever, we seek all the possible effects that can by it be produced; that is to say we imagine what we can do with it when we have it. Of which I have not any time seen any sign, but in man onely [. . .] In summe, the Discourse of the Mind when it is governed by designe, is nothing but Seeking [. . .] a hunting out of the causes of some effect present or past; or of the effects of some present or past cause.[13]

It must be seen that the difference here (which is time as the human–animal difference) is the difference at the heart of the human animal and not that between a human part and another part, the 'beast'. This is because this distinction cannot function here—the animal part of man *is* the 'beast'. This is why I speak of the human animal endeavouring, like Hobbes, to distinguish between what is animal (bestial) in it and what is human. Hobbes understood perfectly well that the man whose trace he was following, in order to bring him to the republic, since there is no republic of beasts,[14] is not to be found in nature. More exactly, since this being

---

13. Hobbes, *Leviathan*, p. 96.
14. See what we could call the 'postulates of humanity' that Hobbes enumerates (see ibid., Chapter 17, in particular p. 225) where he resorts to the parable of the bees to assert that the hive is not a republic. It is astonishing to see that this already venerable truth is still not known by everyone.

is obviously a being of nature, coming to political society requires that it separate itself from its natural (bestial) animality. This is the allegorical meaning of the state of nature where the *human condition* is that of the beast, attached to the given present of nature: 'In such a situation', says Hobbes,

> there is no place for Industry because the fruit thereof is uncertain, and consequently no Culture of the Earth, no Navigation [. . .] there is no Knowledge of the face of the Earth, no Account of time, no Arts, no Letters, no Society; and which is worst of all, continuall feare, and danger of violent death. And the life of man, solitary, poore, nasty, brutish and short.[15]

The famous description, in fact, refers to the unfortunate life of the hunted animal, whose thought cannot gain access to the concept of time but only to the imaged representation of the present moment. It is thus a question of the natural given, since, says Hobbes, 'only the *present* exists in nature.'[16]

In Hobbes' reflections then, we have the primordial elements of the historial of sovereignty: the measurement of time and space operates in the sphere of what will soon be called 'civilization' (agriculture, industry, navigation, art and letters, etc.) so that this sphere which is open to the action of the human animal[17] is the sphere of morality, the vast historical space of development where the peoples and nations of the as yet indeterminate and multiform mass of the natural multitude will emerge. Since, as Hobbes says, nature dissociates men[18] it will fall to history to associate them in peoples, to particularize nations. This is a work that will unfold in history (because it *is* history itself) and is the work of sovereignty—each

15. Ibid., p. 186.
16. Ibid., p. 90; emphasis in the original.
17. We note in this passage that Hobbes never uses the word 'humanity' but prefers, for example, *humankind*.
18. Ibid., p. 186.

man will leave the multitude and will be grounded in a people obeying a common law—which *the genealogy of morals* will examine in the following chapter. Each man will undertake his favourite moral and industrious activities without fear of war or violent death, under the protection of the historical State. Above all, each will contribute in his part to the edification of the world spirit, so revealing itself as a singular actor in the cunning of history, that victory over finitude.

c) History is the name given to the process of the self-constitution of a people— history as the coming of freedom

The principle of sovereignty is an essential and constitutive framework for the modern historial—no *history* without sovereignty. Sovereignty refers first and foremost to the origin of historical duration, because it announces the freedom of a people where there is just the multitude submitting to nature. If there is no history without sovereignty, then the people are the first personage of history, in and by which history is made. It is what is *alive* in what constitutes our history, as we Moderns understand it. 'Great men' or heroes may exist but these are not the bearers or instigators of the spirit of the people. The meaning of history, what makes history not merely the formation and transformation of materiality but work and achievement, proceeds from the collective subjectivity of peoples, their will and passions. Just as for the Moderns humanity is not a zoological category, so 'people' is not a demographic category. It is not the ancient *demos*. The people are not a countable population, not even number, since they are not the multitude who will speak.

The historiality of modern becoming would be incomprehensible if the bearer of meaning were not designated by the philosophy that, so to speak, finds its justification within it. If historiality were incomprehensible it would mean that history itself, the ensemble of practices, the ensemble of what is said and done, would be deprived of meaning. Nevertheless, a meaningless history is *not* history—it is merely the movement of matter. By contrast, our history presupposes a philosophy of meaning and spirit. History properly speaking is a spiritual configuration, it is the space where a world is prepared, a space which is a *time*. It is the birth of the world in time and it would be a contradiction pure and simple, an absurdity, to reject this characterization of modern becoming because that would mean that the world lacks meaning. Would we dare to say that the person building a house acted without knowing the meaning of his action? That would be to say that nothing rational or meaningful was ever effected or built in history. Isn't there, by contrast, the most pervasive conviction in common sense and opinion when we think about historical events that history is the milieu where something happens, and that milieu is time?

It is precisely because *something* is in the process of taking place (has taken place or will take place) that we apprehend this time as the time of history and what comes about there as 'historical'—that is, as having more or less importance in the unfolding of something. Hence, it cannot escape us that this something has a meaning, that it suits us or not. Furthermore, it might turn out that we directly take part in what is happening, in being actors in a particular event—for example, the defence of somewhere besieged by enemy forces. But I do not need to be under fire to be in history—I just need to be at my place in the factory, or working in the fields or taking my kids to school. To the extent that something is being produced—being done and taking place—then a history is involved, because every individual action converges on a final goal which the individuals involved in producing it need not be conscious of. In any case, the Moderns who are thrown into history reassure themselves that history is good, that it is a spiritual configuration, by considering that the ensemble of completed actions forms an organized totality. This is the living world of a people and the effect of its thought and action. We said that just as the builder thinks about his work while he is working, so also the people think about their work as they are making history. The best illustration of this (and we will come back to this passage at a more appropriate time) is the democratic practice of the formation of the law by the universality of citizens of a people, an act that founds the republic and hence its history. This is why historiality is the thought of a people when this thought is instituted in the State. The *modern State*—in other words, sovereignty—is the administrative and juridical body in which the thought of a people becomes effective and actual, and hence productive of historical meaning. What is at work in modern history is what the people will— the sovereign State organizes and orders the world of the people as a living world. History is a spiritual configuration because the people are presupposed as its spirit, and perhaps as its soul. Modern belief holds that history becomes living history through the people. It becomes the anticipation of the future, the comprehension of the present as the origin of a future, its beginning. The people are not just an actor in history, they are the agent of its spirit and thought, and if historiality is the thought of the people, history—that *something* that is always coming and taking place—is the process by which the self-constitution of a people is concretely effected. From this point of view, philosophy does nothing but announce the thought of the people in the form of the concept.

Such a movement—*the act by which a people is a people*—finds reflection as the very movement of spirit—it is collective subjectivity in process of being formed. It is the movement where what Rousseau rightly calls *the collective moral self* is born. The act through which a people is a people is the act by which the *collective moral self* comes into the world, or, better, brings the world to pass as historical world. It is Rousseau who, more than anyone, must be recognized as the inventor of the world spirit. He shines a clear light on, and creates the most developed philosophical concept of, reason in history as it is achieved by the Moderns—*freedom*. It is spirit as the subjectivity realized by a common *moral self.*

German idealism adds nothing substantial to Rousseau's discovery but effects its ultimate philosophical transfiguration, of which Hegel's *Phänomenologie des Geistes* (*Phenomenology of Spirit*, 1807) is the unsurpassable monument. From *Leviathan* to *Du contrat social ou Principes du droit politique* (*The Social Contract*, 1762) it is the moral(ity) of history that is discovered in the person of the subject that incarnates and embodies it—the people. It is history as the process of the moralization of the multitude. This is modern historiality whose agent is the people. If becoming is moral(ity), its envelope is politics, because it is effected in the sovereign State, the State of the people, so that the self-constitution of a people becomes the very meaning of history—the modern assumption about the people consists of the irresistible birth and development of the *sovereign people*, author and agent of modern freedom.

That is why democracy—or at least the version that the Moderns have been waiting for ever since Rousseau, that is, *national* democracy—appears to be more a political regime where the 'people' are directly or indirectly legislator *and* subject. Democracy is the form in which the morality of the Moderns is embodied such that the becoming of the modern world is revealed to be the movement by which the old worlds of tradition disappear into the *past*. A meaningful history thus unfolds in the rupture with tradition, from which, however, Modern Times are not entirely liberated (there is always something of the old in the new). The revolutions that punctuate modernity aim to separate them definitively from tradition. The sovereignty of the people and the advent of democracy have no other meaning than the advent of a humanity finally emancipated from the servitude of the old world. It becomes necessary, then, to recognize what is at work in the modern becoming of the people—with the assumption of the sovereign people, history is the assumption of the *freedom* of humanity. It is the people who realize the project of the separation of what is human from what is not—the animal, that is nature. This at any rate is the modern historial assertion—the people thought philosophically as *a moral self* become the bearer of the *idea*. They are the incarnation of the *Idea* of which the State is the guardian and philosophy the prophet—the idea of freedom as *Idea*.

The Universal and the Particular: the Case of Rousseau

The modern State is the State of a people (even if it is not always the State of the people), which means a people made up of subjects or citizens. From Bodin to Rousseau via Hobbes, philosophy constructed the form of modern freedom in the person of its moral support, the people and its historical instrument—the sovereign State. If we limit ourselves to Rousseau,[19] we find:

> If we ask in what precisely consists the greatest good of all, which should be the end of every system of legislation, we shall find it reduce itself to two main objects, *liberty* and *equality*—liberty because all particular dependence means so much force taken from the body of the State, and equality because liberty cannot exist without it.[20]

It is obviously only in democracy that liberty comes to pass, which means that democracy puts into practice the thought of thought freedom, because it is the people who think. The philosophical proposition originating with Rousseau, *it is the people who think*, in no way puts the people at the origin of the law; rather, it

19. We know that Bodin, who was the first to conceive of the principle of sovereignty, had at the same time to conceive the sovereignty of the people, which gives rise to the theory of what he calls the 'popular State'. But it is Hobbes who clearly distinguishes people and multitude in the context of his endeavour to found sovereignty *philosophically*. Thus he makes Rousseau's radical equation possible: *sovereignty = people*, an equation that gives a definitive term to the profane mystery of sovereignty.

20. *The Social Contract*, Book 2, Chapter 11, p. 225 (emphasis in the original), in Jean-Jacques Rousseau, *The Social Contract and Discourses* (G. D. H. Cole trans. and introd.) (London: J. M. Dent, 1923).

means that the subject who thinks is what we call 'people'. Put another way, it might be the case that a democracy is so only in name. That is why Rousseau refused any representation of the will, without denying thereby the representation of Power. The will, that is, the faculty of thinking the law, refers back to the people, although Rousseau is at pains to assert that not every particular thought (will) is the law, which is why no other subject than the people in a body can think freedom. This is the reason why the representatives, or *a fortiori* the government, cannot be declared the legitimate sovereigns because they are not the body of the people but only constitute a particular body. The problem of freedom goes beyond the question of the single, sovereign legislative will—it puts into question the relationship of universal and particular. This relationship is at the heart of the question of history, that is, of man's becoming human. It is the question of the passage from the state of nature to the moral and political state. Passing from the state of nature to the State *tout court* is not a simple moral and political event, a sort of passage to the ethical life. Rather the passage to the ethical life, as rupture with natural existence, is the entry into history such that it is an entry into the realm of freedom. It will be asked: what does the free life consist of? The reply is: in the access of the individual to the universal. So that history, that vast element in which the human animal is transfigured into a political animal, acquires its meaning in acknowledging its constitutive essence. It is the site of the advent and achievement of *freedom*. That is, the reconciliation of the singular (the individual) and the general, that is the fabric of the free, authentically *human* life, because what is human is what is capable of conceiving a world and of creating it so that what is universal is at the same time particular.

When Rousseau invents the people, that is, when he invents them as sovereign, it comes down to showing that *sovereign work* is the historical constitution of the world of freedom. The sovereign work of the people, as Rousseau describes it, is to think freedom *as universal*. Such a thought (as thought by the people who think) only has a place in history, pure profane becoming human of the world. Freedom becomes a true idea if and only if it is the work of the sovereign people. Therefore it cannot be the thought (or work) of any particular body, still less of a single individual,[21] the monarch for example. This shows that a people is by nature historical, but that there is no natural people. A people does not spring forth fully formed and whole from the earth; what springs forth from the earth is not even a multitude but a scattered troop of animals. Rousseau, very modern in this respect, sees in the people a collective being that passes from youth to old age and hence to death. Like an individual, the people is born, develops and dies. A people is never given and a people is never, in itself and by its nature, a *moral self*; it becomes one. The account of this becoming[22] is a narrative of origins, a myth and fable which is the fable of sovereignty, the fable of the world's becoming spirit. It is the fable of the modern historial which unfolds a sequence of events from a foundational event, through which the particular wills its transfiguration into the universal.

The new question that emerges is: what is the foundational event, the originary moment that inaugurates the unfolding of the profane history of the world? And it is a profane history even if some revelation takes place because it is born from a primary event that has taken place in the given course of human affairs. This event is the originary contract—it is the *revolution*. Through the revolution, human animals enter into the realm of their humanity, thus leaving behind their primordial, natural animality. Nothing is more profane than a revolution of which the people are both offspring and instigator. Through the revolution the people

21. That is why in Rousseau's work as in Hobbes', natural freedom is not freedom, because it is only individual, that is, singular.
22. Of which Rousseau assembles the ingredients in Chapters 9 and 10 of *The Social Contract*, Book 2. See section entitled 'Wilderness' in Chapter 3 in this volume.

come to life, and this life is subsequently lived as universal. This is why Rousseau writes: 'Free peoples, be mindful of this maxim: "Freedom may be gained but can never be recovered."'[23] For a people or individual to lose freedom is to fall back into the particular, that is, into quarrels over interests which make the actors lose their sense of the universal and with it the sense of history. The world of profane life is thus not lacking in spirit but, rather, filled with it, and to bring it forth is to bring forth freedom. This is the task of the people—it is the midwife of spirit because it alone thinks it. But this birth of the spirit does not happen without violence. Rousseau finds inspiration in the following lesson from history: in the history of spirit, violence is sometimes the means by which freedom vanishes as well as that by which freedom is conquered. Coming to the universal in the modern fable is a violent process, even if the events are not violent. Hence, as Rousseau himself saw, the revolution is not sparing of violence. The transcendence of the particular in the universal, the act by which a people is a people, marks the origin of States in violence. When a people is victorious over the established order of things, the new law that it announces cannot (or only rarely) be imposed without recourse to force and violence. The universal is not a contemplative thought and the law is not a neutral proposition; the revolution is not role play and history is not a peaceful stroll.

We can see that the theory of the original *contract*—as the Moderns, especially Hobbes and Rousseau, have conceived it, that is, as revolution, turning the human world into a moral world that must be apprehended by its inauguration—leads inexorably to the thought of history as the violent becoming of the universal, a becoming whose motor is the *people*. The revolution is foundational, it installs a world order as an order of a new world, inscribing morality in the thread of history. To do this, the revolution distinguishes historical time from ahistorical times

23. Ibid., Book 2, Chapter 8.

because it opens up a duration that stretches out ahead It is thus the seizure of historical duration as such; in other words, it distinguishes a 'before' from an 'after' in constructing what will henceforth belong to the past. Just as a new continent is discovered, so also a world is uncovered, one defined as old or former. But this ancient continent is also the shore from which one leaves, and it is a people that relegates it to the past, or to oblivion, the old people of the particular—*a* class, *an* order, *a* clan, *a* dynasty, etc. The historical time thus created is that of the old thought of a people as opposed to the new thought of the people. All revolutions that create a time found a people, the 'whole' people, the healthy part of the multitude, the bourgeois, the proletariat, the alliance of workers and peasants, etc. If the revolution founds a new world, it is because it installs the reign of a new people. But whatever people this might be, history is the eternal recommencement of the coming of the people. The modern *people* is the people who bring the revolution, through whom the revolution takes place. It is through the people that fate-ruled or natural becoming gives way to the modern historial of profane life. Because it is the depositary of meaning and spirit, which are one and the same, the people are the central character of history for the Moderns. So the only legitimate violence is the violence of the people, that is, violence aimed at the universal, at the eradication of the particular, or, at least, at relegating it to the past. Violence is legitimate when it transfigures the multitude into a people.

What we call violence, meaningful death on the battlefield, is the process by which a people defines its own identity afresh, designating those who belong to the *true* people and those who are the *false* people. At the moment of its revolutionary foundation, the history in play is a metaphysics of true and false—those who belong to the *true people* are those who can attain universality; those who belong to the *false people* are those stuck in particularity. This difference between true and false is as follows: the true takes part in the foundation, it is originary.

The false is separated from the origin, it belongs to the past. The metaphysics of the true is constitutive of the historical time of the future, without which there is no beginning of morality. Without this, the distinction between what is *human* and what is not becomes impossible. Profane (historical) life is meaningful, spiritual, because it makes a separation between life as universal from life as particular, a separation that distinguishes true from false, the future from the past. Violence thus has to come onto the historical scene. Nevertheless, it is not inevitable, a fatality, and we can no doubt find occasions when the revolution occurs without violence.[24] However, these occasions are rare. If, as we have argued, the revolution opposes the particular to the universal and the universal emerges from peoples and not from god or nature, then we must wait and see whether a people emerge on (or return to) the scene without violence. This is what history has taught our epoch and it taught the same lesson to Rousseau and his times.[25]

The Violence of History

We cannot ask what history is without asking what justice is, because justice is historical to the extent that it is related to violence. In effect, *either* I ask myself how I know what justice is, by reflecting on the metaphysical and practical meaning that must be given to notions of equality and equity. So I treat justice academically

24. This was the case in the fall of the Soviet empire in central Europe, or, in certain cases, a nation's return to itself with the peaceful collapse of its 'ancien régime'. But this has been largely made up for by the intense civil wars that set the peoples of the former Yugoslavia against each other and where violence reached the point of crimes against humanity.

25. 'There are indeed times in the history of States when, just as some kinds of illness turn some men's heads and make them forget the past, periods of violence and revolutions do to peoples what these crises do to individuals: horror of the past takes the place of forgetfulness, and the State set on fire by civil wars is born again, so to speak, from the ashes, and takes on anew, fresh from the jaws of death, the vigour of youth' (*The Social Contract*, Book 2, Chapter 8).

as equity, taking care to relate my investigation to real situations, lived circumstances, or, as they say, concrete cases. *Or* I ask how the question of justice can be posed. It is perhaps unnecessary (or simply not useful) to pose such a question, but if I do, it is less because *I* pose the question, but because such a question *is posed*, not just to me but to human beings in the city. This is only because the question of justice is a concrete one—the being of justice is determined by being posed to me as a question. Why is this so? Because violence stitches together the fabric of profane human becoming in the sense that violence is precisely what is unleashed when the people judge that the present is unjust. What defines injustice is not the fact that the current norms of justice no longer correspond with the abstract definition of equity, for example, but the infinitely more powerful fact that the universal of the moment is *lived* (*experienced*) *badly* by the particular. That is to say, the *freedom* of the moment is ill experienced by the particular, because there is a conflict between universal and particular. Justice is intimately tied to violence for the reason that an injustice is practically always experienced in violence—experienced as violence—and that it is overcome through violence. So justice can be defined negatively as an order of morality which is not experienced as violent, and in which violence is not called on as a means to eliminate this first violence, this injustice. A just order would thus be a negative order like a perfect world, of which we have already observed that it would be a world more or less lacking everything that the real world, however imperfect, contains.

We can see why the question of justice must be brought up here, even if it cannot be resolved now (if indeed it ever can be). It is because justice is posited as the substantial element of the free and organized life, and in consequence, because it has to do with history and its violence. The lack of satisfaction that the present world gives me is the index that the question of justice is posed in history, and from this point of view, it can be regarded as the essential question to which leads every investigation into history. If the question of justice is linked to the question of the meaning of history, it is because it proceeds from a judgement on the *present*, judged as just or unjust, which provokes the thought of a future which would be more just.[26] For example, we can now imagine what it would be for everyone to have enough to live on, while most of our contemporaries have to make do, get by—when they can manage it. The justice of this situation is perhaps one of the more pressing questions of our time. It is in this sense, or, better, in this context, that the question of justice arises. The injustice of a situation, an injustice resented as violence, is such that the terms in which the question of justice is posed mean that it is not just a question but a *problem*. How do we define justice if in fact we accept the existence of injustice? It is necessary to raise this question, since in one way or another we do accept injustice—and violence with it—since we cannot deny that injustice exists and that we live with it *as if* it were inevitable (a fate or destiny). And this *as if* means that at bottom we accept violence because we are incapable of eliminating it. At least we can only think that history is the infinite quest to eliminate injustice. This is the case if we consider that violence is at once what is unacceptable in the present when it is resented as injustice *and* the (revolutionary) action that aims at eliminating this very injustice in the future. *Revolution* is the recourse to violence in order to eliminate violence. Hence, revolution is turned towards the future—tomorrow, justice will reign. So revolution constitutes and installs the historical time of the future as the living time of profane human becoming. From this point of view, history is revolutionary. We cannot say that the Moderns could have (or could) economize on their revolutions. While it might have been desirable, because it would have avoided the crimes committed during their moments of terror, the demand would be in vain. This

---

26. In this sense, any investigation into justice that ignores the historical is condemned to abstraction and arbitrariness, because it ignores the question of violence.

stems from what profane life seeks to unfold as the norms of profane justice. In the absence of an indisputable *given* foundation of common justice within a people and between nations, justice becomes the object of debate or discussion—or struggle. But the discussion—whose final meaning can be nothing other than the universal communication of what is just and its universal acceptance by a humanity finally reconciled with itself in a particular space or everywhere—might have happened on occasion, but cannot happen all the time. One of the contending parties would have to be prepared, finally, to give in to the reasons of the other party. Again, this might happen on occasion but it will not happen all the time. Empirical history reveals this to be a rare occurrence; what usually happens is the recourse to violence and force. The fact that justice is *historical* (and can be nothing other than historical) prevents violence from being eliminated from history, or prevents history from being anything but the temporal sequence of the moments of violence to which human beings resort to establish justice, because the absence of justice is experienced by them as violence.

Under these conditions, it is utopian to reject all violence and dangerous for justice itself. It is potentially dangerous because an unjust order in the world could be accommodated for a period or for ever. A *non-violent* revolution is a risk that cannot be taken given a violent situation that has become absolutely intolerable. We can certainly find examples of non-violent revolution that have emerged from violent situations or subsequent to violence. But history is not made of such exceptions. While I might opt for non-violence depending on my reason and my will, violence, on the other hand, is immanent in things and does not depend on my agreement to be unleashed. In other words, I do not need to be a violent *individual* for history to be violent. But it does require a decision or a series of decisions for war—civil or foreign—to be declared. However, war does not take place because some *individuals* take the decision to wage it but because things are ordered for violence, such that the decision to resort to force is itself part of that order. If it were in the (political) power of human beings not to resort to force, then the latter would disappear from the course of things. But as the wisest of the Moderns have said, men do not form an empire within an empire. That is to say, humanity only makes history in determinate conditions but without knowing what they are. So the quest for justice in the world does not, for example, refer to a decision by Power to place violence outside the law by right. If the reign of law were in itself the reign of justice, violence would be eliminated. Men do not want war. On the contrary, it is peace they desire and they know that peace is organized according to right. But it is precisely for this reason that wanting what is right might require the acceptance of the recourse to violence because an order felt to be unjust is an order of law. When revolutionary violence is unleashed against the injustice of the moment, it is always a revolution against the form of right in force: 'Just law is only an idea.'[27]

The Spirit is Dead

We cannot rely on the *World Spirit* to resolve the enigma of historical justice. Because the world is not ordered for us Moderns by the beyond, profane life, satisfactory human life can be the free life—the *just* life—only on condition that human beings find the means to satisfy themselves within the world of finitude.

---

27. See K. Jaspers, *Philosophy*, 3 VOLS (E. B. Ashton trans., VOL. 2) (Chicago: University of Chicago Press, 1970). Jaspers adds: 'Attempts to win recognition of a "right" law, one that might be known as generally valid, have always been futile. The right law remains a mere idea, not only is it not objectively and definitely known, but its realisation remains impossible. That is why the passionate quest for a reality of law with justice may so easily take the form of revolution, in which the goal of abolishing violence seems to justify the use of it, although the inevitable adjustment to the reality of human masses will produce a new positive order that again prevails by violence. The end in other words, will be a form of existence we had at the beginning, only with other rulers and another content' (ibid., VOL. 2, p. 211).

We have already noted that satisfaction cannot be said to be universal in humankind. Inasmuch as we know the content of the past, and because we are entirely ignorant of the nature of the present, we can confidently assert that justice is not to be found in history. This is why the Ancients sought the key to justice beyond the sensible, where becoming had no purchase on essences, where the forms could be contemplated. In any case, empirical history, the past as known to us, offers the vast spectacle of injustice and its necessary counterpart—those actions taken to establish justice. If there is a sort of equilibrium between justice and injustice, an equal distribution of good and evil, that is perhaps only true from the point of view of God who possesses the key to the profane mystery, apprehending simultaneously the infinite sequence of finite times. But human beings do not know what God's point of view is;[28] even if they did, they would still have to overcome the astonishment and pain produced by an enigma too obscure to decipher and the burden of injustice too heavy to carry. This situation means that the history we experience and find in history books is not in itself the element of justice—most men regard it as a 'vale of tears' where moments of happiness and satisfaction are too rare to be regarded as the norms of becoming. In the best of

28. See Bossuet, addressing a Christian people: 'But, you will say, God often allows the evil to prosper, and lets the just suffer great evils; and even when such a disorder lasts only a moment it is always something against justice. Let us disabuse ourselves, Christians, and today understand the difference between good and evil. There are of two sorts: there are the mixed good and evil, which depend on the use we make of them. For example, illness is an evil: but it will be a great good if you sanctify it with patience; health is a good; but it will become a dangerous evil if it favours debauchery! These are the mixed goods and evils, which partake of the nature of the good and the evil, and touch one another, following the use we make of them. But understand, Christians, that an all-powerful God has a sovereign good among his treasures, one which can never be evil: this is eternal happiness; and he has among the treasures of his justice certain extreme evils that cannot be turned to the good by those who suffer them, such are the tortures of the damned. The rule of justice will not allow the bad to ever enjoy this sovereign good, nor the good to be tormented by these extreme evils; that is why he will have a day of judgement; but as regards the mixed good and evil, he gives them indifferently to each and everyone' (*Le Carême du Louvre. Sermon de la Providence* [Paris: Gallimard, 2001], pp. 119–20).

cases, the present is understood as the transition to a better future that corrects the past. We find few individuals with an optimistic view of history. The *multitude* in general is preoccupied with organizing its finitude in order to acquire a happiness which it never attains, save in rare moments of history when the possibility of an imminent re-establishment of justice is the motive for revolutionary action. The individual might declare himself happy but the multitude never is. The happiness of *all* is not the happiness of one or a few individuals, and in any case history is never measured by the individual but by multitudes.

Only bad faith could make us deny that our perception of things leads to a simple scepticism about the possibility of overcoming the misfortunes of the world—our own misfortunes—and of finally living according to our idea of the satisfied life that is the free and just life. Moreover, it is this contention that leads modern philosophy to develop a metaphysics of history in which, given the finite condition of men and the injustice that is done to them,[29] the transfiguration of natural freedom into political freedom is what brings men to their proper humanity, a passage that takes place in the course of history. From this point of view, if philosophy begins in scepticism (there is nothing to hope for in the human condition), then this is because history is defined as *promise*. What in fact is the promise of history? For the Moderns, it is the opening of the sphere of their future as the advent of their freedom, as the transfiguration of the injustice of nature into the justice of the city. Philosophy begins in emancipation from the law of nature (or divine law) with the aim of constituting the historical condition of men as the promise of liberation and justice. The abandonment of the law of nature as foundation (an abandonment that installs sovereignty) to the benefit of the human law—*the will*—is a reversal of the sign of history, which moves from negative to

---

29. Job furnishes the relevant allegory here, which Hobbes relies on. On this subject, see my introduction to the French translation of *Léviathan*, 'Hobbes, matérialisme et finitude'; in particular, pp. 14–25.

positive. To the unjust condition of nature, philosophy opposes the advent of justice through history. The negative freedom that human beings enjoy in the state of nature—where, since everything is permitted, *death* is meted out and suffered—is transfigured by the sovereign order of the world into positive freedom. If history is promise, then it is the spirit of history that will free the multitudes from the yoke of nature. *What* history brings to human beings is the promise of the future,[30] that is, a metaphysics of time as the transcendence of the present, the appropriation of the future, and the accomplishment of what was only a seed within the origin. History is spirit because it is the seed bed of what men have sown at the beginning of the time that has for this very reason now become history. The modern philosophical spiritualization of history[31] consists of the discovery in the thick darkness of the past, in the folds of the human memory of the world, of a transcendental origin, an a priori beginning from which the historical epic of the multitudes proceeds because they owe to this what they are in their *being* and what they will become in *history*.

If history is spirit, it is not that it is inhabited by a god but that the sacred that it harbours and develops is the miraculous germ of the founding action or gesture of a properly human order, that is, a spiritual one. Human work is manifested in the world as spiritual creation, which is non-natural or outside nature (which is not to say against nature). To put it another way—what is spiritual in the world comes from human activity raising itself above given nature through the creation of a work, a superior human artifice that cannot be reduced to the given of the *res extensa*. This work is spirit. This is why work as it is accomplished in time—since it takes time to make a world—is the spirit of history. Thus we cannot confuse history understood as the genesis of spirit, whose meaning is elaborated by modern

30. Which certain figures in the last century have thought of as the *radiant future*.
31. Hegel: 'It is on the stage of universal history that spirit attains its most concrete reality' (*La Raison dans l'histoire*, p. 74).

philosophy, with a divinization of profane human becoming. Here, the divine is a metaphor of the historical and the sacred is precisely in history, its profane character. The transcendental origin from which spirit engenders itself in the world has left behind both nature and the divine to fulfil itself as human origin. The divine is a creation of men, it is *their* work and the spirit that comes into the world through it is realized and effected in a superior way in the *work of art*. This bears witness to and proves that man is not just an element of nature but spirit. He is beyond nature because he imitates when he needs to, negates it and above all knows it. For the Moderns, nature is just *what* has to be known—it is the object of an intellectual appropriation. It is the sphere of geometry; it comes after numbers. These are a priori in men's spirit, like the axioms of geometry. The gods are in nature, or government or creation because the spirit of men puts them there. But, above all, it is in art that spirit best manifests itself—it is the work in which the human spirit becomes concrete, immediately perceived not only by the senses but by the thought that is *thought* where nature offers nothing but *extension*. Philosophy does nothing other than grasp the meaning of spirit, nothing but flush it out from men's lives (as their life itself), from their past, present and future, and think this life as finite duration. Philosophy in other words is the thought of time as the vector of spirit. Here we are within the scheme of the historial, in the founding philosopheme of the modern historial: *Time = Spirit*.

The key to the modern historial lies in the philosophical identification of a transcendental origin from which it becomes philosophically possible to unroll the genesis of what emerges there as seed and to unfold it within the framework of a *universal history*. The creation of spirit on the basis of itself is at work in the *polity*, that circle of men's common being, at once condition of emergence of spirit and its effect. It requires a *res publica* for the *res extensa* to be transcended in spirit, but, conversely, spirit is required for there to be a *res publica*. The disclosure of the world spirit takes place precisely in the world. Universal spirit is nevertheless born at a single time and a single place in a finite world. If spirit is born in a *polity* and not in nature it is because it is freedom and there is no measure of freedom outside a *polity* where liberty is in germ or has flowered. We must uncover spirit where it is hidden away—in Greece—to understand why a particular Greek *polity*—the Athenian *polis*—must be regarded as the transcendental origin of the world spirit or the spirit of *universal history*. When modern philosophy conceives 'Greece' as origin—the famous miracle of *Hellas*—that is, as myth, it is attempting *both* to elucidate the sense of (western) Europe as the spatio-temporal framework of the unfolding of the spirit that originally sprang forth in historical Greece *and* to identify this Europe with what is, for it, the very being of the *World*. So that universal history becomes at once the schema for the unfolding of spirit from historical Greece *and* the schema for the constitution of *Europe* as European expansion over the surface of the *orbis*. To the metaphysical equation of the historial—*Time = Spirit*—corresponds the political equation *Europe = World*. What makes the equation possible in both cases is the term 'Greece' as transcendental origin, that is, the mutation of the historical (Greece) into historial myth (*Greece*).

It would a great misunderstanding to see in the present discussion of what I have called the historial an attempt to discredit what modern philosophy has, implicitly or explicitly, designated as *spirit*. On the contrary, it is a question of understanding how spirit is the concrete category of the historial by which the modern history of Europe comes to be that history itself and how Europeans understand that advent through philosophical thought as what properly constitutes them as *European*. It would be to misunderstand what I say about the historial simply to see it only as a critique in the current sense of the word (a depreciative judgement) seeking to condemn what is. It is more a question of performing a diagnostic examination of the historial with the aim of understanding both *what* has been at work in our 'modern' history (a history that has been largely European because it has been made and understood by Europe) and what is no longer. It is precisely the final significance of the historial that the historial provides an end for our epoch because, as we shall see, for our epoch *spirit* is dead. It has died its own categorical death in the tragedy of a philosophy which, at the very moment it announces the rediscovery of the transcendental origin of spirit, fails to see the destruction of that spirit in the Nazi concentration camps through the return of European humanity to animality. It is also dead because the subject of its production that first emerged in *Greece*—a subject which is the very spirit of Europe—is no longer in possession of its historical temporality (the future) but is, rather, in process of returning to tradition, that is to *its past*. These two deaths of Spirit—the second proceeding directly from the first—mean that the subsequent task of philosophy is to understand with all the means at its disposal what the situation of 'spirit' is in our epoch. This involves looking at (and at Europe) with a medical eye of a practitioner who sees the patient in a *state of crisis* and evaluates the gravity of his *critical state*. To the extent that philosophy has not been swept away with the disappearance of what it believed itself to be, its task is to help clarify what is happening just as spirit is retreating from the world, and, if *nothing is done*, Europe with it. The maximum philosophical absurdity would be for philosophy to decide for or against *spirit*! Philosophy reaches its limit here in registering the *fact* that, for it, the origin is to be found in a determinate time and place called Greece—the Greece of Plato and Aristotle and Pericles. *Greece* is a philosophical fact that is the signature of the philosophical essence of Europe and its 'spirit'.

To witness the birth of spirit, we have to begin with Greece and *Greece*. Spirit is nowhere else more at home than in art and science—their exemplary discovery will give rise to the philosophical model of universal history which is both profane and spiritual based on the history of art. It is Winckelmann in his *History of Ancient Art* who reveals the origin of spirit and forges the archetype of the history of spirit in the form of the history of the *beautiful*, its birth and development, its sublimity and decadence. It is thus a question of the discovery of the *archè*. With

Winckelmann, the historical nature of spirit is articulated as the archaeology of the Beautiful. Winckelmann discovers the origin of spirit as manifest in art essentially in Athens. Ancient Athens is the city where political liberty makes the beautiful possible as such and in general as manifestation of spirit. After the expulsion of the tyrants, and benefiting from a propitious climate, the Athenians enjoyed circumstances that were favourable to the birth of spirit:

From then on, all the people took part in public affairs, the spirit of each inhabitant grew, and Athens itself was elevated above all the other towns of Greece. Good taste being universal, and the opulent citizens attracted to the consideration of their fellow citizens by the erection of superb public monuments, there was an influx into this powerful town, just as rivers flow into the sea, of all the talents at once. The arts took hold there with the sciences: their centre was there, and it was from there that they spread into other regions. The prosperity of the State was the principle by which taste progressed. In modern times, Florence attests to the truth of our proposition: the town having become rich saw the darkness of ignorance dissipate and the arts and sciences flourish.[32]

32. Johan Joachim Winckelmann, *Histoire de l'Art chez les Anciens* (1764), 3 VOLS (M. Huber trans.) (Paris: Barrois, 1789), VOL. 1, pp. 48–9. For Winckelmann, the great creations of ancient Greece are to be attributed to political freedom which, by making possible a certain 'way of thinking' favoured the productions of spirit: 'The people's way of thinking was elevated by freedom, like the noble heir of a vigorous line. Just as a thinking man's soul is more elevated in the open air or on the rooftop of a high building than in a basement or narrow hole, so the way of thinking of free Greeks must have been very different from that of nations governed by despots. Herodotus shows that freedom was the sole source and foundation of the power and grandeur of Athens, which previously, having to acknowledge a master, had not been in a state to lead its neighbours. For the same reason, eloquence began to flourish among the Greeks only when they enjoyed freedom: hence the Sicilians attributed to Gorgias the invention of rhetoric. It was freedom, mother of great events as well as revolutions and jealousies among the Greeks, which sowed the first seeds of noble sentiments from then on. Just as the spectacle of the vast surface of the ocean and enormous waves crashing against rocks enlarges our soul and turns it away from petty concerns, the vision of men and things of such greatness could not lead to the con-

Since the Greeks had established the definitive canons of the beautiful, Winckelmann's archaeological history reveals how that an evolution had first been prepared in Egypt, developed among the Etruscans, and reached its sublime flowering in Greece, after which it sank into decadence, that is to say, a loss of the origin.

> Greek art transported onto a foreign soil could not take root in a countryside where it no longer benefited from the soft influence of its natural climate. Obliged to serve the pomp of courtly life, it lost its grandeur and its spirit under the Seleucids and Ptolemies. Art fell entirely in Magna Graeca, where it had flourished with the philosophy of Pythagoras and Zeno of Elea, in the midst of numerous free and rich towns. In the end it perished entirely under the armies and barbarism of Rome.[33]

Hence the judgement he makes of modern art:

> I speak about the natural disposition of nations for art in general, and I do not claim to contain that talent in the countries of the South, nor to deny it to the countries of the North, which would be altogether refuted by the experience of every age. Holbein and Dürer, those fathers of Art in Germany, certainly worked with genius: their works make us see that had they followed the example of Raphael, Titian and Correggio, and had been able to study and imitate the antique, they would have become as great and perhaps greater than these outstanding men.[34]

What history teaches, then, is that once the ultimate form of beauty had been laid down in Greece, history becomes perfectly intelligible, conforming to a

---

ception of anything mediocre. The Greeks in the flourishing state of their republic were thinking beings who had already had twenty years of reflection, and that at an age when we had barely begun to reflect ourselves' (ibid., VOL. 2, pp. 13–14).

33. Ibid., VOL. 3, p. 32.

34. Ibid., VOL. 1, p. 52.

greater or lesser extent with the *archè*, that form or *eidos* whose seed was sown in a particular place in space and time and which makes it possible to identify an evolving spirit, which either progresses or decays.

Closer to our own times, we find a metaphysical perspective that aims at the 'destruction' of traditional ontology so as to rediscover its *archè*. This is Heidegger's attempt in *Being and Time* to refound fundamental ontology on its originary basis (Parmenides), after which spirit had been more or less in decay, the object of forgetting. Just as Winckelmann had already perceived the importance of the Greek language in the birth of spirit in Greece,[35] Heidegger saw in the Greek language the very source and origin of philosophical thinking, as he saw the German language as the contemporary source of the renovation of spirit. If, as Heidegger would approvingly proclaim at the worst moment of our Europe (of our spirit), it was down to Germany to be the Greece of the Moderns, this was because of a claim that the history of ontology would make the thinker of *Being and Time* bring forth. He writes:

> We have shown at the outset not only that the question of the meaning of Being is one that has been attended to and one that has been inadequately formulated, but that it has become quite forgotten in spite of all our interest in 'metaphysics'. Greek ontology and its history—which in their numerous filiations and distortions, determine the conceptual character of philosophy even today—prove that when Dasein understands either itself or Being in general, it does so in terms of the 'world'

---

35. 'Philosophy itself was taught in public for the first time in the same town by Athenagoras, who opened his school in the 75th Olympiad [. . .] a little time before, Simonides and Epicharnus had completed the Greek alphabet; but the letters they had finished were only introduced into public affairs in Athens in the 80th Olympiad, after the expulsion of the Thirty Tyrants. Such were the preparatory circumstances, so to speak, that led to the perfection towards which Art advanced in great bounds' (ibid., VOL. 3, pp. 16–17).

and that the ontology which has thus arisen has deteriorated to a tradition in which it gets reduced to something self-evident—merely material
for reworking, as it was for Hegel. In the Middle Ages, this uprooted
Greek ontology became a fixed body of doctrine [. . .] With the peculiar
character that the Scholastics gave it, Greek ontology has in its essentials
travelled the path that leads through the *Disputationes metaphysicae* of
Suárez to the 'metaphysics' and transcendental philosophy of modern
times determining even the foundations and the aims of Hegel's 'logic'. In
the course of this history certain distinctive domains of being have come
into view and have served as the primary guides for subsequent prob-
lematics: the *ego cogito* of Descartes, the subject, the 'I', reason, spirit,
person. But these all remain uninterrogated as to their Being [. . .] If the
question of being is to have its own history made transparent then this
hardened tradition must be loosened up and the concealments it has
brought about must be dissolved. We understand this task as one in
which by taking the *question of Being as our clue,* we are to *destroy* the
traditional content of ancient ontology, until we arrive at those primordial experiences in which we achieved our first ways of determining the
nature of being [. . .]36

This opening of the great work of thought which is *Being and Time* refers
directly and explicitly to Greece as the origin, so that the meaning of history—of
ontology but of history *tout court*—is elucidated. History is the loss of meaning,
and, to pick up Winckelmann's term (which Heidegger does not use), history is
something like a decadence, a falling away, in any case a 'hardened tradition', a
covering over of authentic meaning ('concealment') which justifies Heidegger's
project—a 'metaphysical' project—to restitute the origin and at the same time

36. Heidegger, *Being and Time*, pp. [22–23] 44–5.

restore the 'meaning of being'. The restitution that Heidegger seeks to achieve passes naturally through the 'destruction' of the 'tradition', which, we have just said, consists of a rediscovery of the *archè*, freed from the concealments with which history has covered it. In this huge operation which can only think the question of Being at the cost of a radical recommencement of *thinking* itself, what is at issue, from our point of view, is what becomes of *spirit*—whose Hegelian formulation Heidegger 'destroys' at the end of his work.[37] So the recommencement of thinking in *Being and Time*, to the extent that it is embodied in a 'destruction' of the ontological legacy—which is a veil thrown over the origin—rests on a 'history' whose meaning is the loss of spirit, and, in consequence, the subsequent necessity for its refoundation at the moment where the unveiling of what has been covered over is finally effected. It is not clear what human significance the return to the origin—that is, its archaeological extraction by philosophy—would have if the present could not enjoy, in the same way that a buried object—which men have forgotten because it was covered up by history but have finally rediscovered—might be shown to the public. The concrete understanding of *Being and Time*—as with every foundation of thought—demands that the work be understood as part of the living world. In this sense, there is no doubt that the 'destruction' of ontology in the sense that Heidegger gives the word refers not to an annihilation but to a rebirth. This presupposes that history thus thought as forgetting must in some fashion be forgotten and replaced by something new. Spirit can be reborn only from ashes and *Being and Time* is this metaphysical bonfire. Because

37. Ibid., Section 83. For Hegel, says Heidegger, 'Because of this spirit *must first of all fall* "into time"'. It remains obscure what indeed is signified ontologically by this "falling" or by the "actualising" of a spirit which has power over time and really "is" outside of it' (ibid., pp. [435] 485). Heidegger had previously specified his critique of the *spirit that falls into time* as follows: '*In analysing the historicality of Dasein we shall try to show that this entity is not "temporal" because it "stands in history" but that, on the contrary it exists historically and can so exist only because it is temporal in the very basis of its Being*' (ibid., pp. [376] 428; emphasis in the original).

he is the executor of its will, Heidegger knows that the world spirit has come to its end; he knows that he is the Hegel of his times and that he is the administrator of the Absolute Self Knowledge of Spirit. He knows—and this knowledge is the very condition of his problematic—that the fate of the European spirit born in Greece is in question at this opening of the twentieth century, after a world war which concretely universalized the spirit of the world at the same time as it announced its fulfilment in a Europe that had been destroyed. The destruction of metaphysics, that is, the self-knowledge of Spirit as having completed its self-production, is not a speculative operation carried out by a single thinker but the construction of history as *past*, and, at once, the seizing of the historical moment—Europe after 1918—as the starting point for the rebirth of spirit.

Being and Time is thus spirit's reveille, something that can only be the work of the German people. At this end of the modernity of spirit, there is a properly German *Dasein*, as there was at the origin of ancient times a Greek *Dasein*. For Heidegger, the German *language* is the new support of this renovated spirit. The question of beginning, this new origin, is thus *the* fundamental question of spirit, the stakes in the history being played out:

> But isn't the beginning by now two thousand five hundred years behind us? Hasn't human progress changed science as well? Certainly! The Christian theological interpretation of the world that follows, as well as the technical mathematical thought of the modern age have separated science both in time and its concern for its beginning. But, this does not mean that the beginning itself has not been transcended, and even less brought to nought. But if indeed Greek science is something great then the *beginning* of this great thing remains what is greatest about it. The essence of science could not even be emptied out and used up as is happening today, despite all its results and 'international organisations', if the greatness of the begin-

ning does not *still* endure. The beginning still *is* and does not lie *behind us* as something that was long ago; but lies *before* us [. . .][38]

What Heidegger calls the 'command of the beginning' is the injunction to spirit to be reborn in Germany, a task—a *destiny*—that falls upon the German people, particularly on the student body—that wise youth of German *Dasein*: 'If we submit to the distant command of the beginning, science must become the fundamental happening of our spiritual being as a people.' Heidegger's search for the meaning of Being is intimately tied up with the rebirth of the spiritual world, the authentic element of the greatness of a people. What is important then is to define spirit in itself and to identify its bearer. Spirit is

primordially attuned, knowing resolution toward the essence of being. And the *spiritual world of a people* is not the superstructure of a nation, no more than it is its armoury stuffed with useful facts and values: it is the power that most deeply presents the people's strengths which are tied to earth and blood, and as such is the power that most deeply moves and profoundly shakes its Being. Only a spiritual world gives the people assurance of greatness. For it necessitates that the constant decision between the will to greatness and a letting things happen that means decline, will be the law presiding over the march that our people has begun into its future history [. . .][39]

38. Heidegger, 'Self-assertion of the German University' (May 1933) (Karsten Harries trans.), in *Martin Heidegger: Philosophical and Political Writings* (Martin Stassen ed.) (New York and London: Continuum, 2003), p. 5; emphasis in the original. We should recall that Hitler's seizure of power was in 1933.

39. Ibid., p. 6. Heidegger thus sums up the authentic rebirth of spirit in German *Dasein*, enumerating the links of a people to its soil and blood: 'The bonds *by* the people, *to the destiny of the state*, in a spiritual mission are *equally primordial* to the German essence. The three services that stem from it—Labour Service, Armed Service, and Knowledge—are equally necessary and of equal rank' (ibid., p. 8).

The Graeco-German injunction of the return to the origin is for us, the European survivors of two world wars, the stumbling block of the world spirit. Such an 'injunction', which aims at a rebirth, turns out to be more the sign of a history informing us that Spirit is *dead*. For those who, having escaped the war, were deprived of their *life* in the supreme violence of the extermination camps are dead to the historial—they are dead, in the last instance, to a *spiritual world* which philosophy had not built for them. Outside spirit, they were only non-human—pure and simple *res extensa*.

CHAPTER 3
Genealogy of Morality, 1: The Historial People

The sovereign State and its world of morality can be essentially understood by elucidating the meaning of the term 'people'. The ethics of the modern world can be understood in terms of a single question: *What is the people?* This is a different question from: *What is a people?* A people is either the population of a country, that is, the totality of individuals who have a territory in common, or the totality of individuals who have a name in common (the Palestinians, the Americans, etc.) by which they designate themselves and by which they are generally known. In determining what constitutes *a* people, name and territory are not givens that individually and in tandem refer to the same human reality. All the individuals of a people need not have a common territory, and there might be minorities living outside the territory where the great majority of the people in question live. For example, I might belong to the people known by the name of 'Palestinians' without living in Palestine, or be an American without living in America. If we reduce the question '*What is a people?*' to its essential structure, eliminating its particular determinations (linked to space and time), we are to go back to what originally determined such a people not just to *be* but to be *known* (identified) as being this people. The question '*What is a people?*' takes us back to the fundamental question, the first, precisely originary question—that of the native, the *aborigine*. What happens then to the question we posed at the beginning, '*What is the people?*', under these conditions? This question is different from the second one because it cannot be reduced to that of the aborigine. Rather, it is a matter of the negation of the aborigine even if we have to begin with him, but only in the sense that he is finally erased. *The people is the* historial *elimination of a* natural *people*—'tribe' or 'horde' in a state of nature.

The Aborigine

When the powers engaged in the voyages of discovery (that is, Spain, England, France, etc.) 'find' these native or natural peoples, they also begin to ask whether the populations encountered in the course of their expeditions are susceptible to legislation, that is, capable of being civilized. Is the native properly human? The reply to the question: 'Is he savage?', that is, is he *open to legislation,* will be constitutive of his being, will decide his essence—'human or non-human?' Questioning the *nature* of the aborigine already raises the suspicion of non-humanity. The aborigine is a priori a tribe or horde outside humanity while the people are the living body of humanity. Hence, the question of whether the beings that the Europeans find in the Americas (or in other parts of the *orbis*) during Montaigne's era—find in the way that you find an object that has been left on the ground—are capable of participating in civilization. For the Moderns, participation in humanity is not a given condition. We are not born *human*, but become so—the way a tribe properly becomes a people—in the course of a struggle against what is not human, against the natural. The term 'humanity' does not refer to a definable zoological group, like the vertebrates or cold-blooded animals. Humanity (like the individuals who are part of it) is an ensemble defined by *morality*, the *policed* life, that is, an ensemble of virtues whose unity and common context are what the Moderns call 'civilization'.[1] The being of the aborigine, then, can only be properly defined by the figure whose being no longer belongs to aboriginality; it is necessarily conceived and constituted by the very thing that is its negation—the civilized person. Its fundamental condition is the one we have just indicated—the aborigines or natives are those whose capacity to be civilized is doubtful. Perhaps they can, but this has to be verified. Their humanity is only *possible*. This is why a people (a 'tribe') is not moral ('civilized') by nature, but becomes so under certain conditions and through certain procedures. Moreover, there are tribes designated by the civilized as incapable of being civilized. So if it is in the nature of the aborigine to raise doubts about their eventual moralization, then their nature is elucidated by those who think themselves as moral (virtuous)—the Europeans.

---

1. Rousseau gives a good illustration of what modern moral philosophy understands by the policed life: the yoke of legislation that is civilization. In the chapters on 'The People' (*The Social Contract*, Book 2, Chapters 8–10), Rousseau examines the conditions under which a people are 'a fit subject for legislation' (Chapter 10). In the course of his examination, he uses the terms 'policed life' and 'civilized' indiscriminately, as we can see in his analysis of whether the Russians are capable of being civilized: 'There is for nations, as for men, a period of youth, or, shall we say, maturity, before which they should not be subject to laws, but the maturity of peoples is not always easy to recognise [. . .] Russia will never be really civilised because it was civilised too soon [. . .] [Peter] saw that his people was barbarous, but did not see that it was ripe for policing: he wanted to civilise it when it needed only hardening' (Chapter 8). It is this thematic of the capacity for a horde to receive legislation, its aptitude for civilization—the virtuous morals of the *policed life*—that is constitutive of the people properly named and defined—a definition elaborated in opposition to the uncivilized and savage horde: the aborigine in person.

What then has been the subsequent definition of the aborigine, a *necessary* definition since it decides whether the aborigines belong to humanity or not? That definition was given in a scholarly study commissioned by the United States government from a professor of international law, Alpheus Henry Snow, in 1918: 'The aborigines are the members of those uncivilized tribes living in a region when a civilized State extends its sovereignty over it and who have been inhabiting it since time immemorial; also their uncivilized descendants living in this region.'[2] This is not Snow's personal definition of the aborigine but one which is *de facto* current in the practice of international law as applied to colonization; or, rather, if such a definition had existed, it would have been the one that Snow laid out in his report.[3] Be that as it may, Snow highlights the definition of the doctrine that founds the practice of the international law of colonization—*aboriginism* or 'the doctrine according to which the savage races can be civilized and therefore should be respected'.[4]

2. Alpheus Henry Snow, *The Question of the Aborigines in the Law and Practice of Nations, Including a Collection of Authorities and Documents. Written at the Request of the Department of State* (New York, London: 1921), pp. 3–4. Snow's work is remarkable and pioneering; he completes his definition: 'As far as its connection with the law of nations and its putting into practice, the term "aborigine" is first of all a term belonging to that section of general public law which is neither strictly national nor strictly international and which concerns the relations between a State, which is known to be one of the civilised States, and the uncivilised tribes that it has under its sovereignty. Aborigines and colonists must be distinguished, these last including the citizens of civilised States living in the region. The relations of aborigines between themselves, with colonists and with the colonising State must necessarily become the object of a special regime established by the colonising State with the aim of preparing the aborigines for civilisation and of opening up the resources of the country for the use of the civilised world [. . .]' (ibid., p. 4).

3. Snow rightly notes that his work (commissioned by the Department of State on 29 April 1918) is novel, and specifies that he: 'found no treatise on the question, not even a chapter in a work on international law which would have served as a model. He was therefore obliged to develop the subject and put together texts and documents according to his own judgement.' Snow discharged his task remarkably well: his work is extremely rich not only in the quality of documentary sources that he brings together (nineteenth-century government and administrative sources, both French and British) but also in the analyses that he offers.

Three constitutive elements of the being of the aborigine must be emphasized. The first is that the aboriginal horde is not civilized (a-morality); the second
is that the aborigine is not a citizen(a-civility);[5] finally the category of the aborigine is a category of the law of peoples—*jus gentium*—or, rather, of international
law—*jus inter gentes*—in that it founds sovereignty as a principle of domination
and discrimination. This last point is crucial because it provides the basis that differentiates the modern morality of the people (the sovereign people) from the
behaviour of the uncivil horde, or uncivilized 'savage race'. Just as the 'people' presupposes the real or symbolic annihilation of the tribe or horde, so also the 'civilized' presupposes the annihilation of the savage, those living in the *state of nature*.
It is in this sense that the thematic of the aborigine is essential to the modern constitution of morality. The aborigine found most notably in the American Indies,
but also on the islands of the Pacific, in Africa and Australia, offers the paradigmatic figure of the savage, whether noble or evil. This multitudinous figure
allowed the Europeans to understand themselves as belonging to the moral regime
of *civil life*. The savages, by contrast, belonged fundamentally to the realm of nature,
even if they possessed some trace of civilization attesting to a minimal social order
or even law—even if those morals were not those of a civilized people.

The emergence of the people by the negation of the aborigine comes about
firstly by the perception of an essential state of incivility, whose criterion it is
important to emphasize. This is found in an equation which is absent in the aborigine but present in the conqueror—civilized people = Christian people. The
place of savagery, the mark of nature in the aborigine, is that he is heathen. It is
always baptism and participation in Christian values that attest to the humanity of
a people and the civilization of its morals. The word 'aborigine' itself indicates this

4. According to the *New Standard Dictionary*, 1913.
5. See NOTE 2: the aborigine must be distinguished from the colonist.

heathen condition—a condition, which can nevertheless evolve into proper faith. But this is what is connoted by its systematic use in the official juridico-political documents and texts of the colonial powers. The word definitively entered the diplomatic vocabulary of international law in 1837, in a British report that William Gladstone put together for the Select Committee on Aboriginal Tribes that the House of Commons established to scrutinize colonial affairs. Before this date, Snow remarks, the term 'aborigine' was used only sporadically and designated 'the native uncivilized individuals of a territory in a determinate region'. Following Gladstone's report, the word became the legal term in use in legal and diplomatic depositions with which the civilized States of Europe dealt with uncivilized tribes or hordes. It is within this context of semantic fixation that we find the equation civilization = conversion to Christianity. Gladstone writes that the Select Committee was authorized

> to evaluate all the measures that need to be taken with regard to the native inhabitants of the countries where British positions are established and the neighbouring tribes, with the aim of assuring for them the proper observation of justice and the protection of their rights, the promotion of the propagation of civilization amongst them and leading them to receive the Christian religion peacefully and voluntarily.[6]

The Select Committee claimed that the 'aboriginal question' did not just involve the national interest of each of the colonizing States. On the contrary, it was a question posed at an international level because it involved common regulations for all the civilized Christian States, notably those concerning the protection of savage peoples affected by contact with those States. Both parties had rights and duties, and it is precisely in order to determine these that the 'aborigi-

6. Snow, *The Question of the Aborigines*, pp. 8–9.

nal question' was posed within the framework of the law of peoples. This is why the definition of the aborigine is worked out with extreme precision and a series of semantic equivalents is established[7] within the texts. All of them have the same sense and define the same moral and political problematic whose aim is, where possible, to elevate the indigenous tribes to the knowledge and practice of Christian virtues. However, as we will see, this moral transfiguration is not simply a goal in itself, because the transfiguration of the natives into a civilized people is, first of all, linked to the interests of the civilized State—the exploitation of the wealth of the territory and its occupation by that State's nationals.

However, we need to continue Gladstone's exploration of what is involved in civilizing the natives, that is, of civilizing them by converting them to Christianity. In his report we read:

We must be attentive to the effect of equitable exchanges and Christian education on the heathens. Unfortunately, if examples in this sense are less numerous than the contrary ones, they are no less significant. And if we consider the examples before us, we will have the proof that every human tribe is open to the remedy and that, in reality, if the latter has been only partially applied, its benefit has been received in every part of the world. So that, if the greater part of the available elements attest to the ravages caused by the Europeans, we have seen enough to show that these nations whom we have contaminated at the same time, have been led to religion and civilization. Independent of our obligation of conscience to transmit the benefits that we enjoy, there is abundant evidence that it is greatly to our advantage to find agreement with the civilized rather than with the barbarous. The savages make dangerous neighbours

7. 'Aborigines' (for which, Snow tells us, the French use *indigènes*) are equivalent to the following: 'savages', 'barbarous peoples', 'heathens', 'uncivilised nations', 'tribes', natives' (ibid., p. 10).

and consumers who bring little profit and if they remain in the state of under-evolved inhabitants of our colonies they will become a burden on the State. We must once more express our conviction that there is an efficient means to put an end to the morals that we have brought about and to spread the benefits of civilization: it is a matter of the propagation of Christianity along with the future protection of the civil rights of the natives. We have observed that simple encounters with the civilized prepare the savages for the reception of the Christian faith and for that kind of civilization that can only be to their advantage and to ours. Once more we see the evidence that good attempts are made to instruct the savages in the arts of the civilized life, with the aim of bettering their condition and of leading tem gradually to the truths of the Gospel.[8]

If the ideology of civilization is inseparable from the Christian moralization of the aboriginal, civilization is nevertheless substantially related to the material conquest of the *extension* (*of the land*) and the submission of the tribes *found* there.

Wilderness

The morality of modern States begins and is consolidated in the European project of dominating the wild extension of the *orbis* and of making it, and the populations who live there, their sovereign territory. In so doing they transfigure the

8. Ibid., p. 11. However, certain 'savage races' are not amenable to being led to civilization. Such are the aborigines of Australia, who, according to an official report submitted in 1840 to the British Prime Minister, are not capable of being civilized although they are 'as intelligent and capable as any other human race'. And the report continues: 'They are subject to the same feelings and the same desires and passions as other men: nevertheless because of numerous aspects of their personality, they are totally different to the others. And if we consider the particularity of their laws, it seems not only impossible for any nation submitted to them to rise above the savage state, and no race, however gifted and civilised it be, could long remain in a civilised state were it submitted to the dispositions of such barbarous customs' (ibid., p. 209).

orbis into world and found the morality of modernity. What we call 'civilization' is this process of the moralization of extension, the passage from *wilderness* to the world, the transfiguration of the savage into the civilized and of congeries of tribes into a people. The wilderness, savage and desert extension, is hardly without inhabitants; on the contrary, it is inhabited but, for the conquerors, the people who live there are themselves an element of the wilderness, merely a modality of the *res extensa*. Modern philosophy in describing their condition as that of life in a state of nature produces the concept of the aborigine considered from the European civilized point of view. In this perspective, the colonial model of the aborigine serves philosophy as the element with which it founds the central concept of morality, *sovereignty*, and the figure who bears that morality, the *people*. The people is the historial agent par excellence, the moral body that is constituted by negation of natural extension. It is what Rousseau, expressing an ideal version of the moral sense of the Moderns, closer to its principle and essence, understands as the *common self* which is a *moral self*. It is, properly, the living soul of the modern world, the site from which its rule and law are enunciated.

From this point of view, the *people* and *extension* are the two pillars of the modern historial—its conditions of possibility. It is through them that spirit comes to the Moderns and the *orbis* is transfigured into world. Unsurprisingly, therefore, Rousseau, following in the tradition that stems from Vitoria and Suárez, but expressing the matter in his own inimitable style, devotes three chapters of his *Social Contract* to the elucidation of the nature of a *people*, and he begins with the problem we are familiar with: *What people, then, is a fit subject for legislation?* This question—which haunts modernity—bears on the *capacity* of any multitude to accede to government by law. Since for Rousseau the law is the *general will*, the people must be constituted for there to be law at all, because, as we know, the general will *is* the will of the people. Behind the question of the possibility of the law, therefore, lies the question of the sovereign, since the people is the sovereign and sovereignty is the *thought* of the people that thinks, and what is important is that the people exist. To make *the* people exist means to differentiate it from *a* people (tribes or multitude). So before the contract or pact can be formed in the primitive clearings of Modern Times, the originary number—the multitude—must be unified somewhere in extension. In other words, material conditions are necessary for the people to be able to pronounce on the nature of the law and so engage in policed life. First, human animals have to be fit subjects for legislation. Then a part of the *res extensa* must be determined as the terrain and territory of their existence. Rousseau's originality lies not so much in the discovery of these givens of civil life but in the statement of what is the essence of the people so constituted—the *moral self*. For Rousseau, the subjectivity that is common to a multitude which has become a people can only be conceived and historically experienced if there is a proper proportion between the *number* of a people and the *extension* of its territory. Territorial expansion is at the heart of the modern invention of the people. It structures the thought of the people as sovereignty and the historical being of the people as sovereign.

We are right to understand the modern State as territoriality. On the other hand, what is not stressed is that the State constitution of extension requires as its very condition of possibility the problematic of the aborigine without which Rousseau's *moral self* would not exist. Modern politico-moral philosophy articulates a theory of *contract* according to which human beings in a state of nature associate with one another by leaving that state to pass into civil and political society. But this philosophical figure would be incomprehensible if, following the indications of the authors themselves, we tried to see it as a simple speculative form, without historical reality, that sought to grasp the origin of the State of sovereignty. On the contrary, to grasp its profound significance, it is a matter of relating the contractual model to aboriginism, which means that there cannot be a single philosophical discourse of sovereignty offering a logical account rather than an historical one. However, in reducing history to the logic of the concept, philosophical logic does not grasp the concept of that history. Instead, we have the idea that savages engaged in the business of survival abandon their savagery because they intellectually prefer to preserve their life in association rather than be exterminated. But this idea simply masks aboriginism by (natural) law and right and, additionally, by the apparent miracle of law and right working together and thus rendering the passage from nature to history possible. In other words, philosophy speaks about contract at the very sites of temporal and spiritual conquest.

If no modern philosopher of natural law has escaped this substitution of contract for conquest,[9] this is because this substitution *is* modernity itself, with the people as its spirit and extension (*wilderness*) as its material. As Rousseau clearly saw, the sovereign, that is to say, *the people*, is this alloy of material and spirit which forms the platform of the morality of Modern Times: 'It may be added that there have been known States so constituted that the necessity of making conquests entered into their very constitution, and that in order to maintain themselves, they were forced to expand ceaselessly.'[10] The *necessity of conquest* is linked to (and justified by) the obligation imposed by natural law on every individual, whether singular or collective, to preserve his life—*to maintain himself in being*. Nevertheless, this does not appear as the substance of the social contract (or pact) proper to philosophy, since the philosophical schema consists, precisely, in replacing it by the

9. Which obviously does not mean that philosophers and theorists ignore conquest; not only do they not ignore it, but, with very few exceptions (Pufendorf) they also justify it. From Grotius through Locke to Vattel, the *liberalism* of the Moderns consists in appropriating lands and extending their sovereignty over the human beings living there, when the latter are not exterminated or reduced to slavery.

10. Rousseau, *The Social Contract*, Book 2, Chapter 9, p. 221.

logic of contractualism. In other words, it is philosophical logic that constructs the notion of *natural law*; in substituting the contract for conquest, it presents the contract as the form of the origin of sovereignty. If aboriginism is absent from the philosophy of natural law, it is in order to separate conquest from the constitutive act of the people—with the latter being 'instituted' by a willed agreement. If *self-preservation*—the essence of natural law for the Moderns—is always present, regardless of its modes, as the *motive* for the contract. On the other hand the means of effecting self-preservation, that is conquest, is always absent. The latter is never evoked by the philosophy of natural law when it deals with the contractual origins of the sovereign State; it is only evoked as a crucial issue of colonization in the theoretical and practical context of the *jus gentium*. More broadly, it becomes the object of a debate on the question of war and peace between sovereign States constituted concurrently by the acquisition of newly discovered territories and the subjection of the aborigines found there. This is the keystone of modern natural law— conquest and its acknowledged necessity, stated philosophically in the form of the substitution of contract for conquest, or, what amounts to the same thing, the substitution of the (sovereign) people for the aboriginal tribes.

The genealogy of morality is thus linked to the development of the natural law of self-preservation, the natural law of conquest. It is because this law has substantial significance only in the historical and philosophical context of aboriginism that it inspires the modern invention of the 'people'. At the same time, sovereignty as the form that gives being to the State (Loyseau) and the 'definition' of the modern *res publica* (Bodin) reveals its essence—it is the *form of individuation of historical peoples*. Being this very form, sovereignty must be understood as the element of morality of which the people is the agent.

It is within the context of aboriginism that we can reflect on the reference to natural law as it is constructed by modern philosophy—every being has by nature the right to act so as to preserve itself. Its liberty here is total, and merely responds to the obligation that this same nature imposes, that of staying alive. In this sense, nothing distinguishes a people from a single individual; both are agents whose *freedom* is dependent on a kind of equilibrium which they must establish between, on the one hand, the law which constrains self-preservation, and, on the other, the law which opens up the limitless sphere of the means for that self-preservation. The freedom of the people is, in fact, what Rousseau has in mind when he asserts that constituted States are led to 'the necessity of conquests', so much so that this becomes a part of their very constitution. What is the State, then? It is the people organized—unified—into a moral body, the people as a *moral self*. The necessity for conquest, then, is at the heart of morality because freedom hangs upon this necessity. If we follow Rousseau, then the formula for the freedom of the people is to be found in the appropriation of extension, an appropriation that cannot come to fruition without the subjection of the aborigine to the plans of the conquering people. It is, says Rousseau, a matter of finding the right relation between the number of the people and (its) extension. To institute a people, that is, to consti-tute it as a free (collective) individual, is to establish such a relationship without which the sovereignty of the people would be illusory and the existence of the lat-ter 'short and uncertain'. The modern appearance of the sovereign people presup-poses a just appreciation of necessity, which involves conquest, if required.

Rousseau elaborates the paradigmatic figure of morality better than any other modern philosopher, when he produces the axiom: people = sovereign. This is also why, in inventing the people that would accommodate modern natural law, he finds in the relationship between number and extension—people with territory—the key to the 'force' of the sovereign, or, better, sovereignty as force. There are all sorts of conditions for 'instituting a people', he says, and the aim of this institution is to confer on the sovereign figure 'the maximum of force'. Rousseau thus does not escape from the model of the natural right to self-preservation, substantially linked to aboriginism, and constructs the 'people' by reference to conquest:

> A body politic may be measured in two ways—either by the extent of its territory, or by the number of its people, and there is between these two measurements, a right relation which makes the State really great. The men make the State and the territory sustains the men; the right relation therefore is that the land should suffice for the maintenance of its inhabitants, and that there should be as many inhabitants as the land can maintain. In this proportion lies the maximum strength of a given number of people; for if there is too much land, it is troublesome to guard and inadequately cultivated, produces more than is needed, and soon gives rise to wars of defence; if there is not enough, the State depends on its neighbours for what it needs over and above, and this soon gives rise to wars of offence. Every people, to which its situation gives no choice save that between commerce and war, is weak in itself: it depends on its neighbours and on circumstances, its situation can never be more than short and uncertain. Either it conquers others and changes its situation, or it is conquered and becomes nothing. Only insignificance or greatness can keep it free.[11]

It is quite remarkable that Rousseau determines the condition of a people that 'keep[s] it free' as that of the right to self-preservation that belongs to every living creature in nature. If the people in the State are not comfortable in a territory, that is, if there is not enough for an adequate life, then it has no choice but to subjugate or be subjugated—onquer or be conquered. Thus self-preservation refers back to the freedom (or autonomy) by which a people exists as a people, in 'great-

11. Ibid., Book 2, Chapter 10, p. 222.

ness', legislating itself through its own law—if necessary by imposing its freedom on others. The theme of conquest is thus not incidental but a necessity emerging from the very constitution of the State, from the very act by which a people becomes a people. But, in Rousseau's language, 'the act by which a people becomes a people' is the social contract itself, and this is the case in every contractualist theory which distinguishes the natural multitude (the aborigine) from the instituted people. It is only the rhetorical device of 'natural law'—the right to preserve my life—that allows philosophy to posit the existence of a contract without making the place of conquest explicit or even by considering conquest as a contract! In fact, what philosophy calls 'contract' is, rather, as I have already pointed out, a substitution for conquest, so that the people can only assert themselves through an 'act' which *necessarily* places them in relations of conflict (war) and exchange (trade) with another people. But this other people is not a 'people' because its territory and wealth are coveted; it is not seen as a people by the aggressor, but only as a horde of aboriginal tribes, a pack of savages. When they are defeated, they will submit to the domination of the victor and will be deprived of their goods, and, in the first instance, their territory. But the conqueror, precisely because he is thrown into the conquest of the other, is no longer really constituted; if he were—that is if he were 'free' and therefore sovereign—he would not suffer 'the necessity for conquest' as Rousseau says. This shows that what is at stake for the two sides—victor and defeated—is the very being of the 'people' and of its corollary, the State. In other words, the people is instituted as people only through the relationship that it establishes with another people—the people only exists in the theoretical context of the *jus gentium*, and in the historical context of the colonial conquest by which modern Europeans have transfigured the *orbis* into world, their world.

The 'Perfect Right' *of Peoples*

The philosophical element of this transfiguration is the conceptual system of natural law, that is, the thinking through of the eminently modern principle of self-preservation without which sovereignty, understood here as the form of individuation of the 'people', is impossible. With respect to our question here—that is, how *the* people is thought of as *this* people—one of the essential tendencies of modernity is to refer to the 'natural law' by which every natural creature is constrained to preserve its own life, its being, a constraint that is inscribed within the very order of nature to which everything is subject by the simple fact of *being*. In this sense, nature itself wishes there to be a common order of nations (peoples) such that the society that these nations form gives rise to an ensemble of laws and duties that affects each of them, without exception. An excellent example of this tradition is Emmer de Vattel. His importance has less to do with the originality of his thought[12] than with the extraordinary fortunes of the work that interests us here—*Le Droit des gens* (*The Law of Nations*, 1758), which became a required reference for the historical constitution of international law after it came out.[13] Vattel's first postulate posits the exis-

---

12. Vattel was content to give (elegant) shape to a tradition that began with Vitoria, was systematically constructed from Grotius to Pufendorf, but was not for all that absolutely homogeneous.

13. Emmer de Vattel, *Le Droit des gens, ou Principes de la Loi naturelle, Appliqués à la Conduite et aux affaires des Nations et des Souverains* (*The Law of Nations: or, Principles of the Law of Nature, Applied to the Conduct and Affairs of Nations and Sovereigns*) (Geneva: Slatkine, 1983 [1758]). With more than 25 impressions in French, the work has been translated into German (2 editions), English (13 in Great Britain, 12 in the United States), Spanish (7), Greek (2), Italian (2), Polish and Japanese. Benjamin Franklin said of it (letter of 19 December 1775 to Charles W. F. Dumas, Vattel's American publisher): 'I am very obliged to you for the charming present that you made of the edition of Vattel. It arrived at a good moment, while the circumstances of a nascent State make necessary frequent consultations on the Law of Peoples. In consequence the copy that I have preserved [. . .] has been continually in the hands of members of our Congress which is currently sitting, and who are very happy with your notes and preface, and entertain a high and just esteem for their author.' Cited by James Brown Scott, series editor of *Classics of International Law*, in which Vattel's work appeared in NO. 3 as *The Law of Nations or Principles of Natural Law*, 3 VOLS (Washington DC: Carnegie Institute, 1916), VOL. 3, p. viii.

tence of a 'Nature' not otherwise defined. From this he deduces a 'General Law' of sociability among human beings: 'each feels within himself that he cannot live happily and work to perfection without the help and commerce of others. Given that Nature has made men such, it is a manifest sign that she destined them to converse together, to help and mutually secure each other'. 'Nature' refers to that determination by which human beings assist each other in need, and hence form societies. From this follows the statement of the 'General Law': 'Let each man do for others what they have need of and that he can do without neglecting what he owes to himself'.[14] The 'Common Creator', the instigator of the designs of nature and its order, has thus arranged things so that necessity impels men to associate. This association or, as Vattel says, the 'universal Society of Humankind' manifests itself in the union of the individuals of a people into civil society with the aim of forming a State, a 'Nation apart'. This union of individuals, united in and through necessity is a source of obligations between members of the same union. But, above all, the individuals remain subject to the obligations that they have towards the rest of humankind as a consequence of the 'Institution of Nature'. Appropriating the 'natural law' tradition, Vattel claims that individuals have 'handed over their rights and given their will to the Body of Society' and henceforth this society has duties towards other societies:

> This society considered as a moral person since it has its own understanding, will and force, is thus obliged to live with other Societies, or States, as a man was obliged before these Establishments to live with other men, that is following the Laws of Natural Society established among Humankind: in observing the exceptions that can emerge from the difference between subjects.[15]

14. Ibid., Section 10, p. 6.
15. We can observe in Vattel's passage that he is saying nothing at all new, but is making an adroit synthesis of fundamental principles of modern natural law, taking the part of those who hold that the tendency of human beings is to associate into a body politic, and he shows himself here

Modern morality, that is, the system of rights and duties of a social body, understood as in Rousseau as a common self, that is, a *moral self*, proceeds from the voluntary association of individuals, who, having handed over their 'force' to the entire body, form a particular people (or a nation) led by the sovereign State. The connection between morality and sovereignty produces a moral particularism that no instituted people can or should escape from. This is the significance of this 'Universal Society of Humankind', as Vattel calls it. Hence, the question posed is this: *What is the aim of this society of nations?* Vattel's answer to the question he himself formulates reveals the historical and philosophical horizon within which the Moderns have determined their concept of the 'sovereign people'. This horizon is given by the *jus gentium* (hence the title of Vattel's work), so that, as we have seen, philosophically the fiction of the social contract or pact disguises as an agreement of wills what, historically, is the differentiation of peoples or nations through a process of conflict. In this process, some peoples constitute their territory (that is, draw frontiers), proclaim their sovereignty (institute their State) and, finally, found their own particular morality (their Law and their laws) within a society of nations that the Law of Peoples regulates according to the dispositions of 'Nature'. In other words, the genesis of the people refers less to a work of self-foundation by which individuals unite their multiple wills into a *single* will, than to a regulated division (usually by force) of humanity in the *orbis* into a multiplicity of sovereign peoples.

to be a disciple of Pufendorf and of his remarkable theory of 'moral beings', according to which the State is a moral person which contains all the rest such that State sovereignty is like something that acts as a support for the will: 'Bodily substances', writes Pufendorf, 'necessarily presuppose a Space, where they place their existence, so to speak, and exercise their physical movements: we also say that *Moral Persons* are in a certain *State*, in which we conceive them as contained to deploy their actions and produce their effects. We could thus define the State as a *Moral Being which supports the others*' (*Le Droit de la nature et des gens*, I, 7, Section 3 [Caen: Université de Caen, 1989; originally publsihed in 1732]). On the significance of this theory in regard to sovereignty, see my *Le Dieu mortel*, pp. 88ff.

It is the form of this process of *division* (not union) that Vattel reveals in the *Droit des gens* as he discusses the aim of natural society, a discussion in which the author unwittingly inverts the historical to the benefit of the historial—the substitution of contract for conquest through the thematic of self-preservation. We read: 'The first General Law, which the very aim of the Society of Nations reveals to us, is that each Nation must contribute to the happiness and perfection of the rest with everything in its power.'[16] 'Perfection' must be understood here as the capacity for autonomy, independence from external influences and internal self-sufficiency with regard to needs. So it must be understood that it is the duty of every people or nation to assist its neighbour to allow it to attain happiness and perfection. Assistance being mutual, each and every nation benefits from it. This is the natural game of nature, if we can put it like that—by helping our neighbour we help ourselves. Put another way, the particular constitution of a people as a moral self requires communication with others, with another moral self and in this exchange or 'commerce' the designs of nature are manifested. So that the aim of nature in arousing *via* necessity and need the 'Universal Society of Humankind' is to allow the constitution of particular peoples or nations. This is what stands out from the explanation of this 'first General Law':

> But given that its duties towards itself bear incontestably on its duties towards others, a Nation owes first and foremost to itself everything that it can do for its happiness and perfection. (I say what it can do, not just physically but also morally, that is to say what it can do legitimately, in all justice and honesty.) For when it cannot contribute to the good of another without essentially damaging itself, its obligation ceases and the Nation is absolved from rendering this office.[17]

16. Vattel, *Le Droit des gens*, Section 13, p. 8.
17. Ibid., Section 14, p. 9.

Morality presupposes as its very condition the subjection of the duty of assistance to the other to the prior duty of self-preservation. So altruism is dependent on the egotism of nations.

One might use Vattel's account of the law of peoples to claim that it is only already constituted peoples and nations who communicate through commerce or force. Hence, one cannot say (as I do here) that the general context of the emergence of the sovereign people is the philosophical substitution of contract for conquest, since the historical condition of conquest is that peoples and nations are *already* established in a State. That would be to forget what is essential to Vattel's teaching—the *law* of a people is to conquer, so long as it maintains its obligation to *self*-preservation. In other words, in what he calls the *perfect right* of conquest— by force—the self-constitution of a people works according to the law of peoples. This thesis prepares the second 'General Law'. 'Nations being free and independent from one another', Vattel writes,

> since men are naturally free and independent, the second General Law of their Society is that each Nation must be left in peace to enjoy this Freedom, which it holds from Nature. The Natural Society of Nations cannot subsist if the Rights that each have received from Nature are not respected. No Nation wishes to renounce its Freedom, and it will break off all commerce with those try to make it do so.[18]

Through the second 'General Law', nature has conferred 'rights' on each nation (just as on each individual) such that none can renounce without renouncing their own preservation. This has the consequence that the 'commerce' which nature has organized with the aim of human beings mutually assisting each other, cannot be stopped by a nation without contravening the law of peoples—and its

18. Ibid., Section 15, p. 9.

fundamental obligations of assistance. It is because the freedom at issue cannot be denied without destroying that same law of peoples. Thus we are faced with an apparent impasse—nature puts an obligation on nation (A) to help another (B) to arrive at 'perfection' and 'happiness', but this obligation might be contrary to the freedom of that nation not to assist its neighbour, if coming to the aid of B endangers the capacity of A to preserve itself and to provide for its own happiness.

This dilemma might be an impasse in the law of peoples if Vattel did not introduce rhetorically the notion of '*perfect right*'. 'Perfect right' has to be understood as 'the right to constrain those who do not wish to satisfy the obligation that falls upon them'.[19] The principle of 'perfect right' is applicable if an obligation (which is the obverse of a right) is not respected. Thus perfect right is the right to constrain an individual, singular or collective, if he/they do not submit to their obligations as agents of the 'Universal Society of Humankind'. In fact, what is at issue is a right which produces effects within the sphere of nations, that is, of moral persons. In this sense, it is an essential element of the apparatus of morality that 'Nature' establishes within the framework of the law of peoples. This refers back to the juridical material that 'Nature' puts at the disposal of peoples in formation so that they are constituted into particular sovereign States. Here we are at the heart of what natural law calls *contract*. For there to be a contract, however, there has to be equality between the contracting parties. Up to now in the schema of 'perfect right' that Vattel has outlined, we have only the game of rights and obligations or duties that correspond to them and the assertion of the freedom of nations within the 'Society of Nations' of the *orbis*. For the rhetoric of contract to confer the appearance of reality on this, it is necessary for nations not only to be declared 'free' but also to be declared *equal*. In effect, there is a disposition of nature that, having made individuals equal, similarly anticipates the equality of nations:

19. Ibid., Section 17, p. 10.

Since men are naturally equal, and their rights and obligations are the same, stemming equally from Nature, Nations composed of men and considered as free persons who live together in the state of Nature, are naturally equal and have from Nature the same obligations and the same rights. In this regard, power or weakness makes no difference. A dwarf is as much a man as a Giant: a small Republic is no less a sovereign State than the most powerful Kingdom.[20]

This proclamation of equality, where the strong is the equal of the weak, is a fundamental and foundational principle of the traditional law of peoples and international law. The formal equality of sovereignties with each other in principle is not up for discussion, and Vattel, like his predecessors, does not dispute it. Precisely because nations are protected by the law of peoples which renders them at once free and equal, a powerful sovereign state is excluded from legally appropriating and subjugating a weaker sovereign, just because it has the power to do so. Moreover, if a nation is weak, there might be an *obligation* on the stronger nation to support the weaker in its efforts at self-preservation which it is subject to like the rest. But a nation respects this obligation, if, and only if, it does not contradict the freedom to appropriate by force another's territory and the wealth found there, should this appropriation be necessitated by the regulatory principle on which the whole edifice depends—self-preservation.

This is in fact what has taken place in modern history. The law of peoples, which was recognized in the late Middle Ages and revived in the period of the conquest of the New World and the formation of empires, is altogether constructed from the perspective of the appropriation of new territories and their wealth by the dominant European powers. The *jus gentium* gives way to a *jus inter gentes* and

20. Ibid., Section 18, p. 12.

international law, that is, a an inter-state law, since it tries to establish the rules by which European States are constituted as colonial powers. The most percipient historians of the formation of international law[21] have seen its foundations in the discussions of the 'Second Scholasticism', that is, the utilization of Thomas Aquinas in the juridical and political elaboration of the justification of conquest. But the real birth of the modern law of peoples, they claim, happens with Gentili and Grotius, and the latter gives the most systematic elaboration of the *jus gentium* since he rigorously constructs its basis in sovereignty. Nevertheless, Gentili's removal of any theological reference in thinking through the *jus gentium* is crucial; this effects the modern revolution which shifts the foundation of law, all law, from God to the people, that species of terrestrial god. That is why the *people* become, as we have already said, the central figure of morality; consequently, the law of peoples cannot escape its empire, and with good reason—in theoretical mode, it accompanies the historical formation of modern 'peoples'. Henceforth, it is the will of nations (peoples) which orders the *orbis* to produce a *world*. And the morality of this world, like its geometry, is not an affair of a god but of men. The 'Natural Law' invoked by men like Vattel is defined by philosophy not theology— it aims to produce a world according to a profane plan and to recognize an order within the history that is being played out at the very time when philosophy is producing its definitions. It is a matter of the sovereign order of the world, whose agent is the people. This is what the genealogy of morals reveals: at the very moment when the colonial question is posed and with it the absolute *simultaneity*

21. On this subject, see the fundamental work of Richard Tuck, *The Rights of War and Peace: Political Thought and the International Order from Grotius to Kant* (Oxford: Oxford University Press, 1999), which renews in a profound way the understanding of modern natural law; and Anthony Pagden's 'Dispossessing the Barbarian: the Language of Spanish Thomism and the Debate over the Property Rights of the American Indians' in Pagden (ed.), *The Languages of Political Theory in Early Modern Europe* (Cambridge: Cambridge University Press, 1987), pp. 79–98.

of the double genesis of the modern State—internally and externally—the people in sovereignty appear to replace the aboriginal multitudes of the Old and New Worlds. From the sixteenth century onwards there is a division of the multitude, which gives birth, slowly but irresistibly, to our own peoples and nations. An order of sovereignties is put in place whose profound significance is the self-constitution of each of the modern nations and peoples. It is the emergence and development of *common selves* philosophically reflected on as *moral selves*, the vast historical and philosophical process of the individuation of historical peoples. It is remarkable that the modern revolution, in engendering some peoples, permitted others to be exterminated through legal conquest. So that here we see the aborigine as the negative of the people, the savage as the negative of the civilized man, the Indian as the negative of the European. From this perspective, Vattel's vast treatise reveals the modern negativity through which the individuation of historical peoples was effected.

This modern process of negation, realized in the production of nations and the genesis of historical peoples, constitutes the essence of sovereignty and its order in the world as world. Or, rather, it reaches its culmination in Europe. To properly grasp its profound significance and reason, we must continue to examine the genealogy of morality that is embodied in the *people* as understood by modern understanding: the very body of morality, the people as *moral body*. This is to go back to its origin, to what makes any morality possible by the very negation of what is opposed to it—natural man, the aborigine.

Modern Negativity

We can in no way understand how the modern 'people' comes to be the leading actor in morality (for, as we have just said, it is its embodiment) if we do not see it as the site of an abstract 'general will' and the author of the law, in other words, if we restrict 'the people' to being nothing other than a figure of practical political rhetoric. However, if the people, in the sovereign State, is the ultimate subject of *thought*, it is because morality is the thought of a civil, juridical and political order that only a subject liberated from pure nature, that is, a subject emancipated from the *res extensa*, can conceive, and precisely, *will* in its truth. The will of the people presents itself as the truth of the profane State. The order of morality that the people establish is only the will of the general (as Rousseau puts it) since it proceeds from the negation of the particular and only the people can be sufficiently radical. If the people in sovereignty *is* the body of the generality—the only agent capable of a *thought* of the universal—it is because its being is the negation of the singular, the very particularity of a *natural* people: the aborigine in person.

We thus have to understand the modern notion of the people through the modern determinations of the historial: to relate the idea of the 'people' to the constraints (*nécessités*), so to speak, of the *world spirit*. For spirit to rise above extension, it is important that the natural human animal—the original savage—be elevated above given nature, something that can only be carried out by the transfiguration of the savage into the civilized man. Or, put another way, by his abandoning his primitive animality. Such an abandonment is figured by philosophy as the passage from nature to the city, the passage of the multitude to the city. *Spirit*, in effect, does not come to the savage multitude solely through the virtue of nature. On the contrary, spirit is anti-nature—it is negativity itself at work, the sign of the human in the animal. There is no spirit in nature, which is why the Moderns find only the multitude there and not the people. We have seen[22] that the historial always proceeds from a certain relation to the origin, a relationship through which human beings construct their present and future. That is why the thought of the people—which is the people as *thought* (will, which is law)—

22. See section entitled 'The Origin' in Chapter 2 in this volume.

necessarily moves by reference to the aborigine, that other of the people: if the origin is present in the people, it is precisely in the explicit form of its negation. Accordingly, a *meaningful work* is possible which the Moderns thematize as the *work of civilization.*[23] The historial construction of the people, its advent as living body of spirit, requires the original animal to be relieved of its given natural being. This can only be carried out in one of two ways: either education into the world spirit or exclusion from the world spirit, in other words extermination. *Education* or *extermination* are the alternatives of the modern historial from the point of view of the foundation of peoples and the advent of nations as the Europe of modernity has produced them in the course of the process called 'history'.

We can see that the notion of the 'people' is absolutely crucial to the modern landscape of morality. It is its substrate, because the people becomes in substance what it *thinks*. To think morality—and to live morally—is to think what the people think and to live according to the will of the people. This thought and this life are politics itself. Being the fabrication of the world of morality, there is only political life in reference to the spirit of a people, if one holds at least to the sovereign order of the world as conceived and constructed by modern Europeans. However, it would be wrong to think that the historial constitution of the people only referred to the historical period of the conquest, to the colonial period of empires whose construction saw the extermination of the aboriginal peoples, or, at best, their *dressage* with a view to christianizing their morals. On the contrary, the moral idea of the Moderns as elaborated within the principle of sovereignty (understood as the principle of individuation) also involves the contemporary negation of the aborigine, or, of his updated figure, the foreigner. There is no 'people' that is homogeneous and absolutely *one*. The people is the foundational fic-

---

23. A work which includes the conversion of the aboriginal tribes to Christianity, as we have seen.

tion of the sovereign order of the world because it is the (fictional) subject of morality, the permanent artifice, ceaselessly recreated. In it, the multitude is defined and thought not as that multitude—*number*—but as people, that is a *transcendental unity* which defines a border and characterizes the radically foreign, so that total alterity provokes extermination. European modernity testifies to this. The modern historial constitution of the people does not designate a situation that is over and done with, one in which peoples and nations have been individualized into definitive, homogeneous entities, which are absolutely one and perfect, so that our period no longer witnesses exclusion or extermination. So it is useful to understand by *people* the moral body as it is philosophically conceived and politically lived in the historical order of sovereignty.

The self-constitution of a people, in other words the practical advent of the *common self*, is not the result of a spontaneous and total growth of a being whose every determination would be given *ab initio* in and through nature. There is no *spirit* in nature, we have said. The people of modern man is an artifice constructed all of a piece which emerges from a history that can only be apprehended by force. And this, in the context of sovereignty, is never anything but *spirit* coming to the 'people'. So what we call here the *historial people* is precisely this emergence, in the course of a 'history' of the subject of morality which thinks its own subjective individuality, its *self*, under the category of spirit. In this sense, the famous 'spirit of a people' is altogether paradoxical—it is a non-fictional fiction. It is a fiction because the people as subject is a (philosophical) fiction whose significance is to separate the multiple from the one, as you separate the wheat from the chaff. But it is not a fiction because it is lived as though it were real, as the very reality of the 'people', as its substance and character. The people thinks itself as the unity of a common self, so that the multiple is considered as what would destroy this very unity. This is the crucial meaning of the modern thematic of the contract—the reduction of the (natural) multiple to the (civil-moral) *one*. But this reduction[24] is never achieved, because the people never think that their unity is achieved and definitively constituted. The sense of self of a people that thinks its own identity pushes it to differentiate itself—by force if necessary—from its neighbour or in general from what it perceives as being a danger, a threat to its common *self*. To be fully understood, the modern people must be reflected on as this *one-multiple*, that is, as the tension between these two poles, which is permanent because always recreated. I set aside the question of knowing if such a tension, which produces force and violence, is *properly* modern, because it seems to me to be undecidable. On the other hand, we can make the following assertion: modern sovereignty is the principle of power, the means by which force and violence—even the conception and realization of extermination—have been the engines of individuation of historical peoples. The great *negativity* at work in modern history is the division of the European multitudes in order to think and establish themselves as people: they divide themselves from and oppose each other as they search for and discover their particular identities in the negation of other identities. The division of the great number is the very negativity of history, its essence, while unity is its result—an eminently paradoxical result because it is never attained in practice. *The one* is the fantasy of morality.

Properly viewed, then, sovereignty *is* negativity itself. The assertion of particularisms has been made possible through it. However, if the people think its identity in the form of the (particular) unity of a common self, it sees no contradiction in asserting its particularism in the form of the universal—only it (the people) can elevate itself to the consideration of the universal, which it expresses in the universality of the law. The permanent tension of the one and the multiple of which the (sovereign) people is the site produces the modern paradox—a particular peo-

24. Which I define elsewhere as the 'ordination of the multiple to the one'. See my *Dieu mortel*.

ple whose *spirit* is declared to be universal.[25] The experience of negativity is nowhere more advanced than in Europe, so that Europe alone comes to the knowledge of the historial, that is, to the knowledge of particularism which teaches peoples that they are only particular. It has been possible for Europe to come to such knowledge because of its experience of war in the twentieth century which, precisely in producing *world* wars, revealed to Europe that it had ceased to be the *world* and the embodiment of the universal.

It is thus philosophically *possible* that a return to the multiple might take place in Europe. If such a possibility exists,[26] it is because Europe has traversed the historical field of sovereignty, has experienced the negativity that made it possible inside and outside Europe, for organized peoples—who live according to the particular rules of their particular morality—to be constituted. Above all, it is because the peoples who compose Europe have attained—or at least this is the tendency of their present existence—*peace*. It is because they have renounced the negativity that belongs to sovereignty that the return to the multiple—to the *multitude*—can be thought philosophically. The condition of such a return (not to the natural multitude, but to the civil multitude) is that morality—the form of free and organized life—rest on some other foundation than that of the historial people.

Friday: the Nation's Ward

Modern negativity is the instrument of the historial, that mechanism of spirit which comes to the world through the people. The result of negativity is the passage from the *orbis* to the world—the European passage of sovereignty reflected on by the agents themselves as the transcendence of given nature and the eleva-

25. We know that the French Revolution, in contrast to those of England and America, claimed in its time to reveal to the *world* the historical model of moral universalism.
26. Which is the hypothesis this *Inquiry* is leading towards.

tion to spirit. The historial is the thought of a world as the world of spirit, whose agent is the people. The transfiguration of the *orbis* into world consists of the introduction of morality into extension; it is the passage of the *res extensa* to spirit. It is stated philosophically in the assertion of the reign of reason over brute materiality, in the declared superiority of calculation over *passions*. In the course of this process, Europeans divided themselves into particular peoples by the *education* (*dressage*) or the *extermination* of natural humanity.

Behind the invention of the 'sovereign people', we find the European adventure of *the conquest of peoples*. Undoubtedly we must see the model of conquest in Robinson Crusoe's fabulous adventure, that is to say, the threefold foundation of the *world* by Europeans: the discovery of virgin extension, the subjugation of the indigenous people found there and, finally, their colonization by sovereign empire. These three figures are exemplary of Europe's expedition beyond its borders and its fixing in an elsewhere that becomes what we call *world*. The *world* is in fact created by Crusoe, who fabricates it *with a view to his own preservation*— his island became his kingdom. Robinson will leave a *people* there after the extermination of the cannibal savages and the brigands—none of these can form the people of a republic. Once he gets over the misery of finding himself in the middle of extension as a result of some evil fate (or capricious god), Robinson gathers his forces together and begins to conceive of future projects:

> as soon as I saw but a Prospect of living and that I should not starve and perish for Hunger, all the Sense of my Affliction wore off, and I began to be very easy, apply'd myself to the Works proper for my Preservation and Supply, and was far enough from being afflicted as a Judgement from Heaven, or as the hand of God against me . . .[27]

27. Daniel Defoe, *The Life and Strange, Surprising Adventure of Robinson Crusoe of York, Mariner*, [. . .] *Written by Himself* (Oxford: Oxford University Press, World's Classics, 1983 [1719]). And Robinson later specifies: 'It is thus that I took for my Survival all the measures that Human

But though he had wanted to come across another human being for a long time, he is faced with a difficult test when he does so—these men, the natives of a neighbouring island, may not be absolutely human. When the cannibals arrive on his island to devour their victims, they inspire terror in Robinson but they also lead him to a fundamental consideration of justice. Like Job on his dung heap, Robinson perceives a strange human animality which makes him consider moral questions:

> What Authority, or Call, I had to pretend to be Judge and Executioner upon these Men as Criminals, whom Heaven had though fit for so many Ages to suffer unpunish'd, to go on and to be, as it were, the Executioners of his Judgements one upon another. How far these People were Offenders against me, and what Right I had to engage in the Quarrel of that Blood which they shed promiscuously one upon another . . . it is certain that these People do not commit this as a Crime, it is not against their own Consciences reproving or their Light reproaching them. They do not know it be an Offence, and then commit it in Defiance of Divine Justice, as we do in almost all the Sins we commit. They think it no more a Crime to kill a Captive taken in War, than we do to kill an Ox, nor to eat humane Flesh, than we do to eat Mutton.[28]

If Robinson refuses to wage war on the cannibals, it is only out of prudence:

> Upon the whole I concluded, That neither in Principle or in Policy, I ought one way or another to concern myself in this Affair. That my business was by all possible Means to conceal myself from them, and not to leave the least Signal to them to guess by, that there were any living Creatures upon the Island: I mean of humane Shape.[29]

Prudence could suggest and you will see in what follows that they were not entirely devoid of Reasons. I did not foresee however, anything more that might inspire Fear' (ibid., p. 140).
28. Ibid., pp. 171–2.
29. Ibid., pp. 172–3.

Nevertheless, if it is primarily the principle of *Preservation and Supply*, self-preservation, that prevents Robinson from waging war against the cannibals,[30] his encounter with a *natural man* brings together two beings who are utterly foreign to each other. On the one hand, Robinson is the embodiment of civilized man—Christian and calculating; on the other, Friday embodies man in the state of nature—cannibal, heathen and naked. Hence, the moment of their encounter, as Defoe writes it, is the subjugation of the savage to the civilized man. If Friday (a specifically *pagan* name because cosmologically *natural*) submits it is because—like Robinson elsewhere—he is afraid. What is common to them both, when they are together, and when in each other's presence again, is the fear of being killed. *Fear of death*, and the fact that a victorious Robinson spares Friday's life, become the two figures of the foundation of a social and domestic order that colonization will in time produce in the following forms: occupation of territory, its re-population, the development of stock-raising and agriculture and the exercise of sovereign authority. The last pages of the novel—which is more the narrative of the *fable* of the humane, English conquest of extension as opposed to the more vicious Spanish conquest—reveal a Robinson back on *his* island, that is, administrator of his 'empire'. No longer just as master but as sovereign and unleashing a policy of rationally regulated colonization. Robinson bids goodbye to the various survivors of the last combats on the island (reconciled English and Spanish pirates) and instructs them to multiply and increase the population and the goods of the land.[31]

30. Crusoe elsewhere seizes the occasion to recall that the *extermination* of the American Indians was the work of the Spanish, so that, for Robinson's part, the extermination of the cannibals would have been of the same nature: 'the rooting them out of the Country is spoken about with the utmost Detestation and Abhorrence by even the Spaniards themselves, at this time: and by all other Christian Nations of Europe, as a mere Butchery, a bloody and unnatural Piece of Cruelty, unjustifiable to God or Man' (ibid., p. 172).

31. 'From there I touched the *Brasils* from whence I sent a Bark, which I bought there, with more

The submission of the savage to the civilized man seems to be the alternative to extermination: the English method of conquest as opposed to that of the Spanish. In any case, what is essential here is that the mutual recognition of Robinson and Friday is not one between equals:

> [H]e came a little way and stopp'd again, and then a little further and stopp'd again, and I cou'd then perceive that he stood trembling, as if he had been taken Prisoner and had just been to be kill'd, as his two enemies were. I beckon'd him again to come to me, and gave him all the Signs of Encouragement I could think of, and he came nearer and nearer, kneeling down every Ten or Twelve steps in token of acknowledgement for my saving his life [. . .] and then he kneel'd down again, kiss'd the Ground, and laid his head upon the Ground, and taking me by the Foot, set my Foot upon his head: this it seems was in token of swearing to be my Slave for ever [. . .]32

In the process of 'recognition', two peoples (or nations, Defoe says) confront each other—one as master, the other as slave.

This is once more to take up the schema of *aboriginism* as the development of the law of peoples enacted in its most general tendency and inspiration—the European conquest of extension is required by the self-preservation of the peoples of Europe. If combat occurs, the aborigines lose their lives unless they submit to the conqueror, that is, accept their reduction to slavery. But the reduction of the defeated does not signify an absolute loss of freedom for them, because their con-

---

People to the Island, and in it, as well as other Supplies, I sent seven Women, being such as I found proper for Service, or for Wives to such as would have them. As to the *English Men*, I promised them to send them some Women from England, with a good Cargo of Necessaries, if they would apply themselves to Planting, which I afterwards perform'd' (ibid., p. 306).

32. Ibid., pp. 203–04.

dition as a conquered people means that, on the contrary, the victors have duties towards them. In the genesis of the morality of modern peoples—the conquerors—the education of the defeated is the consequence of, and in the end, the guarantee of the conquest and its success. It is by leading the conquered peoples to civilization (in other words, to 'the truths of the Gospel' and rational calculation) that the conquering people constitutes itself. Without the seizure of land, without the appropriation of an extension which is half empty of people and culture, the European peoples would not have constituted themselves: according to the very rationality of conquest (that is the *law of peoples*) Europeans undertook the colonization of the *orbis* and its fashioning into a world with the aim of their own constitution. In other words, according to this logic, the self-constitution of a people requires expansion abroad, which can only be achieved at the cost of the extermination of what is not itself, or at best its subjection. This means that there is no 'people' that exists in and for itself and has emerged completely fashioned from some place or other. The logic of the *world* is irresistibly that of conquest and submission, which leads Snow to state that, in the language of international law, the aborigines are the wards of the nations—they are considered *children*.[33]

Conquered peoples are like troupes of Fridays, and it is the *duty* of conquering nations to elevate them to culture and spirit by allowing them to break with the state of nature they find themselves in. The native must be understood as someone who is imperfectly human—the incompleteness of his humanity follows from his belonging to originary nature. This is not to say that he is without morals—it is to say that this (natural) morality is not the *good*. It is an immoral morality, because, as Robinson says of Friday and his fellow cannibals, *he does not know what evil is*. Undoubtedly, Robinson embodies a moral world while Friday, who eats his enemies, is the figure of immorality. He is totally other, so *other* that he returns

33. See Snow, 'Chapter 3: Aborigines as the Wards of the State Which Exercises Sovereignty Over Them' in *The Question of the Aborigines*, pp. 38–9.

Robinson's own image as a man to him as he faces a being that has not entirely achieved humanity. Robinson thus has a *duty* to educate Friday—which he does.

Modern conquest produces slavery, a servitude that the slave cannot escape by work. He escapes it by moral civilization, that is, by entry into a moral body, by participation—thanks to education—in the categories of the good as his masters define and conceive it *precisely when and where* they carry out the conquest that ensures their self-preservation. This is why the question of the savage, or more generally of the *aborigine,* is at the heart of the formation of modern peoples and nations, throughout modernity from conquest to decolonization. It is the essence of a people because it relates to what is not a people (or nation) but to tribes and hordes. The passage to common morality (that of the *common moral self*) is, by definition, the breach with natural morality. It is thus in the act of founding morality—the system of notions and concepts that constitute a civil and political order—that the *effective condition* of the existence of a people is to be found.

That is why, as we said at the beginning of this chapter, there can be no people without the negation of the horde: no nation without the negation of the tribe. It is in this sense that the discourse of the *law of peoples* does not generate the rules that govern relations (war and peace) between nations or extant peoples that must be related. The *law of peoples* is the foundational discourse of these peoples and nations; it is, we might say, the discourse of their recognition, the mutual recognition of the victors of their conquests. It governs the sharing out of these conquests and hence institutes the victors' sovereignties. For this discourse to be the discourse of sovereignty it must be uncontestable, for what is at stake in conquest is just this: that the victorious power be recognized as the sovereign power over the conquered extension—territories and population. Sovereignty is thus won *at home*—French power, British power, American power—and gives birth to a French nation, a British one, an American one by the conquest of what is *foreign*.

The modern territorial State and its *people* are thus born from the conquest of extension, such that a right of sovereignty must be established as the right of war and peace between *sovereign powers*.[34] What is external conditions what is internal—foreign affairs. In other words, affairs that concern *foreigners,* are the condition of home affairs. Modern States are constituted at home by their power in the world outside. In this vast movement that I characterize as the *modern negativity* of sovereignty, it is the peoples and nations of Europe that are formed, as an American 'nation' is being formed now.

Once the United States of America is constituted, in fact, there is no substantial difference between the internal constitution of American sovereignty and sovereignties in Europe. The difference *in our time* stems merely from this—while the American nation is still in process of formation, the nations of Europe have come to an end of the process of formation of sovereignty.[35] However, I have just noted, in the nineteenth century America knew the same process as the European powers in the foundation of its own sovereignty. What the American nation knew in the nineteenth century, once liberated from English colonialism, the Europeans had experienced since the sixteenth century. What is at issue is the foundation of the *nation* (or the *people*) through the constitution of the space of sovereignty as a particular space of morality. To bring about a *common moral self* (to go back to Rousseau's vocabulary), as we have seen, presupposes the drawing of an essential difference between the moral and immoral, the people and the horde. For the Americans, this difference consisted of the determinate division (in the course of the nineteenth century) between master and slave, an original operation by comparison with Europe, since the Americans thought their *nation* by means of a divi-

---

34. Grotius formally establishes such a right in his fundamental principles, and Vattel presents a synthesis of it.

35. What has culminated in Europe—*sovereignty* or the relation to the other as negativity—is still in the process of constitution among the Americans, as, elsewhere, notably in Russia, India and China.

sion within itself, so to speak, between what was part of the American *common moral self* (which had been imported from Europe) and what was a foreign *nation*, even if not absolutely so—the Indian nations. What Europeans had experienced since the construction of their empires—reputedly savage peoples living outside Europe who were subjugated or exterminated—Americans had experienced in an identical fashion, but *internally*. In the United States, the *aborigine* was internal so that the construction of the common moral self came down to posing the question of the status of the aborigine, that is the Indian, in relation to the American *nation*. They are internal *foreigners*. The case of the Indians refers back to the *law of peoples*[36] or, rather, the American situation of the Indians attests to the determination of internal law—*morality*—by the external.

In effect, this is what is signified by the 1883 decision of the United States Supreme Court to declare that the *Cherokee Nation* was not a State:

It is accepted that the Indian territory forms part of the United States. It is in this form that all our letters, our territorial treaties, our history and our laws conceive it. On the occasion of all our encounters with foreign nations, in our commercial relations and in all our attempts to meet the Indians and foreign nations, the latter are considered as belonging to the jurisdictional limits of the United States, and are subject to those constraints that are imposed on all our own citizens. They acknowledge themselves in their treaties as being placed under the protection of the United States; they admit that the United States will have the unique and exclusive right to regulate trade with them and to direct all their affairs as they understand them [. . .] Even if the Indians are recognised as having an indisputable and thus unchallenged right over the territories they occupy

---

36. Hence Snow's inquiry, commissioned by the American government, into the status of the American Indian in international law.

until that right be extinguished by a voluntary cession to our Government, nevertheless there must be serious doubt about whether the tribes who reside in the interior of the recognised frontiers of the United States can be strictly speaking designated as foreign nations. They should be more properly designated as domestic dependent nations. They occupy a territory over which we enjoy a title independent of their will, which must take effect in the matter of possession when their right of possession ceases. As they wait, they are in a state of pupilage. Their relation to the United States resembles that of ward to his guardian. They await protection from our Government, and rest in its bounty and power: they call on it to free them from their needs and address the President by calling him their *father*.[37]

Thus we cannot understand the birth of a people or nation—the birth of a common moral self—without referring to that scarcely human part of humanity whose participation in the citizenship offered by morality is a problem from the start. In fact, the process of foundation here, both in American and in Europe, is to make the native, the aborigine, what he naturally is not, that is a part of morality. The foundation of a people requires that the *natural* has nothing to do with the nature of a people and that the originary nation is not—by its very nature—part of that artificial nature created by arms and the law, which subsequently becomes the only nature, the only norm of morality. This is what follows in exemplary fashion from the European experience of conquest and its obvious imitation in the foundation of the United States of America by confrontation with the Indian nations. Just as Europeans regulated the citizenship of the aborigines they found in the course of establishing their colonies, the Americans had to pronounce on the status of the citizenship of the Indians. In other words, the being of a people (or nation)—what it is *to be* American, English, French—is not decided, so to

37. Snow, *The Question of the Aborigines*, pp. 38–9.

speak, in an endogenous fashion through a social contract by which the natural multitude constitutes itself as *one* people and *one* nation. On the contrary, it is in the permanent confrontation with the aborigine (at home or outside) that the *self* of a people or nation is constituted in history. We can thus see that the people is a creation of the modern historial, that fable of endogenous foundation by which the people comes to be in history, as the very subject of that history, a history which must henceforth be understood as the advent and development of spirit, the transfiguration of the natural *orbis* into a spiritual, meaningful world.

In order to grow rich, the peoples of the modern world had to find their virgin extension, whether inhabited or not, whose appropriation was authorized by a right of conquest elaborated by circumstance, for their own self-preservation. This is why self-preservation, or, to put it in other words, the solid foundation of a common moral self in which each individual participates as *citizen*, has as its condition the possibility *of having to fight for the extension. Finitude* here takes up its rights, so to speak, such that the invention of the people, that is the declaration of its sovereignty within the historical State, is always the radical separation of self from its other. What Europeans finally found in America was their own being, that is, the force and power to constitute themselves in Europe itself as sovereign, sovereign peoples and nations. This is just what America discovered in its foundation—it discovered that its own existence presupposes the elimination, or in any case the subjugation, of the aborigine,[38] or, rather, it discovered that its *very foundation* consisted of this presupposition.

38. 'The native tribes', we read in a judgement of the United States Supreme Court in 1846, 'which were found on the continent in the period of its discovery, have never been recognised or treated as independent nations by European governments, they have not even been considered as the owners of the territories they respectively occupied [. . .] From the very moment that the government of the United States was put in place up to today, it has exercised its power over this race informed by a spirit of humanity and justice, and it has endeavoured by all its means in its power to enlighten it and increase its welfare, and, if possible, to save it from the consequences of its own vices' (ibid., pp. 43–4).

The Spirit of Morality

In the spirit of the *jus gentium*, suitably represented here by Vattel, there is a kind of natural society of nations which would be endangered if a member of this society did not respect its common rules and customs. There is a universal rule of morality here, that is, an immanent law that regulates the natural order of civil affairs that human beings must submit to, or run the risk of destroying the order itself by not doing so. Vattel thus takes care to define precisely the rights and duties of 'Humankind' with regard to the imperatives of the morality that is upheld by this society of nations. The foundational principle of morality thus understood is submission to the *natural obligation to cultivate the earth*. Vattel expresses it as follows:

> Agriculture is not only to be recommended to the Government for its extreme utility; it is also an obligation, imposed on man by Nature. The entire earth is destined to feed its inhabitants. But it will not be enough, if they do not cultivate it. Each Nation is thus obliged by Natural Law to cultivate the land which falls to its part, and it only has the right to extend itself or to resort to the help of others, when the land it inhabits cannot furnish what is necessary. Those Peoples, such as the ancient Germans or some modern Tartars, who inhabit fertile lands, but disdain the cultivation of the land and prefer to live from raiding, diminish themselves and do injury to all their neighbours, and deserve to be exterminated, like ferocious, dangerous animals. There are others who, by fleeing from work, only wish to live by Hunting and their Herds. This could be done without contradiction in the First Age of the World, when the earth was more than sufficient in itself for the small number of its inhabitants. But now that Humankind has multiplied so much, it could not continue if all peoples chose to live in this manner. Those who still maintain this leisured way of

life lay claim to more land than they need for honest labour and they cannot complain if other Nations, who are more industrious and applied, come and occupy a part of it. So, while the conquest of the policed Empires of *Peru* and *Mexico* was a glaring usurpation, the establishment of various Colonies on the Continent of *North America*, might, if contained within just limits, be entirely legitimate. The peoples of these vast regions traverse them rather than inhabit them.[39]

We have to distinguish between grand politics and principles in Vattel's discourse. Like all his contemporaries and like many people afterwards, Vattel condemns the extermination of the Indians by the Spaniards, notably during their conquest, but, on the other hand, he casts a favourable eye on the English conquest of North America. The English conquest is in fact 'extremely legitimate', since it is 'contained within just limits'. Nevertheless, the principle remains that it is important for States to conform to the obligations of Nature, to the extent that the finitude of extension confers the *right* (which he calls, as we know, 'perfect right')[40] of conquest with the aim of self-preservation and self-subsistence, if a people cannot satisfy its needs in place. We cannot, then, without contradicting the dispositions of nature, oppose this right; if that is accepted, there will be a place for all nations to intervene, with resort to force if need be, against the infractor. In other words, a nation cannot oppose, *de jure* or *de facto*, the exercise by another nation of its *perfect right* to survival, if it is in need.[41] There is thus a rule

39. Vattel, *Le Droit des gens*, Section 81, pp. 78–9.

40. See NOTE 19.

41. Whence Vattel's assertion: 'The Laws of Natural Society are of such importance to the health of all States that if we were accustomed to trampling them underfoot, no People would manage to preserve and be at peace at home any measure of wisdom, justice or moderation that it could grasp. All men and all States have a perfect right to things without which they could not survive: since this right corresponds to an indispensable obligation. Thus all Nations have the right to suppress by force anything that openly violates the Laws of Society that Nature has established

of the law of peoples that allows a State to acquire territories beyond its boundaries in two required orders: *domain* and *empire*. We understand by this that a State has the right to constitute a property (*propriété*) and exercise its sovereignty (will) over it with the aim of its own self-preservation, that is, the self-preservation of its population.

It is thus in relation to the *finitude* of the human condition and the means which it has at its disposal to satisfy its subsistence that a State, to face up to this finite condition, possesses by nature a right to expand its sovereignty. The ultimate significance of this disposition of the law of peoples is that the *morality of a people*, as its very existence, is dependent on the most immediate materiality: the territory and its goods. Hence Vattel's justification of conquest, linked to the obligation, as we saw, to cultivate the land.

> We can see it [the nation] now established in a Country, which becomes its own good and its residence. The Land belongs to men in general: Destined by the Creator to be their common habitation and their nourishing mother, all have from Nature the right to live there and to take from it the things that are necessary for their subsistence and that are useful of their needs. Humankind having multiplied tremendously the land is no longer capable of furnishing of itself and without cultivation what is necessary to the upkeep of its inhabitants; and it cannot receive an appropriate cultivation from vagabond peoples to whom it belongs in common. It is therefore necessary for these peoples to attach themselves to some part, to appropriate portions of land, so that, untroubled by their toil and enjoying the fruit of their labours, they apply themselves to making these lands fertile, to give them their sustenance. This gives rise to the

among them, or directly attacks the welfare and safety of this Society' ('Introduction' in *Le Droit des gens*, Section 22, p. 13).

Rights of *Property* and *Domain*, which justifies their establishment. On their introduction, the right common to all men is restricted in particular to what he possesses legitimately. The country a Nation inhabits, however it was transported there, whatever the families who compose it, being spread over this Country, and whether formed into Bodies of Political Society; this country, I say, is the establishment of the nation; it has a proper and exclusive right to it.[42]

As we can see, by the law of peoples,[43] the occupation of extension with the aim of subsistence, in other words, the cultivation of the land, is the foundation of all morality. A cultivated extension, seized from the hands of its lazy inhabitants, only occupied in hunting and gathering, and raised from its original state of *wilderness*,[44] is the justification for the colonial enterprise, but also founds the morality of a nation in freeing it from need, in fact, from finitude. The colonial enterprise is a doubly moral one: at the same time as it permits the population of a State in formation to guarantee its existence, and hence to give body to the *people*, it also allows a congeries of wandering tribes to be raised to civilization. For the conquered tribes, the seizure of their lands offers them the possibility of being raised to morality by participation in the natural community of nations, in other words the opportunity to escape from their own natural condition. It integrates a humanity up to this point outside history (because imperfectly human) into this very history, so that the sovereign order of the world replaces simple finite extension. The invention of a *history* is thus made possible, a *universal history* of which a single humanity is the object, while *peoples* are its subjects and agents. We are no

42. Ibid., Section 203.
43. It is a question of an indisputable given of the law of peoples, and Kant, for example, is Vattel's disciple in this matter.
44. See Snow: 'Leaving them [the Indians] in possession of their lands is to leave the country in a state of wilderness, or in other words, *in a state of nature*' (*The Question of the Aborigines*, p. 36).

longer in the biological cycle of pure nature, but in the becoming human of humanity, which is the advent of morality. The question of the *legitimacy of conquest*,[45] a question which haunts the European understanding of modernity, is thus resolved by universal history, that vast movement by which nature, as what men do not know, raises them above their own nature in creating a moral community regulated by law among them. Universal history, because it is the receptacle of spirit,[46] becomes the element in which peoples and nations are formed by acceding to morality. It is in relation to a universal community of civilized nations—the unified body of humanity—that the particular morality of historical nations develops, which constitutes the *people* as common moral self. The structure of morality would be unintelligible if it were not related to its fundamental element—the people and its active will in the sovereign State.

Nevertheless, although morality belongs to the people, it remains the case that the spirit of morality, which is in effect 'the spirit of the people' (as German

45. Vattel asks himself: '*Whether it is permitted to occupy a part of a country, where there are only nomad peoples and in small numbers.*' It is another famous question in the main prompted by the discovery of the New World. It is asked, whether a Nation can legitimately occupy some part of a vast country in which there are only found nomad peoples who because of their small number are incapable of inhabiting all of it. We have already remarked in establishing the obligation to cultivate the land, that these peoples cannot assign to themselves exclusively more land than they have need of and can reside in and cultivate. Their loose inhabitation of these immense regions cannot become a true and legitimate possession: and the peoples of Europe too confined at home, finding a land which the Savages have no particular need of and make no current and sustained use of have been legitimately able to occupy it and establish their colonies there. We have already said, the Land belongs to Humankind, for its sustenance: If each Nation wished from the start to assign for itself a vast country, but only to live off it from hunting, fishing and wild fruits, our globe would be insufficient for the tenth part of the men who inhabit it today. We thus do not discard the views of Nature, in confining the Savage to the narrowest limits. However, we can only praise the moderation of the *English Puritans* who first established themselves in New England. Even though they were provided with a Charter from their Sovereign, they bought the land they wanted to occupy from the Savages. This praiseworthy example was followed by *William Penn* and the Colony of Quakers that he led to Pennsylvania' (*Le Droit des gens*, Section 209).
46. See Chapter 2, 'The Historial or the Spirit of the World', in this volume.

philosophy would put it in the aftermath of the French Revolution), is first of all the spirit of the *jus gentium*. The people exist morally within a State so constituted that the condition of possibility of this constitution is the existence of the people. It is Rousseau who is the central reference here. His concepts articulate the two elements of morality: the general will, in other words thought experiencing itself in the State, and the moral self, in other words the *subject* of this thought as experienced in the State. In the doctrine of sovereignty, already clearly stated by his predecessors, the thought of the people and in consequence its morality (in the form of the *law*) cannot be disputed; it must be respected absolutely and we must submit to it absolutely. There is one and only one *individual* who can by definition not submit to it—that is the people itself, the sovereign in person. We know the celebrated formula of the contract and the 'sanctity' of its terms: 'At once in place of the individual personality of each contracting party, the act of association creates a corporate and collective body, composed of as many members as the assembly contains voters, and receiving from this act its unity, its common self (*moi*), its life and its will.'[47] The advent of the social body, the passage from the multiple to the one, to the extent that it occurs in the historical and philosophical context of sovereignty produces 'a simple being, an individual', as Rousseau says a few lines later. What is the ontological condition of this 'being' then? It is to be immovable for all, intangible for each, and absolutely perpetual (as Bodin wants to say of the sovereign). The virtues of its being are thus those of its will: immovable and perpetual. For, since this 'simple being' is the *sovereign people*, it is contrary to its very nature that there exist a law that it cannot break—it would be as if the will ceased to be the will because the subject who wills ceased to will. It would be as though there could exist, without internal contradiction, a will that did not will: at once and in the same relation, being and non-being.

47. Rousseau, *The Social Contract*, Book 1, Chapter 6, p. 192; translation modified.

What we have to understand by the people, then, is this collective body, this unified moral self that is considered by others to be an indissociable whole. However, we have seen that the contract is the compensatory fiction of conquest. This is verified here. When Rousseau deals with the sovereign, he specifically mentions that the body politic, the people embodied in the State, forms a great *whole*. The people is, properly speaking, the living totality within which, or rather by which, the scattered individuals of the multitude aggregate together in a *collective moral self*. But this belonging to the whole creates obligations from which the individuals/citizens as *subjects* cannot withdraw. Or more correctly, they can always do so but they do not have the *right* to do it. The difference that exists between the people, considered as such, and the individuals (considered as subjects) is that only the former has the right to change its will, that is to say, to revolt against the law which it founded itself. In other words, the sovereign, and only it, can change its opinion, that is, its morality. By contrast, the individual subject cannot do so without committing a crime. The question thus posed is this: at what moment does the *sovereign people* change its mind? In what philosophical and historical circumstances does the *self* of the people (the people as *self*) abolish its own law and denounce its own morality?

The reply to this question requires a prior examination of the following problem: if we presuppose, as we do here, that Rousseau formulated sovereignty as close as possible to its concept (as Lavoisier *defined* oxygen, before Priestly discovered it) because he had conceived the people, the question becomes: how does the people know it *is* the people—that is, the sovereign people? Because the being of the people is not given in nature but proceeds from history, then it is in this history itself, in the general becoming of materiality, that we will find the origin of the people. However, history is not what it still is for many of our contemporaries, who conceive of it as a sort of divinity that arranges things to their advantage, when they feel that 'everything's going OK', or to their disadvantage, in the contrary case. History is only the totality of what happens and has happened and does not constitute a given meaning, legible in each event. So, if the origin of the moral self—the people as the subject of the ethico-moral totality—is historical, then it is because peoples are constituted in relation to one another in conflicts where human beings oppose one another. Peoples are constituted in war, and recognized through it. The people is the subject of morality in the historical State because it is a *violent synthesis*. It confers spirit on becoming. Since God and the gods have left the scene, no doubt terrified by their own creations, or at least uninterested in what is in play, without the people, becoming would be like the natural repetition of the same. In Europe we are given to saying that spirit was born here and has developed in the course of the centuries down to our own time. But this is to read the distant past of the origin through the modern prism of the spirit of the people and the people as spirit. History so understood, the material becoming of materiality, only becomes the accomplishment of a work (civilization) for us Moderns in the universalization of spirit. Spiritualization is the globalization of the European spirit, so that this history is the element in which peoples are recognized. The invention of the people, the unique foundation of the modern State and its morality, is the invention of the history of the world which is the world of spirit. Within the world it is a meaningful history that is at work, through which peoples, these moral selves, are made singular and individual. No people as the spiritual nourishment of history is simply given as one *being* among the number of *beings* in nature. That is why a people is created in the face of another, which is recognized as this people and recognized as such. But recognition is not a literary figure: its ink and flesh are human. The self-constitution of a people requires that it be recognized by another, and the vast, constantly regenerated movement of recognition down to our times is the movement of war and peace, but this now appears to have come to its close in its general movement within Europe. A people only comes to be during the conflict which opposes peoples to each other, as if the stakes of the conflict were the place that a common moral self understands itself to have in the globalization of spirit. In this *spiritualized* history, violence—war and revolution—is the means by which peoples and nations are born, or at least the condition of their advent. In other words, what a people has in common, what philosophy had previously designated as the *common being* which the modern State is charged with governing according to law, comes to pass only through trial. And if we must understand this advent of the common in reference to a *spiritual* history, it is not because spirits govern it and gods preside over its movement. It is only that, in modernity, the people reveal its meaning, by that very fact become not simply the people but the *historial people*, without which, so it seems to modern man, there would be no history but only becoming without end, and certainly without reason.

In this sense, the distinction that we currently make between internal and external politics lacks any relevance here. Clearly, the internal situation of a nation can entail, or in any case determine, the facts of external politics. The French Revolution and the following destabilization of Europe as a whole is often invoked as an example of this. It has been said that the necessary condition for the revolutionary war after the French Revolution was the passage from subject to citizen.[48] This is to employ an otherwise unobjectionable sociological explanation, but this does not do justice to the fact that the *citizenry* in question is not atemporal. That an event inside a nation has consequences externally does not mean that internal politics is the determinant of foreign affairs. On the contrary. The dynamic of citizenry might be plotted from the declaration of the sovereignty of the English Parliament in 1689, to the revolutions in America and France, and onwards to the

48. Eric Weil, *Écrits et conférences*, VOL. 2 (Paris: Vrin, 1991), pp. 241–2.

revolutions of the nineteenth century, the revolutions of 1848, and then those of the twentieth century. Such a revolutionary sequence includes successful revolutions, defeated ones, and even counter-revolutions. The citizenry who determine that 'a people is a people' is not an isolated, national production even if it is engendered in one determined country or another. Citizenry is constituted by a process that enters into the self-constitution of a historical people and, as such, cannot be assigned to a single country. Citizenry or citizenship is the implication of the individual and of everyone in a determinate place in the advent of peoples. The advent of a people cannot be thought simply as an event of 'internal politics'.

In human affairs, on the contrary, there is a simultaneity of the internal and external. Things do not happen at the same moment, but they do happen in the same time. The duration and territorial space in which events are played out are both more or less extended. It is a characteristic of the sovereign order of the world that in constituting particular entities, modernity has fashioned relations (if not links) between nations such that one event—a revolution—cannot simply be the revolution of the country in which it occurs. If we consider the historical movement of the sovereign order of the world, we see that sovereignties, those foundations of particularisms, are the backdrop of an order of universalized violence. It is no fatality that has led the twentieth century to globalize war just when sovereign nationalisms have given modern States the ideological and technical arguments to justify extended confrontations, and dominated their management, so to speak. The pre-eminence of the 'inside' over the 'outside' is an illusion stemming from sovereignty itself. As Carl von Clausewitz observed, when a nation takes up arms, this 'people' or 'nation' does not exist in and for itself—rather a people made up of soldiers becomes conscious of itself, so to speak, as a citizenry.

The illusion of sovereignty does not have to give rise to violence—war and revolution. Peoples and nations are constituted by human actions. But such a constitution does not work through a *sui generis* production. This is the historical illusion of sovereignty: creating the thought that the people in its State posits itself in itself by an act of self on self, by its will to be *one* rather than *multiple*. There is also a second illusion: that of philosophy, which elevates the first to the dignity of the concept in inventing, thanks to the social contract, a hitherto unknown figure in the fable through which spirit speaks. With this figure, history becomes universal: it extends to a world, which thus becomes the space of the expansion of spirit. It is this world that the law of peoples describes: it describes the vast movement of the creation of peoples by other peoples. It is the saga of peoples conquered and defeated; it states their rights and duties, each having its place and its task to accomplish within the universal. The sovereign order of the world is governed by law, but only after it has been built by wars and revolutions. Thus the social contract exists in the world, as much war as revolution—it is the (philosophical) sign of *negativity*.

Whatever it is, in Europe the curtain has come down on the play, whose script philosophy wrote. The historial people who played the principal character has now withdrawn from the scene. The callow, pre-philosophical imagination of an end of history (in a new and popular style) is not however on the agenda. The play is over, but not for everyone, and for the Europeans, *the time of the multitude* begins. However, before examining a possible morality, we first have to continue our inquiry into the genealogy of morality through an analysis of the *political self*.

CHAPTER 4

Genealogy of Morality, 2: The Political Self

The 'Little King'

The modern idea of democracy rests on the belief that morality, and *justice* in general, comes closest to its concept and aims when it emanates from the individual who has become a 'citizen'—a 'little king', Bodin says.[1] But it must be understood that this *little king* is only a king because he is sovereign—like every king. The sovereign individual is thus the beginning and final term of the thought of thought freedom (*la pensée de la liberté pensée*). So the genesis of the *little king* makes phi-

1. Bodin judges that 'the end of these popular states is the banishment of virtue' because democratic sovereignty consists of dividing sovereignty into a multitude of 'little kings', which dissolves sovereignty itself: 'But there is a still greater plague in popular Republics, which is the impunity granted to the wicked, because they are citizens' (*Les Six Livres de la République*, 1583 edition [Darmstadt: Scientia Verlag Aalen, 1977], p. 943).

losophy contemplate the difficult figure (because paradoxical or properly unthinkable) of a subject which is at once both master of itself—its thought and its action—*and* subordinated or subject to itself. The writer who could be said to have done most to define, perhaps even to invent, sovereignty during his epoch thus discovers the autonomy of the subject almost incidentally, by chance. However, is it truly by chance that such a discovery of a contradictory subject occurred at the very moment that democracy—still called the 'popular State'—is being theorized for the first time in the context of sovereignty? At the point when Bodin uses the expression 'little king', it is obvious that the question of democracy is anything but a new one. This is a trivial statement but it *does* mean that the question of democracy is posed in a new fashion by reason of the very novelty of sovereignty. It is now thought in terms of autonomy, the obligation that an individual (whether singular or collective) contracts for itself. We should note here that if sovereignty is something new in Bodin's work, it is not because it springs whole *ex nihilo* from the spirit of a political writer of genius. We might say that Bodin's notion of sovereignty goes back to a tradition based in Roman antecedents, the principate to be precise. Bodin himself refers to it, and, although, he expressly declares that the Emperors were not sovereign,[2] it remains the case that sovereignty retains some trace of its origins in Imperial Rome.

The novelty comes from somewhere else—from the place where the sovereign *individual* turns into the *sovereign subject*. Even a summary chronicle of this eminently 'modern' figure would probably take its origins back to Ockham's nominalism. The individuation of the *name* opens up the terrain to the individuation of the will, as well as to the individuation of power and thought. What is remark-

---

2. 'The first Roman emperors were not sovereign', Bodin says, 'but only leaders and first citizens, which they called *Princeps*, and this form of Republic was in appearance Aristocratic, in fact, Monarchical, and was called first in dignity, honour and standing: although in truth, most of the Emperors were tyrants' (ibid., p. 144).

able, however, is that we owe it to a philosopher jurist to have intuited in the 'little king' the democratic citizen—the enigmatic power of an individual master of himself *and* subject to himself. However—and this is central to the genealogy of morality—self-obedience is first thought in relation to the subject of the 'sovereign people', and then, and only then, does the thematic of self-obedience become concerned with the individual. This is the passage from one extreme of sovereignty to the other—from Bodin, who rejects the autonomy of the sovereign, to Rousseau who asserts the autonomy of the citizen. In fact, Bodin writes:

> In both Republics [monarchy and aristocracy] there are two parts: that is, the one or those who hold sovereignty, on the one hand, and the people on the other, which creates difficulties between them over the rights of sovereignty, which vanish in the popular state: for, if the prince or the lord who holds the state is obliged to keep the laws as many think; and they cannot have a law not approved by the people or Senate, the law cannot be broken without the consent of one or other of the holders of right: *which would not happen in a popular state, since the people are a single body and cannot put obligations on itself.*[3]

As for Rousseau, his proposal is too well known to need recalling: to obey oneself is to obey no one. 'Obedience to no one' is the crucial stake of sovereignty and democracy. While Bodin sees in it the ultimate argument for the refutation of the popular State, Rousseau by contrast finds that it is the irreducible foundation of democratic sovereignty. We have thus passed from the practical impossibility of democracy (Bodin: democracy is destructive of democracy itself) to its absolute reality (Rousseau: sovereignty *is* democratic or there is no sovereignty at all).

Such a transformation—whose stakes are autonomy or freedom—takes place in philosophy and history within modern natural law. This leads us to forget that

3. Ibid., p. 143; emphasis added.

the question of autonomy, in relation to its principle, is not the question of the individual as such but the question of the people within which the individual finds its place. To do this, we must move from Bodin to Grotius, who gives body to Bodin's invention of the individual sovereign explicitly and in a theoretically revolutionary way. While Bodin did not reason in terms of natural law, with Grotius the individual is originary, to the point that every *right* is a power of the individual. 'Right', he says, 'is a moral quality, attached to the person, by virtue of which one might legitimately own or do certain things'.[4] The power attaches to a person and what is merely an intuition in Bodin's *little king* becomes the rational constitution of the subject of right (which the history of ideas designates as 'subjective right'), a transformation of the juridico-political problematic which we are justified in calling 'modern'—if we must stick with that word. From this assertion must follow, naturally so to speak, modern democratic theory in which the citizen is master of himself—a free little king—because he exercises his proper 'rights' and enjoys them sovereignly. In fact, it became impossible to think the State in general without at the same time thinking its origin in the individual-subject (his will), the possessor of 'natural rights', or better the *proprietor* of these rights, without thinking the democratic quality of this State, that is, without thinking it through sovereignty. The democracy of sovereignty is the unavoidable end of the invention of subjective rights,[5] its aim and its culmination. The pinnacle of this process of the advent of the free subject is attained in the ideology of the 'Rights of Man', the ideology of the liberal democratic State which is disposed to inscribe into its constitutional charter a declaration of the rights which it undertakes to guarantee to individuals. In any case, just as Bodin only evokes the citizen–little king as the

4. Hugo Grotius, *Le Droit de la guerre et de la paix*, 2 VOLS (Jean Barbeyrac trans.) (Amsterdam, 1724 [1625]), 1.1. Section 4.1.
5. That is why a nation of subjects of right like the United States has a tendency to present itself to the world as having a mission to spread its 'democracy' over the surface of the *orbis*.

effect of the sovereign people, so Grotius, as we will see, first thinks the people in its State, its nation, so that the individual of 'subjective right' is *not ab initio* the particular but the collective subject. This is the model of the singular subject. It is in this form—the position of the singular as subject by derivation from the collective—that democratic natural law is inaugurated.

Hence, it is necessary to briefly rehearse the theoretical movement by which the individual comes into being—it is evidently the passage from the natural (savage) individual to the civilized (political) individual. In other words, it is important to bring out how through the motif of purely biological, pre-political existence, the philosophy of sovereignty comes to conceive the citizen as juridical subject. Far from thinking the individual politically—the *political self*—the modern proponents of 'natural right' have made such a thought impossible by replacing it with the commodities of the juridical self—the subject of right in person. In that case, every moral and political question of our time (whose stakes and terms the present work attempts to analyse) leads to this: in the current context of the European world where sovereignty has reached its culmination, is it necessary to think the renovation of the democratic principle as the passage from the juridical subject to the *political self* and hence as the refoundation of the *res publica*?

What is One's Own and What is Common

The little king is the unsurpassable horizon of democratic sovereignty—in other words, if we think democracy as the 'sovereignty of the people' (or any other equivalent statement), we cannot think the citizen in any other way than in the form of the sovereign self. This is what the discourse of sovereignty reveals in its theoretical figures which pass from Bodin and Grotius to Rousseau *via* Hobbes[6]

6. Although even Rousseau would make a show of regarding the one as 'troublemaker of despotism' and the other as 'paid sophist'. In reality, Rousseau only took to their logical conclusion—

and others. This is a process whose description in the material body of the philosophical narrative takes the form of an account that is *at once* historical and non-historical—the fable of natural right. We have just emphasized that for Grotius every right is a power of the subject, but it must be understood (which is not always the case) that this 'subject' is either a singular individual or a collective one. The right in question belongs to a single self *because* it first belongs to a collective self. In reality, modern thought about right(s) following Grotius does relate the *jus* to a subject, on condition that it is conceived both as a State (a people organized into State sovereignty) and as particular citizen, the singular individual of the multitude. In this sense, if Grotius effects a theoretical revolution it is precisely because he reflects on right as the property of a single and common subject.

The modern *sovereign self* which reaches its culmination in the little king of our contemporary democracies was born in the originary historical context of European colonial expansion and in the philosophical advance of a thought of *freedom* envisaged as the existential element (or milieu) of a subject that was autonomous and the owner or master of itself. Hence, the recourse to the fable of natural right, as Grotius first developed it. The right of the singular individual is thought on the model of the right of the collective individual—the single self is reflected on in the form and model of the common self. It is in thinking the right of State sovereignties in formation (and in competition in war) in the context of the historical conflict of conquest and the theoretical controversy that gave rise to Grotius coining his celebrated thesis: '*Right is a moral quality, attached to the person*'. What is at issue, he specifies, is a *faculty of the person* which is 'right properly named'. This leads on to 'power': 'We have power,' he says, 'either over ourselves, which we call *Freedom*, or over others, which is *Paternal Power*, the *Power of a*

the 'general will'—the theses of natural law that were first stated in Grotius and Hobbes, so that his democratic absolutism wants nothing in relation to the so-called absolutism of Hobbes and Grotius; he completes it and brings it to a culmination in the 'sovereignty of the people'.

Master over his Slaves, etc.[7] So freedom is 'power over ourselves'. First of all, it has to be understood that modern thought about right(s) relates to the individual (either singular or collective), that this right is 'freedom', and finally that it is a question of the freedom of a 'person'—itself singular or collective. Thus we cannot be content to say that Grotius' theoretical novelty consists of relating right to the individual if we understand by that a particular person endowed with individual freedom. In other words, Grotius does not think right on the basis of the singular individual as if he had in mind a *sui generis* individual which would serve as the basis of a reform of what heretofore had been understood as *jus*. This discovery, posited a priori so to speak—right as a moral quality of the person—would provide the basis on which a general theory of the *jus gentium* could be elaborated. This would found the system that emerged from the legal heritage from Victoria to Gentile in the light of its fundamental revolutionary position, revealed to it by grace, so to speak. This is an academic perception of the formation of modern political right,[8] that is, of the modern development of the system of political philosophy within the idiom of natural right. It displays the academicism of an infraphilosophical genre—the 'history of political ideas'—which sifts 'ideas' one after another, picking out artificial and abstract entities (which can be easily committed to memory by the public) like 'subject', 'Right of Man', 'nature', 'civil society', 'power', 'individual', etc. These give rise to each other, oppose one another or complement each other, in a vortex of ideas, whose movement is energized from within. In our case, the effect produced by the history of 'ideas' is to give an image of political right or its philosophical construction, in which the narratives of natural right are also fables. These provide a *mise en scène* in which individuals who desire society as much as they are strangers to it by nature eventually associate with one

---

7. Grotius, *Le Droit de la guerre* I, 1, 5, 2; emphasis in the original.

8. In the sense of a system of the philosophical principles of sovereignty as in Rousseau, who gives his *Social Contract* the subtitle 'Principles of Political Right'.

another in common groupings under the direction of absolute sovereigns (or those that are not), making sovereignty singular or unitary. In this perspective on ideas, Grotius' *idea* produced the idea of the individual (those Crusoes) and his or her rights, and, on that basis, were deduced its consequences in the order constructed between peoples and nations. However, if Grotius' *subject* is first of all the common subject (as, in fact, is the case)—a people organized as a sovereign State—and the singular subject (the particular individual) is only a deduction or extrapolation, then sovereignty—the State in person—is not the effect of a contract (of whatever form) produced by the will of individuals, as the fables of both the theorists of natural law *and* the academic historians of 'ideas' would claim.

Various consequences flow from this. The first is that the basis of the modern fable and the fiction that it develops is the fable of the individual. It is the fable of the autonomous and free 'subject', which founds the social body in which it lives, that is, enjoys, suffers and finally dies. With this fiction of the sovereign, particular or private individual, the fiction of the sovereign State, understood as the effect of the will of free individuals, disappears—the State is not the form of the consensus of particulars because sovereignty does not result from a contract but from conquest.[9] The second consequence of Grotius' subject being originally the collective subject—the State in person and as person—is that the single self is only a derivation from the common self, or, in other words, the private is only a particular modality of the public, its particularization. It is in this perspective that modern morality develops, so that the corollary of this second consequence is that the modern nation of citizenship and the democratic sphere this refers to become highly problematic. If citizenship and democracy are problematic, it is because their foundations in the private individual and his will have been considerably weakened. If in democracy the individual is that figure who only obeys the law

9. On conquest, see the preceding chapter, 'The Historial People'.

which he has imposed upon himself (autonomy), an obedience that is his very freedom, then democracy must be altogether rethought outside the sovereignty of the individual, since such a primary and founding individual does not exist. In these conditions—if confirmed—the fact that democracy has to be rethought in its concept becomes a necessity since from Bodin to Rousseau, the theory of autonomy—of self-obedience—constitutes its foundation and aim. From this point of view, these two authors can be related to one another, since, as we have already seen, their respective accounts form, so to speak, the two extremes of a model of sovereignty whose common theme is the subject's obligation towards himself. If Bodin and Rousseau have something in common[10] it is the following. When the former declares that sovereignty of the people is 'legitimate', he condemns it, as we know; by contrast, Rousseau finds in Bodin's argument of the moral and political impossibility of a people's self-obedience the very rationality of democracy and the final resolution of the enigma of sovereignty. It is in self-obedience that each individual of a people attains himself as a free individual. But to move from Bodin to Rousseau requires Grotius and his subjective right. It is through Grotius and Hobbes that Rousseau manages to democratically fasten the buckle of sovereignty, so that for Rousseau democracy appears as the truth of sov-

10. This has remained largely unperceived until recently, to the point that it is astonishing to see that generations of students have read Rousseau through Robert Derathé's interpretation, for example, who, like others afterwards, manages the *tour de force* of not mentioning Bodin in his commentary on Rousseau, whose notion of sovereignty is nevertheless directly inherited from the author of the *Six Livres*. While Derathé is relating Rousseau to his predecessors (Grotius, Hobbes), he does not go back as far as Bodin, who first conceives the *sovereignty of the people*, of the 'legitimate' forms of sovereignty as he puts it. It is also striking to see that Derathé attaches no importance to the structure of the *Social Contract*, which is intelligible only on the basis of the canonical distinction that originates with Bodin between sovereignty and the exercise of sovereignty. See Robert Derathé, *Rousseau et la science politique de son temps* (Paris: Vrin, 1974). On these questions one will in future have to consult the indispensable work of Jean Terrel, *Les Théories du pacte social. Droit naturel, souveraineté et contrat de Bodin à Rousseau* (Paris: Editions du Seuil, 2001).

ereignty. The people *alone* is sovereign—no other sovereign is possible or legitimate. This flows from Grotius' invention: if everyone obeys himself, and hence
obeys no one, it is because Grotius has, first of all, thought the individual himself
on the model of the people unified through State sovereignty, having rights and
powers, and which, by that very fact, forms a homogeneous unity later thought as
a sovereign person.[11] There is a homology between the individual of the multitude
and the State as an individual.

This is why such a particular individual does not exist—that is as *sui generis*
subject with original rights so that through this very *property* it would be at the
origin of the *res publica* in general of which it is citizen or subject. We see this in
Grotius in his treatise, *De la liberté des mers* (*Freedom of the Seas*, 1703)[12] where
he refutes Portugal's claim to the appropriation of their conquered lands, a claim
that the Portuguese base on a triple justification: discovery, Papal donation and
occupation. Grotius has no trouble in demonstrating that none of these titles is
legitimate, so that Holland has every right to trade with the natives in the lands
that have been discovered. The aim here (both for the Dutch whose cause Grotius
defends, as well as for himself in demonstrating a theory of the right of peoples)
is the break-up of monopoly and the opening up of routes to exchange. He rests
here on the ancient theory of the universal right of communication or exchange
that Vitoria established. However, Grotius produces innovations in distinguishing
the common from the singular or private—it is, in fact, by making a detour
through a theory of property (*propriété*)—the nature of what is *one's own* (*propre*)—that he is led to think a State (the Dutch state, for example) as an individual, a collective individual or people. In other words, the Portuguese State and the

11. However, the articulated theory of the person-State is developed by Pufendorf. See Chapter
3, NOTE 15, in this volume.
12. Hugo Grotius, *Mare liberum—De la liberté des mers* (1609) (A. de Courtin trans.) (Caen:
Université de Caen, 1990 [1703]).

Dutch State are two individuals having their own rights, so that it is necessary to distinguish what is particular to each and what the two have in common. A theory of property is thus mobilized to found a doctrine of exchange (trade) as a particular chapter of the *jus gentium*. Or rather, to be accurate, of the *jus inter gentes*, because the parties in question are particular nations, in other words individuals. The right of the individual—which is the right to property—is thus revealed in the form of the right of nations to free exchange. To found the law of peoples, or international law, is to recognize that the subjects of this law or right are collective subjects, endowed with what Grotius later describes as 'moral quality'. These subjects of right or law, inasmuch as they are agents of law (and partners in trade), are States possessed of sovereignty, our better, possessing sovereignty,[13] that is to say, the right of sovereignty and the use of this sovereignty. What then is *one's own*? It is defined in his writing on the freedom of the seas: 'Something is one's own if it belongs to oneself and cannot be another's.'[14] This specification allows us to distinguish the common from one's own in proceeding to the individuation of the common domain. In fact, says Grotius, 'God gave nothing to this or that person, but everything to Humankind; and in this sense, nothing prevents many people being at once, and so to speak *en masse*, the masters of the same thing.' How we have passed from what is common to what is not, and hence to what is 'one's own'—in other words to individual property—is what Grotius seeks to explain with

13. In his treatise *Le Droit de la guerre et de la paix*, Grotius explicitly defines sovereignty on the basis of property: 'there are two *subjects* in which sovereignty resides, one *common*, the other *one's own* . . . the *common subject* in which sovereignty resides is the *State* [. . .] the State is thus, in the sense I have just specified, the common subject of sovereignty. But *the subject that is one's own* where sovereignty resides is *one or many persons* depending on the laws and customs of each nation: in a word the *Sovereign*' (ibid., 1, 3, Section 8, pp. 3–6). And Grotius is more precise: 'It is necessary to distinguish in the matter of Sovereign Power, as well as in the matter of Property, *the primary act* from the *secondary act*, that is the right and the use of the right' (ibid., 1, 3, Section 24).

14. Grotius, *De la liberté des mers*, p. 677.

the aim of refuting the Portuguese claim to their conquests. It is by occupation, that is, by use. The use of a common good makes you its owner, when this good can be appropriated; this is the case with land, when it is inhabited or cultivated, but not of the air which we breathe, which remains indivisible by nature. Which leads Grotius to say:

> So, as the principle of use consisted in the corporeal application of things, so it is therefrom, we have said, that property derives, just as it seemed good that, by a similar application, things appropriated for use finish up by belonging to it completely. It is what we call *occupation* applying this word to things that originally had been held in common among men.[15]

It is the individuation of what is common that gives birth to the clear notion of the individual proprietor of a right to use a thing. In detaching the thing from its natural state (*natural*, in fact, since originally, says Grotius, things and bodies were held in common in universal nature), or rather from the natural community, the thing becomes the particular person's good and henceforth his property. It is through property that the individual comes into the world—as proprietor.

It is in these circumstances (where appropriation follows use) that Grotius finds a compelling argument that allows him to deny the Portuguese the *right* to appropriate exclusively for themselves the fruit of their conquest. They do not have sovereignty over the things they have conquered, since they make no use of them. We see the germ of an idea of a common good of humanity as the foundation of an order between peoples and nations, that is to say, between collective subjects unified under a 'common subject'—the sovereign State in person, whose 'proper subjects' (*sujets propres*) they are.

15. Ibid., p. 678.

However, in the course of the controversy generated by the commercial and philosophical polemic that Grotius unleashed, we gain an indirect glimpse of the particular or private individual—the proprietorial self. In fact, Grotius reconstructs the genesis of the distinction between public and private—what belongs to the commons and what is one's own—in the abandonment of the natural and originary constitution caused by trade:

> So [that is, through trade between men] republics begin to be instituted; and we divide into two kinds those things already separated from the universal commonality of men: some are public, that is belonging to [*propres*] the people (because this is the natural meaning of the word); others are private, that is belonging to (*propres*) particular owners. For what is surplus, *whether public or private, occupation proceeds in the same fashion.*[16]

This last assertion—public or private occupation is the same—is of the highest importance for modern natural right and 'subjective right'. It means that the private individual, endowed with inalienable human rights (precisely the least of which is not that of property), is a category of the law of peoples. For the law of peoples, the private individual is 'private' because he is deprived of the common. The private is the negative of the public and 'one's own' is to the common as negative is to positive. Grotius also says that the common is what is not owned by anyone, but this is in the sense that, he specifies (relying on the poets, Rousseau will say),[17] what is public does not belong to a people since it belongs to 'human society'. In Grotius, public refers to the law of peoples, so that the category of the individual (the private), to the extent that this is *not* public, is itself a creation of the law of peoples. The private is determined by the public. Property is the agent of

16. Ibid., p. 679; emphasis added.
17. Ibid., p. 680.

this creation. The institution of republics equally relates to the law of peoples, that is, it relates to war or trade. In both cases, however, the status of property must be established, which means that occupation must be proven or recognized. It must also bear a good that can be appropriated.[18] If the law of peoples shows us how republics are founded—the *public* appropriation of what is at first common in nature—we should rather speak about the *jus inter gentes* because this institution of republics is simultaneously the creation of *peoples,* those collective individuals henceforth placed outside 'nature': we no longer have the natural society of humankind but the artificial society of peoples among each other—a society of the subjects of the law of peoples.[19] The passage to the republic is a leap out of common nature considered as the original element from which human beings are separated by the appropriation of what they occupy publicly or privately. This is why Grotius declares that *public or private, occupation proceeds in the same way*, or, in other words, a people constitutes itself as a people through the mediation of property (we will see what its substance is) and being constituted, it institutes individuals as proprietors. Property is the key to the ontology of the individual. The individual who says 'I' is only an *I* because he can say *this is mine* and he can only say it if and only if the public authorizes it. If the I is a *Self* it is through the appropriation of a thing that the *res publica* (the public thing) concedes to him as a private thing—something that is his. *Mine* and *Yours* are categories of the law of peoples, as is the individual.[20]

---

18. Hence Grotius' argument against the Portuguese: no one can appropriate the air or the sea, which are the common goods of humanity: 'The use of the waters is no less common to all today than it was at the origin of the world. Men can acquire no right over them that would prejudice their common use' (ibid., p. 701).

19. Which are as much historical States themselves, constituted by association of subjects of right.

20. This is the limit of the theory of so-called 'possessive individualism': it does not grasp the individual proprietor as a category of the law of peoples because it does not see that private right

We have demonstrated that everything that could become private property, following occupation, is no less capable of becoming public property,
that is the exclusive property of a people. Hence, says Celse, the fact that
the riverbank that formed the frontier of the Roman Empire belonged to
the Roman people. So we cannot be astonished that this same people
could concede to its subjects through the intermediary of the *princeps* or
praetor such and such mode of occupation of the littoral. In any case, this
occupation itself must not be considered as less restrictive than if it had
been private, so that it must only be understood to the limit and with the
reservation of common use by virtue of the right and law of peoples.[21]

Indubitably, Grotius' great idea was to think the individual as proprietor and to
conceive of him as having (owning) certain rights, which constitute him as a
juridical self. But he could do this only by deriving the individual and his rights
from the *people* (nation), itself a proprietor or bearer of rights. He thinks the
individual—the *subject of right*—within the frame of a general theory of property
conceptualized on the basis of the *subject*, but deriving the private subject—the
individual in person—from the common subject, the private from the public.

This allows us to grasp the essence of property, that is, the land, or, better,
extension. The primary thing in nature, extension (*res extensa*) can be appropriated and its division into public or private parcels is the means by which republics
and peoples are individualized. Sovereignty thus does nothing but express the
public property of the *res extensa*, just as it expresses the people as a collective
individual, a *common I or self*. The frontier is coterminous with property, so to
speak, since the parcelization of extension requires closure. The struggle for

is a consequence of the right/law of peoples.' See C. B. Macpherson, *The Political Theory of
Possessive Individualism from Hobbes to Locke* (Oxford: Oxford University Press, 1961).
21. Grotius, *De la liberté des mers*, p. 683.

extension (the fatal limitation of the *res extensa* being the ultimate mark of finitude), and hence the inevitable struggle for existence, is thus at the origin of our
law of peoples as it is the element in the latter's categories in which the thematic
of the individual and its rights is played out in modernity.

So it is henceforth impossible to hold to the schoolboy fable of *modern natural right* which turns the individual and what he owns in free and rational fashion
into the origin of our States. Certainly, nobody believed that one fine primal
morning, natural individuals came together in primitive clearings to elect a chief.
But it remains the case that the fable of original and natural rights is the moral sustenance for the foundation of the republics that philosophy reproduced. There is
more ideology than philosophy behind this imagery. As Grotius develops the first
of his theoretical axioms in the form of a system of thought, he proves not to be
as naive as his distant liberal or libertarian successors ('vulgar' ideologists as Karl
Marx called his economist contemporaries). From Benjamin Constant to Murray
Rothbard a *sui generis* individual was postulated, a bourgeois Robinson Crusoe,
who enjoyed a creative liberty in the modern republic as great (according to some
of them) as the absolute servitude of ancient citizens. The synthetic exposition of
the theoretical system of natural right which Grotius developed in his *Right of War
and Peace* does not give voice to historical human action but to the formal model
of that action.[22] The model understands society by relating contract to conquest
and the private individual to the *res publica*. This is why Grotius reveals the ultimate meaning of natural right—the advent of the public or private *juridical self*—
in the form of the right of peoples perceiving the *res extensa* as the determinant of
the *res publica*. The sovereignty of the common (and private) subject is the
response to the infinite question of finitude:

---

22. As Hobbes and Rousseau among others understood when they had recourse to the model of
the contract.

On the earth itself, assigned as property (*propriété*) to private individuals or to peoples, one cannot bar passage to the people of any nation, so long as it takes place without arms, and is not a charge to the people who allow it, nor can one forbid anyone to slake his thirst by a river. And the reason for this is that the same thing being naturally capable of different uses, the peoples of the earth seem only to have wanted to share out those things which are impossible to exercise without involving the right of property, save in mutual receipt from one another of those other uses whose exercise does not imply the condition of proprietor.[23]

Robinson Crusoe: Bourgeois

This is because the individual who *has* these rights *is* right (law)—the subject of right. But he is not this subject because, so to speak, Mother Nature made him so. From Grotius onwards, the individual existence of the subject (like the existence of the republics themselves) is a construction of the law of peoples and rests on property, which is not a *sui generis* given but the effect of a relation that links the owner (*propriétaire*) to the thing owned. Because possession is not given by nature (human or otherwise) it cannot be thought of as originary—it has to be negotiated. And the negotiation in question is made in terms of the law of peoples, that is, the right to war and peace. At once it becomes clear that the owner of this good (this patch of land) is only properly proprietor if, and only if, he is recognized as such. In this sense, right is the procedure by which subjects engage in mutual recognition. For A to be proprietor, B has to recognize him as such—law is this recognition that institutes A (and B) as a subject of right. There is no subject of right existing by nature and in itself. On the contrary, because the *land* is a given which human beings use for their individual and collective survival, they become its private

23. Grotius, *De la liberté des mers*, p. 693.

proprietors only in the juridical context of the constitution of the *common* wealth. The modern philosophical tradition of natural right (beginning with Grotius) has grasped this, so that, *looked at from this angle*, there must be a considerable revision of so called modern 'individualism' if we understand by this the idea of a radical origin of civil association in the individual and his own right.

The enthusiasm with which yesterday's liberals, and perhaps those of today, proclaim the superiority of modern freedom over that of the ancients is a consequence of this individualist illusion: since individuals, subjects of right, are at the origin of the State, they are its masters, while the ancient City demanded from all its citizens (not to speak of slaves) a complete submission to its aims. This liberal vulgate, emphatically disseminated by Constant, forgets just one thing: that the individual—the subject of right—is a creation of the modern State, the inevitable avatar of the conquest to which sovereignties at war (and at times at commercial peace) were given down to the twentieth century. The individual can become a colonist overseas only if the state allows him to do so, because the conquered land has been pacified and the sovereignty of the conquering State has been established there. The citizen of a European State can appropriate land and men (slaves) for himself only under the aegis of the conquering State. The individualism of the entrepreneur does not spring forth from his will or his rational calculation. The entrepreneur can devote himself to calculation and self-enrichment only because the State that backs him authorizes him to capitalize on his calculations. If the calculating egoism of the entrepreneur is what defines him as an entrepreneur who looks after his own interests, nevertheless his legal capacity to engage in business depends on the public constitution. This is as true abroad, in conquered territory, as within the sovereign frontiers of the metropolis.

So Constant was busily promoting a shopkeeper's ideology based on the fantasy of individual independence which seized the Moderns even as it freed them from the legislative machinery of the ancient City. Whereas, says Constant, the ancients had no private sphere in which to fully enjoy life, and the laws scrutinized their behaviour even in the bedroom, the Moderns are, by contrast, entirely liberated from the tutelage of the collective body. This is because the modern citizen takes no effective part in public life:

> The part that each took in national sovereignty in Antiquity was not, as in our times, an abstract supposition. Each person's will had a real influence: the exercise of this will was a lively and repeated pleasure. In consequence, the ancients were ready to make many sacrifices to maintain their political rights, and their involvement in the administration of the State.[24]

An enemy of the 'sovereignty of the people' which he sees, not without reason, as the source of the crimes of the Terror, Constant blinds himself to the supposed benefits of the individualism of rights[25] in postulating them as *sui generis*. These 'rights' are the very being of the individual and all the individuals of the multitude: 'There is a part of human existence that, of necessity, remains individual and independent, and that is by right outside any social competence. Sovereignty exists only in a limited and relative way. Where the independence of individual existence begins, the jurisdiction of this sovereignty stops.'[26] What is this right that *by right* founds the independence of the modern citizen, what is this right prior to every right, that produces modern freedom where ancient servitude

24. Benjamin Constant, 'De la liberté des Anciens comparée à celle des Modernes' (1819), in *Écrits politiques* (Paris: Le Livre de Poche, 1980), p. 501.

25. 'The citizens possess individual rights independent of any social or political authority, and any authority that violates these rights becomes illegitimate. The rights of the citizen are individual freedom, religious freedom, freedom of opinion, in which is included its broadcast, the enjoyment of property, and a guarantee against any arbitrary [state act]' (Benjamin Constant, *Benjamin Constant: Political Writings* [Biancamaria Fontana (trans. and ed.] [Cambridge: Cambridge University Press, 1988], p. 180; translation modified).

26. Ibid., p. 177; translation modified.

once held sway? It is not clear that Constant needed to answer this question, since in his eyes the truth of modernity was manifest in its beneficial effects. One of the main benefits trade brings is peace. A society of 'independent' individuals promises the enjoyment of inalienable rights. Everyone will be devoted to his occupations, independent of the will of the State, leading to the peace that comes with trade. This is the tableau that Constant contemplated in post-Napoleonic Europe: war was followed by peaceful trade and exchange: 'War and trade,' he writes, 'are but two different means to attain the same end: that of possessing what is desired.' So, the well-ordered (European) world is made up of individuals who desire various goods, and modern sovereignty, by contrast with the ancient version, does not interfere in the affairs of these subjects of right, because these are posited by nature. It follows that, 'war being prior to commerce', modernity can henceforth enjoy peace if and only if the rights of the subject of right are known and recognized. This is in 1819 the high point of the modernist vulgate. The *orbis* does not open up to the 'desire' of free and independent individuals but to the States of Europe, as they pursue their wars of empire, a Europe whose superiority to the warrior Cities of Antiquity, Constant says is obvious:

> The very division of Europe into various States is, thanks to the progress of the Enlightenment, more apparent than real. While each people, otherwise, formed an isolated family, born enemy to other families, now a mass of men exists under different names and in diverse modes of social organisation, but homogeneous in nature. It is strong enough not to fear the barbarian hordes. It is so enlightened that war is a burden for it. Its uniform tendency is towards peace.[27]

27. Grotius, *De la liberté des mers*, p. 495. Hence, as we know (something that Constant could not even imagine in his time, and for good reason), Europe has done violent damage to the defence of modern freedom. Europe unleashed wars, and it is only after its globalisation in the twentieth century and the definitive end of its empires that it becomes possible to speak of a European 'uniform tendency towards peace'.

The history of ideas, which fabricates 'ideas' as a series of autonomous productions, is comfortable with Constant. As a philosopher of the second rank, but
a first-rate ideologist of the liberal-democratic liberalism that still nourishes our
contemporaries, he does not seek to ground his assertions in the logic of the concept but, rather, offers them as *opinion*. Like every ideologue (those replacements
for theologians), he produces the opinion of which he is the product. Rather than
attempting to produce knowledge, he offers justifications for common feelings,
those same sentiments whose counterpart State absolutism designates as *social
freedom*, the idea by which individuals form a 'civil society', distinct from political
society or the State, so that this very distinction protects them (the individuals)
from the dangerous entrapments of sovereignty. In itself, this is a good idea, but
just that, an idea. It can be opposed to another idea, and precede or follow on from
yet another. This opinion (sentiment organized into an ideal) has a clear and even
correct view of sovereignty's potential tyranny. So opinion is founded as a spontaneous solution to *evil*. Constant's liberalism thus offers a solution in the free individual, the bearer of rights, who associates with similar individuals to form a society separated from the State, a force opposing the power of the State. Within this
'civil society' therefore, the individual can freely enact his freedom, that is, undertake his projects (to possess and to work). This capacity, which the individual has
by nature and on his own account, by free creation, becomes part of the order of
morality according to the liberal schema only if it is related to the struggle against
the State. The meaning of civil society is its capacity to act against the State, or to
preserve its forces in the face of the power of the State. In particular, the *law* in this
context is what the State opposes to the *right* of the individual: political power is
contrary to social power.

What is proper to ideology here, just as elsewhere, is the simultaneous production and resolution of a problem, which amounts to an arbitrary definition of
its terms. In the case in point, the autonomy of civil society is derived from the

(perfectly obvious) tyranny of the State. The question is then posed: can the enslaved individual be reconciled with the State through the expedient of civil society? Constant is representative of those who feel rather than think. The idea that civil society exists on one side and the political State on the other is absurd, given that one cannot exist without the other, just as the circle cannot exist without its centre.

The key to the mystery of civil society is to be found in sovereignty, understood as the principle of the State, its form. Just as sovereignty gives form to the State, so also the State gives form to civil society. Under these conditions, it is absolutely correct to be concerned about the state tendency (the 'natural bent' of governments as philosophy puts it) to subvert civil society—the twentieth century has provided a demonstration of this if such were needed. However, from this historical truth we cannot construct a theory of civil society *as if* it led a separate existence. This problematic of *as if* is widespread, from Constant to Marx; it underpins both the conservative theme of the rights of the free individual, barely restrained by law, and the theme of the revolutionary emancipation of a class, not the individual. In both cases, *sovereignty* is misunderstood in its essence—it is neither the concept of the oppression of the individual by the abstraction of the will (general or otherwise) nor of one class by another, two examples of a figure which, properly considered, are the same. The sovereignty that gives form to the State is the form of the individuation of historical peoples (or nations). In misrecognizing the nature of sovereignty, the ideology of civil society misrecognizes the nature of the State *and* civil society itself. It is not because I posit that individuals have rights (the rights of Man) that the State is less tyrannical than it wants to be, so to speak. It is so because the State remains the master of rights. The assertion that the individual enjoys rights within civil society is just words if the State exercises a tyrannical sovereignty. In other words, it is not the pressure of civil society that makes the State pliant—because civil society has no force faced with the armies of sovereignty. The revolution of civil society is not one against sovereignty; it overthrows the government not the State. The slogan calling on civil society to rise up against the State might be popular, but it is no less pre-philosophical and politically demagogic. The ideology of civil society is, in fact, a State ideology, the ideology of the liberal democratic State. It is always the State that tolerates the Rights of Man so that the greater or lesser autonomy of civil society—who thinks them—refers to the *exercise* of sovereignty. Only a democratically exercised sovereignty makes its ideology out of the 'Rights of Man' and places them in the preamble (or annexe) to its Constitution. The rights in question, the rights of the individual subject of rights, are effective and real—guaranteed—only if the State guarantees them. In the same way, they are non-existent (or only exist verbally) if the non-democratic State rejects that ideology.[28]

In its essence, civil society is the *space of the market* or *the marketplace*, and the market is the ultimate cause of civility. This was the case in the thought of the founder of political economy, as it is today.[29] But nowadays, the *space of the market* is transformed into an idyllic space because we can play at being Crusoe. The *Robinsonade* of the petit-bourgeois trader has replaced the foundation of classical political economy. The consequences for the space of the market, the sphere of *universal* exchange, must now be reassessed, especially if we consider this as the

28. The majority of contemporary despotic states, large or small, are ready to declare that they protect the rights of man, but, according to their understanding of the matter, this is just a verbal declaration. Moreover, those same despotic or tyrannical States will accept or reject a liberal democratic State calling their attention to these rights when it wishes to trade with them. The *tolerance* of these despotic States is no different than that of democratic States—both accept criticism only when it is not against their interests to do so. Thus, so long as it doesn't prevent the despot from satisfying his needs, the latter is happy to talk about 'the Rights of Man'—words, words, nothing but words.

29. See my introduction to the French edition of *The Wealth of Nations, La Richesse des nations* (Paris: Gallimard, Folio, 1990).

surface of the circulation of commodities, and civil society as the element within which the multitude of free subjects (producers and consumers) exercise their rights. In both cases, the space of the market is the public environment of private morality, the juridico-political space of *contracts*. The subject of right sells what he produces and consumes what he buys. The means by which these commodities and goods circulate is the contract, so that when a thing is exchanged it is the rights to property themselves which are exchanged through the contract. The thing (commodity) and right (a subject's power) are the material of the space of the market, while the apparent agents are simple supports. This is what the liberal economist explains. When a self, an *I*, goes to market, to buy and sell commodities, it is Master Jacques who buys and sells. He changes role depending on the operation his physical presence materializes; commodities cannot bring themselves to market, they have to be transported and they can only pass from hand to hand if a free *I*, that is, the proprietor of his own (*propre*) person and rights passes them over.

What are the determinations of the being of an *I* such that he will leave home to go and meet another *I* in a public space and agree a contract with him, whereby the first will give a pound of butter (or a monetary equivalent) to the second, who in exchange will give the other a loaf of bread (or any other equivalent commodity)? We might say that *hunger* leads the first to get hold of some good, which becomes a commodity on the market but, once it has been exchanged for another, it becomes an object of consumption for him, a thing which he subsequently owns, which he uses to feed himself and his family. The transformation of a commodity (a product destined for exchange) into a *thing* that is possessed (a consumption good) is an effect of the desire of every being to preserve itself in being, whether it be it a wild beast, a domestic animal, a tree or a blade of grass, or human beings themselves, regardless of their intelligence, wealth or poverty. And

we could even describe this biological instinct for self-preservation as 'natural'—
it is only universal because it is the effect, in sum, of universal finitude. In this
sense, an *I* going to market unconsciously practises metaphysics, since he takes
part in the universal struggle against the finitude to which he, like every other *I*,
is fatally subject. If this *I* refuses to go to market, he will disappear, body, goods
and rights with him. As he wants to put off this necessary end of the self, he gives
himself up to the market to make a series of contracts there. These might consist
of exchanging butter for bread, but they might also consist of exchanging a fleet
of international aircraft for oil or gas. In this case, the *Is* making contracts are
States—but they are always *Is*. The picture of civil exchange will be less incomplete
if we ask what *price* a given *I* is prepared to pay to satisfy the desire for self-preservation, or, in other words, how deep is he prepared to dig into his purse in order
to get a loaf or oil. This is where the circle of the market closes on itself: it is the
market that fixes the price of the market, through competition. Put another way,
if an *I* offers more commodities than another competing *I*, he wins the market.
This consideration leads us to a crucial question: why do some have hydrocarbons
or bread, and others aircraft or butter? The question is: can we say that some *I*
might have everything at once and more besides, a bed, a Rubens, an orchard, a
herd of cows, etc., so that he needs nothing more for his survival and his pleasures? Such an individual would have no need to go to market and make contracts.

It turns out that *nature* is not ordered in this fashion. The economist presents
this by saying that some are by their own nature and right, capable (*en puissance*)
of rearing their herds, which they own, while others have oil under their fields,
which they too own; some know how to make butter and others bread. Since, in
the end, needs are complementary, nature has ordered things well in creating a
public space for the exchange of capacities and talents, complementary virtues
through which the needs of some will be satisfied by the product of the work of

others, and vice versa. Capital has to be made to play its part because the production of commodities requires the accumulation of funds. Our economist, for whom Nature lacks all mystery, goes on to explain that having made an exchange that benefits or 'profits' him, our *I*, rather than spending this surplus, decides to save it. His savings allow him to accumulate capital, which he can invest, especially in the purchase of labour power which nature makes impossible to save and accumulate. In this way, the association of capital and labour allows everyone in civil society to preserve his being, in proportion to his virtues. What we have here, according to our economist, is a design of nature, the mother of wealth who frees us from need—the market is its spontaneous manifestation. So, our economist continues, the 'natural law' which regulates morality is manifested in the market or civil society. In addition, because natural law makes a distinction between the just and unjust, the space of the market is not merely the strict universe of rational calculation and contracts but also the sphere of subjectivity. The *I*, producer and consumer, is a moral being since by the exercise of his (natural) right he contributes to universal wealth. This is only because he respects contracts. In correctly enjoying his right, without trickery, in honouring his word, the strict bearer of the right that he is in his quality as *subject* gains a supplement to the soul that makes him into a moral being. From this point of view, civil society is the sphere of morality—we find only moral beings there, and if, as ever in human affairs, a black sheep turns up, the merchants' *police* and their *courts* will impose good order. In short, market civil society is moralized by the universal circulation of right that some *I*s bring to the market.

Marx was right to condemn this vulgarized representation of political economy produced by economists who had sold out to the market. The idyllic character of this picture—where only singular, equal *I*s are on the scene—still forms the heart of today's dominant liberal vulgate which is unafraid of justifying the alien-

ation of labour power as a commodity, like any other. However, it is not this assertion, the liberal refrain par excellence, which places its author into the camp of the
ideologues; it is, rather, the simple-minded robinsonade of a subject of right as a
spontaneous generation of nature. It is this *embourgeoisé* Robinson Crusoe who
Murray Rothbard emphatically constitutes in his *The Ethics of Liberty*[30] as the
model of the free actor as the heart of the 'free market' of a so-called libertarian
society. The extreme philosophical poverty of Rothbard's account (which he nevertheless presents as a complete statement of contemporary political philosophy)
rests on the postulate of 'natural law': it is the *nature* of the apple that makes it
fall.[31] In the same way there is a human nature which can be elucidated without
difficulty. When we exclaim in astonishment: 'Who is going to establish these supposed truths about the nature of man?' our philosopher economist replies: 'The
answer is not *who* but *what*—man's reason. Man's reason is *objective*, i.e. it can be
employed by all men to yield truths about the world.'[32] Armed with these certainties, our vulgar singer of liberal refrains heralds the final state of the robinsonade
of the free market and its foundation in nature:

> If Crusoe economics can and does supply indispensable groundwork for
> the entire structure of economics and praxeology—the broad formal
> analysis of human action—a similar procedure should be able to do the
> same thing for social philosophy, for the analysis of the fundamental
> truths of the nature of man vis-à-vis the nature of the world in which he

30. Murray Rothbard, *The Ethics of Liberty* (New Jersey: Humanities Press, 1982).
31. Just as it is the nature of hydrogen and oxygen to produce water when they are combined.
Rising to the level of generality, he goes on: 'The world in fact consists of a myriad number of
observable things or entities [. . .] The observable behaviour of each of these entities is the law
of its nature, and this law includes what is produced as a result of their interactions. The complex that we may build up as a result of these laws may be termed the structure of *natural law*'
(ibid., p. 9).
32. Ibid., p. 10.

is born, as well as the world of other men. Specifically, it can aid greatly in solving such problems of political philosophy as the nature and role of liberty, property and violence.[33]

From suppositions to transpositions, analyses to syntheses, Rothbard then undertakes to construct the juridico-economic subject that constitutes our Robinson, from which he will form the general picture of philosophical economy. Through his natural reason, Robinson calculates and chooses, thinks about his means of survival, makes his tools, invents his technologies and amasses his capital. He is endowed with free will, and this makes him devote himself through his own spiritual and mental resources to the creation of the instruments of his subsistence. He ceaselessly scrutinizes his conscience, hesitates and deliberates, doubts and overcomes doubt, decides and conceives, and, finally, elucidates the *nature* of things: 'He comes to know the *natural laws* of the way things behave in the world. He learns that an arrow shot from a bow can bring down a deer and that a net can catch an abundance of fish'.[34] We had thought such naive beliefs firmly consigned to the past and Daniel Defoe, whose own work however had no truck with these robinsonades. Defoe, like his hero, is the first to realize that Robinson benefits from the cultural contributions of his time symbolized by the profit he makes on bits of the wreck. In fact, Rothbard is under the illusion that he has found in Robinson the model of man as what he calls a 'rational being'. But he does not construct 'Robinson's philosophy of right' on this basis, but on that of first individual as constructed within the ideology of the common, vulgar liberal economics that flowers from the nineteenth century onwards.[35] An individual is enthroned—*homo oeconomicus*—as the natural subject of right, freely devoting

33. Ibid., p. 29.
34. Ibid., p. 31.
35. In addition, Rothbard has become a disciple of G. de Molinari, a pompous, polymathic, enthusiast of nineteenth-century ultra-liberalism. One could usefully read his edifying dialogue

himself, by deliberating and choosing in full knowledge of cause and effect, to the rational calculation of the means of his own self-preservation.

The reduction of socially organized economic activity to the complementary actions of a multitude of individuals forgets what the economist of robinsonades is attempting to establish in the first place, i.e., that there is a market, that is, a socialized space of exchange and contracts without which there can be no *I*. Such a space does not result from the adding together of the actions of a plethora of little Robinsons who come to market. If that were the case, violence would be a correct consequence of calculating reason. But savage competition is what makes the market—the free market—impossible. Only some can survive there; the rest are either excluded or integrated into trading groups, which leave their 'free will' no margin for deliberation. In other words, if the robinsonade is in itself philosophically inappropriate, and, in addition, methodologically inappropriate in its aim to give an account of general economic activity, this is not so much because it reduces the market to the (more or less 'perfect') competition of interests which are both antagonistic and complementary, but because it ignores the formation of historical ensembles (territorial sovereignties) as the prior formal condition of existence of the space of the market. This means that it is not the individual—the *I*—which makes the market but the market that makes the individual. It is not the citizen who makes the city but the city that makes the citizen. If the space of exchange is not constructed (and often by civil or foreign *war*) as the space of sovereignty,[36] then there is no economy—family, feudal or otherwise— and no general economic groupings. In other words it is only because States open up markets by conquest and territorialize their authority, pacifying a territory open to their

after the 1848 revolution, which stages an encounter between the dangerously utopian 'Socialist', the feudal anti-bourgeois 'Conservative' and the 'Economist' who dispenses the truth. See G. de Molinari, *Les Soirées de la rue Sainte Lazare* (La Varenne, Saint-Hilaire, Eventura, 2003 [1848]).
36. What Adam Smith calls 'nation'.

sovereign regulation, that individuals are (more or less) free to play the game of *I* (*jouer le jeu du Je*).

Contemporary 'globalization' is only really possible if States (especially politically and economically dominant States) have enough force to transcend their previously consolidated frontiers and conquer markets, so that their settlers, those who hold their State passports, registered at their embassies, can devote themselves to the mercantile deliberation of their private interests. Here Rothbard gets the point of the ideology of *as if*. He acts *as if* entrepreneurs, like a completely fantasized Robinson, open up markets on a desert island, far away from *laws* and *States*. On the contrary, markets require, as their condition of possibility, the existence of a civil society where needs find their means of satisfaction, because the laws of sovereignty make exchange possible, maintain civil peace, without which contracts would be mere words—covenants without swords are nothing but words. We find a pertinent historical illustration of this reality in the creation of a transnational market in Europe after the Second World War. It was only because the States of Europe had pacified the territory of Europe, and each nation had uncontested sovereignty within its territorial space, that a 'great market' could unfold. No robinsonade created this increasingly integrated European economy. Furthermore, the 'great market' constituted by the European Union could not exist without the regulations created by the central European juridico-political system (Parliament, Judiciary and Executive). Robinsonades lead to the Hobbesian state of nature, in which nature is just the universal war of all against all. Behind this adulterated model of the fictional Robinson, whose market is an island and whose inventor is a subject of right shipwrecked there by a storm, there is the disguised and problematic figure of the originary individual, author and actor, autonomous and indeterminate, perfectly free in a state of nature.

Once Again . . . the Little King *and the* Terror

The authentic model of the subject of right is not the robinsonade above, which is merely its vulgarization. Its philosophical foundations lie in the schema of the institution of sovereignty which was inherited (essentially after Grotius) from modern natural right. To grasp what is proper to civil society, it is necessary to turn to the State and its genesis—we see here the formation of the subject of right, the *juridical self* of the little king. The traditional description of the origin of the body politic is a literary narrative—it is a fiction, at times pastoral, at others riven by conflict, which provides a stage setting for the individuals of the multitude who are in a state of physical and moral nudity (they are only dressed out of egoistic care for the self), which is, however, the very substance of what they *have* and the mark of their *being.* The naturalistic fiction of this foundational narrative becomes the fiction of natural law when the relation of being and having is stated in the form of a right. We are thus in the presence of a vast theatre of 'nature', a psychodrama, in which we ourselves are actors. In other words, we play a role, act out a character. The primordial nudity in which the human animal comes into the world is different from the nudity of the animal *tout court,* in that the latter is not recognized *ab initio* as incarnating a character, playing out a role. The simple animal is an individual that exists only in absolute identity with itself; the other is nothing, or if it is something, it is *prey.* By contrast, the human animal is not human only because of its biological configuration—it is human also because the fable of natural law recognizes that he is the bearer of the *jus.* So the state of nature in which we find this character, and where we discover ourselves as the subject of a *jus,* must be regarded as the human condition inasmuch as it is distinguished from the animal condition. The passage to humanity comes about, in the fiction of origins, because, properly speaking, the *jus* is *what being has* and that being is an *I.* We could also invert the proposition—the being of the natural individual is an *I* if the *jus* is what he possesses properly as his own (*en propre*), so that he can say *I am because I have the right*.[37] This means that for me, right is what I have when I am. And I am a self, because the being of this self is having the right. If I do not have this right, I am nothing, or, rather, I am something—I am some *thing*—but I am not human in the midst of other human beings, my fellows.

What is this *I* that is contained in its having? It is the individual of the multitude considered in its given natural condition, as a *human* individual and not just a simple thing or beast. I am not a thing because the thing (inanimate or not) is known not to be with itself in the relation of being to having. The identity of the thing is its immediate relationship to itself without consciousness. If identity is thought in this form, it makes the subject of the identity a simple thing—beast or slave. The reduction to slavery is the reification of the individual without right, his reduction to the state of a thing. Just as the animal, if it is without right, is reduced to the condition of the thing. Such a reduction is, on the other hand, what the human being in the natural law fable escapes from, since, as we have just said, its being is to have something—the *jus*. So that precisely because of this its identity is reflexive, and not pure, immediate equality with itself. The lesson of the fable, in effect, is that I own my own person (*je suis propriétaire de ma propre personne*), *I am the owner of my own body*. The content of the *jus* is a right of property over myself. Which the thing cannot claim—and by definition neither can the slave. Being someone else's property, the slave is someone else's good. Like the thing, therefore, he disposes of no right of his own because the rights that he does dispose of (if he has any) depend on the benevolent disposition of his master. This is the case with Friday. Friday owes his salvation to his submission as Robinson's slave and everything he has he owes to his master—primarily his life.

---

37. As we have seen earlier (Chapter 2, 'The Historial or the World Spirit'), in the natural law fiction, the passage from nature to history is the passage to the human. This comes from the fact that human individuals are juridical selves—they have rights.

The state of nature is thus the situation I find myself in when, among my fellows, toiling in extension in order to find the means of my subsistence, I can say that I am the owner of my body and my person, in other words, when I have a (more or less clear) consciousness of being myself, a self that the tale of origins will define as the subject of right. In other words, my natural condition is that of being a juridical self. I am autonomous. My preferring to live alone or in a troupe has no bearing on whether or not I am a juridical self. In addition, whether I know it or not, all *selves* are like myself—there are only equals who people the extension. They are equal in right because they are owners of their own bodies. I can covet another's body for my pleasures or my needs, and try to appropriate it; I can calculate how to satisfy my desires and try to appropriate the other by creating a stock of slaves to whom I concede only those rights that I wish. If my attempt comes off, I will have things at my service—not *selves*. If I fail, and I manage to stay alive, I will probably be reduced to the state of a thing—a body deprived of self. Whatever the case, the right ascribed to me by the fable of natural law, that is, the right that I *have* when I *am,* is the same for everyone, because it exists by nature and even within my nature, to the point that my own identity as an individual of the multitude is to be the title-holder of this right, to be the figure in which this right is embodied. If this right is not embodied in the individual, then there is no right. If this right is not in my person—a person that the *I* possesses precisely because this is the very fact that creates the right—then it exists nowhere. It might be in some divinity or in the order of things, but that is not what the fable tells us. Rather, it tells us that justice is not in things but in the individual who has right over things because he is their owner.

All of which leads us back to the state of nature. In the state of nature there are only juridical selves, all having the same rights and all seeking to meet their needs. To do this, they group together or associate or try to live (subsist) in solitude. We can think what we like about these groupings and troupes; we might say, as certain philosophers do, that human beings have a tendency to live together and associate, or that their preference is for solitude, mistrust, which is why they live dispersed and separate from one another. This can all be defended, but there is one thing that is indubitable—that they have, by nature, a right. It is this natural right that selves make and that authorizes them to demand from others that it be respected in my person, as I must respect it in theirs.

Looked at correctly, this *natural right* is an entirely social right—it is the condition by which an individual enters into relation with another, whether that encounter is due to some human tendency to associate or the result of chance or necessity. In both cases, my encounter will be of advantage to one or other, or both. Experience will decide. I can in fact make a rational calculation about whether I should engage one part of my property, my body, and the work it can perform, to assure my survival or to some other end. I thus make an exchange in the form of a contract. I am not alone with my partner in performing this calculation. Everybody does it. The state of nature is the situation in which all subjects of right seek to exercise their right so as to achieve satisfaction. This does not mean that if we have a moral norm, every transaction will be moral or just, because it could be immoral or unjust, depending on what morality I have. Some people will see a 'contract' where I see 'theft'. In this type of contract, especially when they are made in large numbers, there are bound to be actors who think, rightly or wrongly, that they have been robbed. They have the subjective conviction that their *jus* has not been respected. There is thus no need to resort to the fiction of natural law to see that the person who is so convinced will do everything in their power to reclaim their right. He will either have recourse to a court (it will then be necessary to set one up) or he will take the law into his own hands (it will then be necessary to set up a police force). The natural right that I exercise vis-à-vis my fellows is a right that I exercise in society.

In fact, given that everyone has this same right *ex hypothesi*, everyone exercises it, one right must necessarily encounter another—'society' is a relationship of right and this relationship is natural. There can be no serious doubt on this question unless I accept that I produce justice myself, which would contradict the idea of a right that is equally embodied in the universality of the individuals of the multitude. We cannot accept both the equality of the *Is* with each other, from the point of view of *jus* (or it is necessary to show why some have by nature rights that others do not) and the idea that my right is diminished by another. If natural right exists only in society, it is because it can only be *effective*—as opposed to being only exercised—if, and only if, there exists a common guarantee by which the integrity of my right is recognized. It is only the courts and the police that allow for such a guarantee. Since these institutions do not exist in the primordial nakedness of the naturalist fiction, they must exist in history.

We can conclude from this either that there is a *jus* which everyone possesses by nature, which makes each into an *I* (a juridical self), and in this case it is necessary for there to be guarantees for these rights to be effective and not merely exercised, or that there is no right, so that in pure nature human beings are simple things—which the fable of natural law/right rejects, in asserting, on the contrary, the irreducible quality of the individual being as a juridical self. In short, it is an internal and absolute contradiction to claim at the same time (which the holders of natural right do) that, in a state of nature outside society, I am the bearer of a right, for the reason that the right, to exist, must be exercised. This exercise necessarily puts equals into social relation. There is thus no state of nature—unless we understand this to be the social state itself.

It is essential to the modern narrative of natural rights that we keep sight of the fact that the state of society—civility—is a state of nature where juridical selves encounter one another. These selves are exclusively concerned with their well-being which they advance through making contracts. The state of nature is the market civil society of contracts. I say 'exclusively' because what I am considering here is the social encounter of selves. That does not mean that this is the only concern in individuals' lives. In *civil society* they are the agents of the market, but not when they return home or when they privately enjoy their surroundings without resort to rational calculation of survival. On the other hand, when an individual leaves home he is in the public square,[38] which is, properly speaking a state of nature. Or we could formulate it another way—what the natural law fable calls 'state of nature' is the *public square*. True, the fable specifies that what it calls 'state of nature' is the pre-juridical (and pre-social) condition in which human beings find themselves prior to the establishment of a common [system of justice]. True, prior to the law, there is no law, so the state of nature thus defined is just this situation, anterior to any law. But this assertion is coherent only because it negatively defines the state of nature as the lack of law, so that the law (and the judge that applies it) is already inscribed in nature. It is there in potential and the exercise of their natural right by each individual of the multitude is precisely what brings this law into action. We are thus forced to accept that the state-of-nature-without-law is the metaphor for the civil society where juridical selves encounter each other—natural individuals acting out the role of right. If the state of nature is the negative of society, it is because the latter is already present in the former. This supplies the answer to the question often posed to natural right: why do human beings voluntarily leave the state of nature? We know that the answers vary, but they are all marked by Hobbesian realism. Human beings associate together in order to impose a master on themselves—without a master they would devour each other.

---

38. This was rightly noted by Bodin in his definition of the 'citizen': 'When the head of the family leaves his home where he commands to treat and do business with other heads of families about what touches them all in general, he loses the title of master, of head, of lord, to become companion, equal and associate of the others: leaving the family to enter into the city, and domestic affairs to deal with public ones; and in place of lord he is called citizen, which is properly speaking nothing other than the free subject who holds citizenship from all' (*Six Livres*, VOL. 1, p. 68).

This reply is satisfying from the realist point of view, but it is a paralogism and we are astonished that it is so widespread. In fact, natural right fabulists always like to recall that the construction of the fiction of the state-of-nature-without-law is a logical elaboration. Which is satisfying. What is less so, on the other hand, is that the exit from this original state is circumstantial, anecdotal even—there is no logical argument for it. Hobbes offers an excellent explanation for this move from the state of nature—it is the fear of death which drives human beings to associate themselves into civil society. He puts his finger on the ultimate human emotion in the face of finitude—it is neither a rhetorical argument, nor a logical form, but a vital given of experience, which is not the state of nature, and has nothing to do with the experience of the historical world. Individuals associate, then, out of fear for their lives—this is the only *real* reason. It is also a given of experience that human beings have need of the law (without having need of a master). The law is what protects right because it guarantees its exercise. In other words, the individual is an *I* because the law allows him to be one. It is the law that makes me proprietor of my own person. If this is indeed a disposition of nature in me, this disposition means that the law is equally a dimension of the state of nature, or what amounts to the same thing—the state of nature is the civil state itself. The juridical self is the modern *zoon politikon*.

What turns the modern human being into the *zoon politikon* is not the cosmic order, nor the divine order of the created world, but self-preservation. This constitutes the human logic of the world in the will, that will which posits the law for self-preservation. The Moderns have become modern through property and ownership, that is, they emerged from a state of nature—natural and divine— through ownership, first of themselves and then of extension. As the separation of the common from the private is first effected on the individual—on his body— and only then on extension, it opens the field to the person, to the figure who holds title to the *jus*—all possession of what is external to my own body is possible only on the previous, express condition of my possessing myself. I cannot say of a portion of extension: *This belongs to me* if this *me*, this self, is not free, that is, in a relation of property (*propriété*) with itself. If I am not the person who, in obeying myself, obeys no one, then I am not free to say: *This belongs to me*. So, in the state of nature in which we Moderns are by nature, there are only proprietors. In the state of nature, the little kings are all proprietors of their own bodies and their own persons, without which they could not encounter each other as equals and engage in exchange for their self-preservation.

Rousseau is therefore right to exclaim in his second *Discourse*:

> The first man who, having enclosed a piece of ground, bethought himself of saying '*This belongs to me*' and found people simple enough to believe him to be the real founder of civil society. From how many crimes, wars and murders, from how many horrors and misfortunes might not anyone have saved mankind, by pulling up the stakes, filling in the ditches, and crying to his fellows: 'Beware of listening to this impostor; you are undone if you once forget that the fruits of the earth belong to us all, and the earth itself to nobody.'[39]

Rousseau here utterly opposes the tradition, whose idiom he nevertheless adopts. He thinks in the terms of natural law while rejecting one of its fundamental axioms, the axiom of property, which nevertheless is constitutive of the subject of right (a matter of the singular or collective individual). But he takes up the fable of the state of nature as a corollary of the *social contract*. Whatever else it might be, the rejection of property seems essential here to elucidate the ultimate significance of the citizen—the little king—in our democracies, and even the nature of

---

39. Jean-Jacques Rousseau, *A Discourse on the Origin of Inequality* (1754) (Maurice Cranston trans., ed. and annot.). (Harmondsworth: Penguin, 1984), p. 42; translation modified.

democracy itself when it is thought in the theoretical context of sovereignty—the status of the citizen is not linked to the status of property. In fact, says Rousseau, the citizen is a *member of the sovereign*. This figure produces an essential rupture with the individual in a state of nature as natural law describes it. While the latter, the bearer of right and *juridical self*, is necessarily in a social relationship with his fellows (as we have seen), Rousseau's 'savage' is solitary, an authentic nomad of the state of nature, so that the post-contractual citizen does not have a relationship with another citizen as individual. In other words, Rousseau's rupture produces through the passage to the body politic not a simple subject of right (juridical self, owner of himself) but a political subject, the subject as *political self*. In rejecting property, Rousseau envisages the transcendence through the 'body politic' of the ordinary state of civility thanks to which the individual in the state of nature becomes subject of the sovereign, not a member of the sovereign. The difference is crucial, because, in the first case, civility is simply *social*—it places subjects of right in each other's presence through the contract of exchange in the social space of the market.

By contrast, the democratic figure of the citizen does not take shape within the market but within a 'common moral self', which makes each individual into a citizen, a 'member of the sovereign', a participant in the universal. In the first case, the individuals exchange contracts among themselves, recognize each other as particular subjects of right; but as simple actors in civil society they do not raise themselves beyond the particularity of contracts of exchange. The *juridical selves* of the tradition from Grotius to Hobbes are replaced by Rousseau's *political selves*, in which the citizen raises himself to the universal while the simple subject remains in particularity. Rousseau is the first to establish a link between the particular individual and the universal. This is not just a social link—inter-individual relations within the space of exchange: civil society or nation—but a link within the 'people'. The citizen is nothing without the people. Rousseau holds that the individual comes into existence politically and morally as the 'citizen' only through his being part of the sovereign people, that is, the universal. The individual accedes to the *thought of the universal*, which is the law itself. The body politic is beyond the social body.

So, the idea of democracy as it is finally elaborated and comes to its culmination in the context of sovereignty consists of the advent of the political self. There is nothing of this kind, as we have seen, in thought before Rousseau; there, sovereignty is the space where individual rights are exchanged. Civil society is a juridical space from which the universal is absent; we only find particulars who are entirely depoliticized because they are only motivated by concern for their own interests. Civil society is a pre-political space, an authentic state of nature. By contrast, sovereignty, that essence of the *res publica*, is external to civil society (as the liberals desire it) in the sense that it makes the free exchange of rights possible. It is thus impossible for it to exist among men without the help of the State in person. If politics is external to civil society, it nevertheless does not lead an autonomous existence, so to speak, relative to the sovereign State. On the contrary, it is only through the army, the police and the courts of the sovereign that the space of sovereignty is a space of internal and external exchange that Smith rightly calls *nation*. Within this *nation*, individuals are not members of the sovereign—they are subject to it, or at least, depend on it. If a thought of the universal is possible in the nation, then it is because it is conceived by the sovereign itself and only by it, something that remains improbable since the universal cannot proceed from the will of a single being but only from all in one, the *people*. Rousseau understood this, thus making the individual not simply a *petit bourgeois* involved in exchange but a little king (*petit roi*) of the republic, who can overcome his singular individuality by raising himself to a contemplation of the universal. This mutation of the juridical self into a political self is the foundation of democracy. If in the state of nature the individual is part of the social body, as a citizen he is a member of the sovereign body politic. It is this double belonging that is foundational for democracy—it is no longer the monarch alone who says, '*L'État c'est moi*', but each citizen who embodies the republic. The *little king*, and only he, can represent his own freedom as the common freedom that exists concretely in him, as in all his fellow citizens, and can therefore say that, in obeying himself, he obeys nobody. When the little king thinks, his thought is that of the people, not because it is identical to it but because it *is* that thought itself, the conception of the *law*.

Hence, it is through the people that the little king comes into the world. This is not a natural individual, a simple juridical self, who by his own efforts is able to raise himself to the contemplation of the universal by effecting this mutation into the political self. When Rousseau says that it is necessary for the individual absolutely to renounce his natural right, this is in order to bring forth the citizen of the people. In order to be *total freedom*, obedience to the law that we are given is necessarily the advent of the little king, *that perfect sovereign self*. Philosophically, it is the thought of the sovereign people that institutes the citizen, not the other way round: historically, this happens in the Terror, as if the guillotine were the instrument by which the people universalize the individual. The political self does not emerge from the juridical self; the petit bourgeois involved in exchange cannot turn himself into the little king, because what determines him in his free existence as a particular individual, a subject of right is not the common but what is his own. Civil society *cannot* of itself accede to the universal,[40] and by nature is not political; only politics can bring me to the universal. Thus, if I am confined to the single civility of exchange, I have no part in the universa; I have only a civil existence, not a political one. The passage to the universal

40. This is what Hegel expresses, after Rousseau and the Scottish economists.

requires a specific foundation to be found in the thought of a people, that is, in the people as the subject of the *thought of freedom*. If freedom does exist in civil society, it is only in the *private* activity of the subject of right. To exist as the thought of *public* morality, as the thought of *public* freedom, it cannot proceed from individuals among themselves but only from all in one, the *people* in person.

The people is thus the ultimate limit beyond which sovereignty as actualized in democracy cannot advance. In other words, democracy is the end of sovereignty, its aim and its culmination. There is in fact an absolute contradiction which sovereignty cannot resolve, a contradiction whose tragic emblem is the Terror. To resolve the contradiction, the Terror inaugurated the reign of the universal in the republic by absolutely eliminating it. The Terror bears witness to the impossibility of reconciling the universality of the thought of freedom as the thought of the sovereign people with the essential and constitutive particularism of this people itself. The administration of the universal by the Terror manifests the impossibility of making it (the universal) live within the particularism of a people. The individual rejoins the universal in *Death*. The victory of the universal is the victory of death. It is only in nothingness that the particular essence of an historical people can historically effect the universal. The thought of a people that thinks freedom as universal can conceive this universal only in the mode of the historial, that spiritual sublimation of the historical. If the people is by its very nature a common self, this common cannot transcend the particular. If it undertakes to go beyond itself, it turns towards the Terror and its avatars. The individual no longer has a value and becomes the plaything of the historial, that is, of sublime goals that can never be attained—save in death.

This does not mean that the individual—the citizen—cannot live freely and peacefully. On the contrary, he can, but outside the sovereignty of a particular people. If the individual's access to the universal, as Rousseau says, is the mark of the democratic life, where to live freely is to obey only the law that one is given, then the individual cannot find peace within the democracy of sovereignty. If Rousseau's democracy leads to the Terror, that does not flow from the idea that *citizenship* is the individuals' passage to the universal. Rather, it comes from another, absolutely contradictory, idea that it is the people who define the universal. Beyond the historical experience that led to the Terror, the universal is defined in this way only by tyrannical States: Fascism, Nazism and Communism have this idea in common—that the people think the universal. The *will of the people* is the ingredient of the modern historial of sovereignty. The people is the universal subject—the 'people' defines who belongs to the people, who is a member of the sovereign and who is not. What is universal in a people can be understood only on condition that the people itself defines the multitude that composes it and takes part in its will, because it (that fraction of the multitude) is capable of acceding to the universal, that is, to *what* the universal in question has as its basic *particular.* What is proper to the people is in fact to trace the border (internal and external) between those who belong to the people and those who do not. It is thus necessary for it to define what particularizes it as *this people*, and not that people. The discrimination of the individuals of the multitude—belonging to the people *or* not—takes the extreme form of *extermination.* And the law which states the form of the universal does so only because it names the particular,

That is why the sovereign people, its essential particularism, is the very limit of democracy—it is the greatest danger that threatens it. So the crucial question for our time is this: from now on, by what means can the *individual of the multitude* gain the universal if, on the one hand, the universal is (as Rousseau discovered) the very essence of democracy, and, on the other, the thought of the universal cannot be the work of the people (contrary to Rousseau) without running the risk of tyranny? How can the *individual of the multitude* live freely and peacefully if the sovereignty of the people can offer him, at best, only the space of the market and, at worst, the bloody despotism of a Terror?

Today this question is posed for Europeans in a particular way because it is in Europe, more than anywhere else on the surface of the *orbis*, that the elements for an answer are to be found. This is the case because the cycle of sovereignty has reached its culmination—after its perversion by tyrannies exercising it in the name of the people, or even 'democracy'—in a period when the division of Europe is in fact no longer pregnant with war but with peace.

CHAPTER 5

European Humanity or The Multitude

Humanity in the Orbis

People in our time could be forgiven for regarding the Kantian vision of *humanity*—the ethical end and aim of the world or the moral disposition within us—as the optimistic dream of a philosopher[1] who was otherwise not prone to naivety. Nevertheless, if an all-too-legitimate pessimism took hold of Europeans at the end of the last century, the idea of humanity as such was not altogether ruled out. Europeans cannot invalidate their idea of humanity without denying themselves as Europeans, simply because what it is to be European is bound up with the ways

---

1. 'There is something within us that we can never cease to admire once we have seen it, and it is what at the same time elevates *humanity*, in idea, to a dignity which one did not imagine in man as object of experience' (Immanuel Kant, *Le Conflit des facultés*, in *Oeuvres philosophiques*, 3 vols [Paris: Gallimard, Bibliothèque de la Pléiade, 1980–86], VOL. 3, p. 865).

that very idea has been conceived in the course of modernity. But if a profound pessimism remains all too legitimate, it is because the experience of the last century or, rather, the centuries of modernity, has led us to think that such an idea has more to do with the verbal persiflage of the State. Or at any rate, we might consider it as a postulate that remains at the level of intention rather than real accomplishment. Historical experience adds weight to the justified pessimism of those who see in this irenic conception of humanity more a moralizing slogan than a maxim of morality. This stems from the fact that the idea of humanity thus conceived refers to an arbitrary and abstract universalism that the concrete history of men, that is, their experience as determined and known, continues to invalidate. Human beings living and dying on the surface of this planet do not form a community. It is no exaggeration to say that nothing today gainsays this proposition. The idea of humanity does not refer to the empirical world of the constitutive materiality of men's everyday existence but precisely to an idea.

Such an idea of humanity as the end of concrete human existence is not by nature given in the historical world; rather, it limns the postulates of the historial. What is not given is its universality. In other words, there is *nothing* in what is given or in my environment to make me think that any such thing exists to give more than verbal substance to a republic of mankind. Nevertheless, Europeans cannot reject the idea of humanity, as their moral aim, so long as they also acknowledge the experience of *evil* and the unspeakable *miseries* that, only a short time ago, Europeans were subject to. Kant could formulate his profound idea of *humanity* only on condition that he excluded from its spirit the very *possibility* that our twentieth century has nevertheless realized *in fact*. If Kant had had the intuition of even the *possibility* of Auschwitz, he would have refrained (or he would have been seized by doubt) from stating the famous proposition in *Religion within the Limits of Reason Alone*:

Mankind (rational earthly existence in general) *in its complete moral perfection* is that which alone can render the world the object of a divine decree and the end of creation. With such perfection as the prime condition, happiness is the direct consequence, according to the Will of the Supreme Being.[2]

It thus may be impossible to renounce the idea of humanity (in Europe or elsewhere), but it is not Kant's sense of the term that is at issue. The discrediting of Kant's idea of humanity finally rests on its revelation as the goal of a banal moralism—the idea of the republic of mankind. In fact, we *know* today (and Europeans *know* it better than anyone) that the human plan for *animality* has slipped into the divine plan for humanity. The idea of a republic of mankind is impossible because it is not an idea but a dream or daydream—it may be appropriate to the vision of philosophers and poets, but it is not at all a proper idea of this world.

In fact, this world has still not managed to uncover or unify the moral conditions of a universal humanity, or humanity in the *orbis*. And it is highly improbable that it will ever do so. Such a humanity would finally achieve peace with itself, not because it rejected war by an act of will or a juridical decision (placing war outside the law, for example) but because the conditions of war themselves would have disappeared. But this is not the case, and the conditions for war are still everywhere in place on the grand scale of the *orbis*. The conditions for war reduce to one: the finitude of extension, that is to say, the life resources of the human animals of the planet. The creation of the conditions for the moral existence of *orbis* humanity (and with it the republic of mankind) depends not on wars being rendered unlawful (supposing there to be an agency capable of making such a prohibition compatible with the idea of the humanity of the *orbis*, which, as we will see,

2. Immanuel Kant, *Religion within the Limits of Reason Alone* (Thomas M. Greene and Hoyt H. Hudson trans. and introd.) (New York: Harper Torchbooks, 1960), p. 54.

is not the case) but on the conditions for war being eliminated from the life of men. Which is meaningless. Because finitude, that is the limitation of extension, is a given, perhaps the only given in human existence, the one that human beings cannot hope to master save in some far distant future. On the other hand, we might think that human beings could succeed, at least in some time and place, in coming to an understanding between themselves about the means and conditions of their common survival. But even that understanding does not flow from their will but from the conditions that make such an agreement of wills and reasons possible. To put it another way, the fact that—here or there—peace reigns (if only in the most elementary sense of peace: the absence of war) must not be seen as a result of an agreement. On the contrary, this comes from the mere fact that at such-and-such a time and place, peace is preferable to war. Humanity in the *orbis* (and the republic of mankind with it) is not a historical possibility in our world— it never has been, and never will be.

The first reason why *orbis* humanity is not at peace is that the universality of the individuals of the multitude peopling the *orbis* do not form a single *societas* by nature. This is for us the given condition of our nature. In effect, human beings associate locally and for a time only with the perspective and aim of bending nature to their ends, that is, the ends of extracting the means of their subsistence from nature. The human multitude of the *orbis*, as such, in the state of nature, is in permanent conflict with extension. Since the material extension of the planet has been discovered, and hence the limits of the extension have become known, human beings have perceived their existence as determined by the finitude of their world. The more infinite space has opened up to their dreams, their thoughts and even their actions, the more the finitude of their world has impressed itself upon them. The more the conquest of finite space, of their own sensible and apprehensible space, becomes possible, the more the infinite nature of that con-quest becomes obvious. Or, rather, the more human technicians conquer extension, the more they grasp that such a 'conquest' is impossible because it is properly infinite. It is from the infinite conquest of finite extension that the impossibility of any *societas* of mankind flows. As does the division of humanity, a division that is not local and transient but substantial and ontological. Before any apprehension of the extension of the *orbis*, human beings were able to imagine (better: think) that the republic of mankind, the *civitas maxima*, the universal republic, was possible. And in a certain way, it was, in effect, simply *possible*. Such a possibility resided in the fact that the moral connection underlying it could be seriously (which does *not mean* successfully) asserted, especially calling on religion as connection. Religion could always be seriously thought as universal, no matter what religion and no matter what obedience. Christianity was, quite correctly, in the wake of those first attempts to think the universal republic, understood as the Christian republic. Thus, we have, so to speak, the syndrome of the empire seized by the truth—the true religion of the true god ought naturally to make the foundation of the *civitas maxima* possible, or even necessary.

Remarkably, at the very moment of the discovery of the finite extension of the *orbis*—notably during the foundation of the empires in America, first of all by the Portuguese and the Spanish—the *civitas maxima* began to seem impossible at the level of thought. The work of the theologians who condemned and attempted to moderate the conquest (Vitoria or Las Casas) expresses this definitively and sees no recourse against it. Yet immediately, as the specialist historians of the *jus gentium* concur, the problematic of its foundation and eventual construction was broached. What is proper to the nascent *jus gentium* is not the construction of a *societas* of mankind but the emergence (via the new, sacrosanct, foundational principle—*sovereignty*) of a regulated division of the universality of the individuals of the multitude peopling the *orbis*. Such a regulation of division functions by the slow constitution of human groupings, the future 'nations', whose historical destiny from those times of discovery and conquest (the sixteenth and seventeenth centuries) has been, materially, to enclose their particularism behind frontiers and identify it morally in a body of ethical values. That is why today it is impossible to dream (or, better, it is not a question of a *dream*) of the advent of the republic of mankind within the universal humanity of the *orbis*. There is no practical possibility of bringing such a humanity about—in order to do so, it would be necessary to reconcile it with itself by leading it to an undivided unity of universal reason itself. But such a world reason does not exist. What does exist, by contrast, is, for the most part, the particular calculations made by individual nations rather than the community of nations working towards the same end. It is because no common end exists for the universality of human beings of the *orbis* that there cannot be a common universal world today (or tomorrow). Our world cannot be directed by will towards the same end, an end which, to be different from the ends that have characterized previous worlds, would be the prosaic satisfaction of the basic needs of life. Such a world of the universal satisfaction of the needs of the human world is not on the agenda. This does not mean that in some indefinite future it might not happen. But human beings wait for and expect nothing from the indefinite. This is because their servitude is ever present and their experience of finitude is that not everyone has their needs satisfied. In this sense, humanity in the *orbis*, considered as such, is barely *human*, if 'human' describes the existence of free and satisfied individuals living within particular peoples who are also free and satisfied.

It is thus with great seriousness that philosophy must renounce the idea of a republic of mankind that I have just described. It must also renounce the very idea of humanity if by that we understand the ideal of a universal humanity finally reconciled with itself and capable of organizing itself, even constituting itself as a republic, or, in other words, a *societas*. The dream of a society of united nations is indeed a dream that philosophy once had and must now give up. However, to renounce the idea of a universal society of mankind in the *orbis* is not to renounce the idea of humanity as such. The idea of humanity remains true in itself, in the sense that it is constituted by a plurality of humanities. The truth of humanity is plural. The reference to a humanity in general is pointless if it means that we forget the life of humanities themselves and their infinite enterprise—differentiated and multiple—of struggle with finite external nature (extension). The American continent is in struggle with nature, but this does not have the same meaning for a North American as it does for someone from South America. Europe struggles with nature, but this does not have the same meaning for someone from Western Europe as it does for someone from the East of the continent. The same is true for Asia and Africa, and we really should speak about Asias and Africas.

The world is not unitary and the human multitudes that people it are not a single and undifferentiated humanity, because humanity in the *orbis* is still (and has long been) entirely subject to the dangerous—*violent*—condition of the state of nature, if we understand by that the human condition of perpetually seeking its own humanity, that is to say, its satisfaction and freedom. Satisfaction of needs and freedom of the body and spirit are the two essential quests of human beings. And in this search, human beings move away or maintain a distance from humanity itself; satisfaction and freedom are in no way states that are attained once and for all. The desires of human beings—individuals or nations—are insatiable, and hence, it is vain to appeal in general to a humanity that is satisfied, in other words, *pacified or at peace*. Peace is not the given condition of human nature. In fact, if we contemplate human experience, we cannot deny that *conflict* (whether leading to open war and violence, or not), or at least competition, is the current modality of life. True, moments of understanding and agreement are not infrequent. Happily, this is because human beings desire peace and act accordingly. So at times they enjoy rest and find satisfaction in it. But it would be too idealistic to assert that this is their ordinary condition. Europe is undoubtedly the best illustration of the natural condition of men—a permanent state of war across an entire continent aimed at constituting groupings of human beings that are finally pacified. And it is precisely in globalizing war that Europe has left the state of war, making it possible to *think*[3] the particularism of the morality of European humanity in its present condition. In the world as it is, only Europe is in this situation—only Europe has left the state of nature, at least in the sense that a legislation of its humanity is possible. This is because Europe's internal conflict, nation against nation, is suspended, as is its conflict with the wider world (at least in the form it took for five centuries: as midwife to its own historical nations). It is because the violence of war has not just produced nations but a European humanity at peace with itself, that Europe has emerged from the state of nature. And Europe is alone in arriving at such a state of humanity at peace.

. . . and Humanity From Europe

To see a sentimental or polemical significance in this proposition—*Europe is alone in arriving at such a state of humanity at peace*—is to misunderstand it. We have shown[4] that the ultimate meaning residing in the materiality of the lived history of Europeans from the end of the fifteenth century can be stated philosophically in the particular freedom of particular nations. The advent of historical nations and peoples, the advent of a collective subjectivity of the freedom of a 'people', happens in and through violence and force, that is, through war. As if war and philosophy (*polemos* and *logos*) had worked together to produce the modern division of European humanity under the banner of sovereignties. As we know, the nations and peoples of Europe (and elsewhere) are not the creations of nature but of history. This is trivial. As we also know, the very history that turned the European continent—but not only it—into the battlefield for the constitution of particular nations brought into existence in the world, and as world, new actors, unknown

3. See Introduction in this volume.
4. See Chapter 3 in this volume.

to previous chronicles—the *peoples* of modernity. In so doing, the Europeans, or, rather, the multitudes of Europe, were thrown into battle and nourished Europe with their lives. It is in this context with their own lives at stake that, so to speak, peoples came to resemble their philosophy—the fable of the state of nature was verified in facts, generation after generation, at the very moment when philosophy was producing books on the matter. And this fable of nature was precisely the fable of the world, because a world was indeed being formed through it and in its terms. What is trivial is no less true, because peoples and nations were well and truly the stakes of this history and the characters in the fable. Today, Europe offers the spectacle of a peaceful world, a world at peace, but, in truth, surprised at the fact, even stunned in the face of this properly unprecedented revelation—for Europe, *war is over.*

In fact, on our current horizon, there is no effective possibility of a European civil war beginning again. War is no longer the order of the day between the nations and peoples of Europe.[5] And, considered in its totality, the greater part of this modern, battle-worn Europe does not perceive the world that surrounds it— first and foremost its European neighbours—as being the site of imminent or tangible danger or a space that it wishes to conquer. In this sense, war has indeed come to an end in the European world, and, in consequence, European humanity enjoys a substantial, ontological peace because its European being has been constituted in the course of the previous years of modernity (and that is what this word means). Even if substantial, such a peace produces a profound *astonishment* for Europeans, accustomed for five centuries to war, and, even more, to death as ever imminent on the fields of battle and conquest. This astonishment may not be

5. Which obviously does not mean that regional or local armed conflicts have been eliminated from the continent. I am saying nothing of the kind. Whether in the Balkans or in Chechnya, such conflicts show that wars that lead to 'crimes against humanity' nevertheless cannot lead in contemporary Europe to a generalized conflict, and to the ultimate globalization of that conflict.

healthy for Europeans. If repeated and constant astonishment in the face of war led them to cultivate philosophical thinking in order to establish the principles of their common being, then their present (and durable) astonishment at peace has so far not led them to a consideration of their present and future moral welfare as European humanity freed from violent death.[6] In other words, I am not claiming that the *given peace* which is the exit from the state of nature is in itself anything other than a heavy burden for the multitudes of Europe. Nor am I claiming that once they have agreed on the *market*, Europeans will ever come to an agreement about the republic, in other words, about *morality*. Nevertheless, this is the condition of their constitution as European humanity. It might be that the struggle to the death that came within a hair's breadth of mutual suicide was their very truth and that peace will turn out to be their swan song. But if that should be the case (something philosophy cannot exclude a priori), it is because their aims were too elevated—a universal humanity of the *orbis* finally reconciled with itself by Europe. It is worth wondering, then, whether this task of promoting universal humanity is not the historial illusion of a profane, all-conquering Europe that clung to the spiritual incense of evangelization to stimulate its conquests and legitimate its spiritual domination. In any event, those times of the spirit are at an end for us.[7] The new time of peace re-poses in a prosaic but crucial fashion the question of ends, not this time as a universal projection of an ideal humanity but as the immediate constitution of the freedom of European humanity. This is not to say that Europe must manage its own astonishment by ceasing to be interested in

---

6. This comes from the fact that Europeans know in some confused way that this current peace, however durable it might be in time (in any case without expectation that it would be eternal), is not for all that the 'perpetual peace' of the philosophers, the peace of reason conscious of itself among men, but that, rather, it springs from the stupefaction born of the discovery that the abyss of death that had opened up in front of them could be the tomb of their very humanity.

7. They are not over, however, for America, for example, which valorizes its designs in the world by the explicit will to lead the *orbis* to the 'triumph of Good over Evil'.

humanity in the *orbis*. However much it might want to do so (and it might not want to do so, which would be fatal for it), the world, that of the *orbis*, will not cease to be interested in Europe—for better or worse. Having alone emerged from the state of nature, Europe must henceforth face other humanities who are still within a state of nature. But while their history set Europeans against each other and against the rest in war, henceforth Europe *de facto* faces the state of nature of the rest of the *orbis*. This is an unprecedented situation, like the peace which it enjoys, and the state of nature in which the rest of humanity in the *orbis* finds itself thus constrains Europe to conceive its own morality in a new way.

Perhaps what we are dealing with here is another example of the cunning of history—five centuries after the conquest of the Americas, Europeans are positioned against the American state of nature. Peace in Europe contrasts with the state of nature of America (the United States); an attack on the territory of America in effect placed the latter in a state of war. But this was not what changed the state of the world in general (nor its world in particular), which was itself also in a state of nature and had to be lived in as such—with the exception of Europe. America's external projection of its power in order to conquer a sphere of influence parallels Europe's previous experience. In realizing that its territory was vulnerable, America experienced war directly, a capital experience in the genesis and formation of a nation's identity. American humanity thus finds itself placed in its turn at the heart of the state of nature about which it had only the vaguest idea, or perhaps did not even suspect existed. Only war *at home* leads a people to know, or at least perceive, its *finitude*. But Europeans have had the experience of finitude for centuries; and peace, without relieving them of it, nevertheless leads them to think their identity and their being differently than they used to do during war. That is why America and Europe are in a process of divorce that must soon be concluded. Politicians cannot just make ritual, even incantatory appeals for a *transatlantic link*—the past link has collapsed and the present makes a new one impossible.

Peace becomes the Europeans' *fatum*, while the warlike course of nature can only continue for the Americans, since, in being at war with the rest, American humanity is, first of all, at war with itself. In America, the internal conquest of extension continues and we could argue about when it might come to a conclusion; but the conquest of peace outside its borders has hardly begun. Conversely, Europe is no longer at war, neither with itself nor beyond its borders. This is the time (and burden) of peace. It is in measuring itself against others that a nation achieves its internal moral constitution, that it discovers its own particularity and comes to a consciousness of its moral self. The experience of the possibility of imminent death—the non-verbal but objective threat of death doled out at home as *thing*—produces the civil thought of morality. That is why America is and resides fully in a state of nature—its condition is that of natural pre-moral life. America is Hobbesian, cleaved to extension, on the defensive vis-à-vis the outside world (non-American humanities), seeking, in and for itself, alone, by its own will to adopt a posture that will inspire respect, distance or dread. Immersed in the natural world (the technological appropriation of extension), it lives in fear. American humanity thus asserts its belonging to the state of nature because it asserts its existence in struggle with the external world and with the rest of humanities. Not yet at peace, American humanity is not yet fully *free* because it does not recognize the freedom of others, just as the others do not recognize its freedom. By contrast, Europe is placed in a Cartesian posture—its metaphysics is no longer that of the natural world but that of the 'new world'. It thus runs the risk that the cunning of the made-up, invented world, which imposes on Europe the new condition of its peaceful life, will leave it disarmed faced with the armed prophets of the state of nature of the *orbis*.

Freedom

What is in play here is nothing less that Europe's freedom, and with it the freedom of the other humanities of the planet. The freedom of the one always depends on the freedom of the others—there is no *moral* sense to be made if Europe, or any other world, were free and some other part of humanity were not. The question of the freedom of the European world is thus no different from that of other worlds, and there would be no advance of morality if Europe tried to constitute itself by itself, independently of the rest. However, it is only within a Europe at once divided *and* at peace that the concept of concrete freedom is thinkable. By concrete freedom, we mean nothing more than the determinate freedom of particular nations, in other words, historical nations, considered as constituted ones. The problem here is thus the following—it is a matter of conceiving the forms in which European humanity can declare its freedom to the world without such a declaration being at the same time an imperialist act or an egoistic one. To resolve this difficulty, it is important to have a prior understanding of what is substantial within it. This is, first of all, to ask why the question of freedom is posed not in the form of freedom in general but practically—as freedom that can be conceived by this or that part of humanity. This is the *particularism of freedom*. Then we have to understand why peace cannot be properly defined and experienced as a universal state of the absence of war but as the juridical recognition of the particularism of freedom—*cosmopolitan right*. Finally, we have to understand how the particular field of European peace makes historically possible the idea of a right particular to Europeans, a *right of the European peoples*.

a) What should be understood by this notion of the particularism of freedom is that only the consideration of the historical will produce a reasonable formulation of the idea that freedom always concerns a particular subject, either individual or collective. In effect, as we have seen,[8] freedom as the self-determination of a subject is concrete if, and only if, it is experienced or lived in the particularity of a people. It is precisely in reference to the constituted particularism of a people that self-determi-

8. See Chapter 3 in this volume.

nation, its actions and its words are possible, and effective. This is the very significance of the modern advent of historical nations. If a nation is a people whose reason and will are self-determined (which, to be its freedom itself, is however only the state of nature of its freedom), then freedom is concretely lived because it is experienced in its particularity. And if, as history shows, this particularism, whether it is in the course of constitution or already fully achieved, is threatened by some internal or external cause, freedom is lost for the people. The defence of its particularism is *historically* the legitimate defence of freedom. From this point of view, the history of the peoples of Europe and elsewhere is the battle of particularisms, even if one or other people, organized as a conquering and victorious people, arrogated to itself the right to conquer another in the name of the universalism of freedom. To such a universalism, real peoples, that is the multitudes, oppose their absolute right to live freely according to the particularism of their freedom. A people suffering under tyranny would be happy to be liberated by another people but would quickly resent the weight of a new despotism if the liberator decided to remain in the liberated country for an indefinite time, on the pretext of bringing aid or clarifying the country's best options. We cannot then grant the least justification to the ideal of a universal freedom that involves powerful nations assuming the right to enact human or divine plans for the good. In this conception, as in reality, freedom or self-determination is the first condition of peace and this condition is particularism.

But a freedom merely attached to the immediate particularity of an organized people would be rapidly confronted by the most dangerous of contradictions. If the freedom of a people is limited to this people and if a people proclaims its freedom—or simply its very existence—unilaterally, without the agreement and recognition of the others, its freedom might be real but could not be concrete. True, a people proclaiming its self-determination of its freedom has the feeling of freedom because in this way it experiences its own particularity. But the feeling remains just that. There are countless historical examples which show that it is dangerous for a people to feel itself free when there is no juridical and material *guarantee* from outside—from the *others*. It is because the other peoples are the external condition of the freedom of a people and its autonomy that the unilateral assertion of its right by a people is bound to destroy its freedom at the very moment that it experiences it. Freedom is only concrete, if, being particular, it is at the same time recognized as the freedom of a particular person. The subject is free on the single condition that its freedom, its autonomy, is posited by the community of subjects (persons) and is the effect of the freedom of all. Concrete freedom is self-determination but it is not limited to that—it is not the finite freedom of nature. True freedom is recognition. In consequence, it is plural humanity in which this or that particular humanity participates, which guarantees the freedom of the latter.

The European experience of the world shows that the denial of the plurality of humanity is largely at the root of wars—civil or interstate. The paradox of this history is fully apparent here and exploits the paradox of freedom; at the same time, it makes it possible to discard the illusion of the humanity of the *orbis* as being the foundation of peace, a foundation that is illusory in not being historical (ideal). What is this European experience of the world? It is, we know only too well, to have recourse to war in order to establish its morality or 'spirit' universally among the human multitudes peopling the *orbis*. It consisted, on the basis of European particularism, of nothing but a single people of Europe globalizing its own freedom by imposing it on others. The effect of this history is thus to have suppressed, in whole or in part, particularism through empire. The world as European empire illustrates the historical paradox of a culture (Europe's) which, obliged to renounce empire and finally establishing itself within the diversity of nations in peace (by a return home, that is, a return to itself), rediscovers particularism as the unique vector of its concrete freedoms. But Europe after its historical trajectory is not in the same situation as before it undertook it: today it finds itself in the peace of the suspension of war. It is thus after denying human plurality that Europe comes to discover itself as particular humanity. To put matters differently, it is because Europe denied the freedom of other peoples (their particularism) in the illusion of the universal that it can today live its own freedom concretely in a different fashion. It can do so, in the sense that it is something *possible*. It is such a possibility that I explore here.

To see the designation of this new, barely formed subject of a new morality of a new world as *European humanity* as an instance of Eurocentrism, would be a profound misunderstanding. If this subject is the author of a concrete legislation of freedom, it is because it has also come to be its object. So the charge of Eurocentrism cannot hold because European humanity thought in the above manner is precisely the critique, even the refutation, of the moral and political Eurocentrism of modern history. In the present theoretical context, the notion of Eurocentrism consists of having constructed the idea of the humanity of the *orbis* on the basis of the worldwide expansion of the particular morality of the Europeans. The projection of European humanity outside itself, that is, the projection of its 'spirit', in order to instruct and lead the world, is the realized form of Eurocentrism. By contrast, European humanity as the subject of freedom is only the subject of freedom because it is also its object: it is the very *person* of freedom to come, and it can be only such in the world of the *orbis* here and now. In addition to the paradox of history (a new Europe turning away from the old Europe without which nevertheless any novelty would be impossible), there is the paradox we referred to above, the particularism of freedom—it is in thinking (and bringing to life) the concrete freedom of its particularism (the particularism of European humanity) that Europe makes it possible to think (and realize) a morality founded on humanity as plurality.

b) The thought of humanity as *plurality* is at the basis of the idea of cosmopolitanism. If, as we have observed, the idea of humanity as an end cannot be maintained as the foundation of action aimed at the life of peace, it is essentially because such an idea is not given within the historical; rather, it is an ideal. This is what is apparent if we consider not humanity in general (since this is precisely what is in question we cannot begin here) but European humanity. It is on the basis of the particular that we can represent the nature of the universal multitude peopling the *orbis* as constituted by particularisms. And the point of departure here is Europe and its particular humanity. It will be asked whether this point of departure is justified. Truth to tell, it already has been, if we want to maintain the spirit of the assertion that Europe's emergence from the state of nature is not an arbitrary one. It is not arbitrary because, to repeat, war has been eliminated from Europe, to the point that we can no longer envisage, even hypothetically, that a conflict that would pit the historical nations of the continent violently against each other might break out. Because Europe is at peace, it is in the European peace that the asked-for justification can be found. But it is true that in Europe peace through the silence of arms is still not peace by right. For it is only in the form of right that humanity can hope to live a peaceful life and emerge as humanity conscious of itself. But even so, it can seem contradictory to want right and, at the same time, the particularism of freedom. If, as we assert here, wanting the freedom of humanity in general is a proposition that has no sense, because, deprived of concrete determinations, it refers back to the ahistorical kingdom of ends, it is necessary to relate freedom (and peace) to its concrete historical subject, that is, humanity as plurality. Not universal humanity, but the particular humanities of the historical world. Among these, European humanity, because of its past experience and present condition, offers an adequate model of the *multitude*. *Humanity as multitude* is the meaning of the idea of the particularism of freedom. It is the idea of life made peaceful through cosmopolitan right. What is important, then, is to posit and even to will diversity, the multiple, in order to think the fundamental elements of a cosmopolitan law which European humanity would promote. In fact, it is because Europe is the terrain of diversity at peace, after having been the object of attempts at unification by violence and force, that it can pursue the path of cosmopolitanism, the cosmopolitanism of *its own world*. And it is because in constituting its particular freedom Europe cannot but found the freedoms of others, that it thus opens up, without egoism or imperialism, the peace of the future. In any case, this is Europe's possibility and this flows from the following: in the present period of the *orbis*, Europe is the only extant force of peace, because it is itself at peace—at peace with itself.

The notion of a *European cosmopolitanism* is in no way contradictory. It can only be seen as such from the point of view of a vague and ideal 'cosmopolitanism' that postulates a *single* world (the world as *continuum*), not whose least defect is that it does not exist in the real world; or if it does, it is only verbally in utopias and dreams. This cosmopolitan world nourishes a philosophical millenarianism which is not the philosophy of the world as it is but as it might be, if it were not just as it is. For the same reason that the republic of humankind is *impossible* (even if we can dream it), cosmopolitanism of the *orbis* is not the idea of the world but the ideal of a world. By contrast, the present period of the European world is that of a European cosmopolitanism, that of Europe as *world*, that is, as republic.

Europe is the image of humanity as multitude, in fact—because there is nowhere comparable in terms of the diversity of languages, cultures, histories, morals and civilities, and especially of peoples and nations. Nothing is more contrary to Europe than the wish to identify its nature, to corral its diversity into some principled unity. Identity seeks to relate a thing to itself in the immobility of a subject that is incapable of reaching beyond itself. The nature that such identity designates is equally fixed in an eternal essence. Identity and nature are foreign to Europe, which is what it is not and repudiates the immobility that would reduce it to an essence. By contrast, Europe is historical, a becoming, never one but multiple, never finished. Not being a unity, the expression of a simple essence, it is by contrast a union, a manifestation of the plurality and diversity of its common being. The fact that its diversity leads to division does not suppress its common being, but it does delay its advent and prevent its completion. Besides we can see in this very division the sign of Europe's loathing of its reduction to the unity of a principle, to the identity of an essence. In the Europe of today, in fact, *union* does not mean that the nations that participate in it according to the treaties in force are in unison or form a simple unity. Above all, *continental* Europe is not on its way to constituting a union—the East and the West are not the elements of the same common totality. They are precisely the places of Europe, its landmarks, its multiple pathways. In the continent's territorial continuity, humanities and their histories are different and discontinuous. And it is from this discontinuity, which emerges from the secular work of what is historical, not the designs of nature, that peace is born.

However, it is far from being the case, here or there, that the peoples are all free and satisfied. This is not the case for one good reason—a people is not a homogeneous collective being, emerging fully formed from nature. In consequence, a people is never complete in its being; if it were, that would be its death. The image offered by a people is always that of diversity and multitude—peoples (in Europe as elsewhere) are the result of multiple intermixings, the effect of constant and constantly renewed migrations and immigrations. In this sense, there is no Spanish people, or British people or French people, etc., that have sprung forth whole and pure from history. This is what the work of history teaches to the multitudes (who often ignore it, however). The 'peoples' they form are something completely different than homogeneous humanities identifiable as essences. This is why the peoples of Europe, even if for the most part constituted as historical nations, are never fully and definitively completed. A people is not a closed form—there are dissidences and migrations constantly in progress, which are the sources of dissent and violence. If, as elsewhere, European humanity has not congealed into the unicity of a given nature, nevertheless it is in Europe that we find the greatest diversity of peoples living and cooperating with each other, the majority of whom wish to live in peace (something concretely expressed in *trade* between people) as a consequence of their common and shared histories, having so often faced each other as adversaries and enemies.

Thus, it is the historical, in other words, the materiality of a secular history, and not the postulates of the historial, that is, the human ends of nature, which creates the common being of European humanity as the common body of the multitude. Having arrived—after a long detour beyond itself in the conquest of the *orbis* whose humanity it shamelessly dominated—at the reconciliation of the multitude at home, European humanity can henceforth be at once both subject and object of the common morality of the constituted nations en route to federation in peace. Hence, in Europe the thought of humanity as *civil multitude* is indeed the basis of a new cosmopolitanism, which itself replaces the political right of particular nations (historical States) by the cosmopolitan right of European humanity. For such a right, whose general and historical principles we will define shortly, belonging to Europe is not determined by belonging to the historical nations. It is not the citizens of States who compose European humanity, but European humanity—the multitudes living under its laws—which institutes the cosmopolitan right of Europe *as new world or republic*. In such a world, there is no foreigner who would be refused belonging to Europe on the pretext that he does not belong to one of the former historical nations. Inasmuch as the desire of any individual to become a member of European humanity is not the desire to belong to one of its old historical nations, such a desire addresses Europe as *a new world*.

c) We have the habit of asking how the peace of law is possible if it presupposes the existence of a law that could compel the sovereign wills of States, while, by its very nature, State sovereignty is free from any constraint within the internal or external order of things. And it is to just such a contradiction that the problem of peace is generally led, that is, at bottom the problem of the possibility of a law or right of peoples (*jus gentium*). But this is only a contradiction for those (still numerous) who remain buttresses that prop up the sacrosanct principle of sovereignty as the foundation of peace and the law of peoples which guarantees its terms. The term contradiction is thus used as if it existed in the state of things—on the one side, free sovereignties; on the other, an impossible constraint or compulsion exercised on them. This point of view is not novel, and it is precisely in examining it in these terms that the right or law of peoples was developed in Europe, notably in Grotius' work and subsequently. Grotius posited sovereign figures, the monarchies in Europe which were in the process of internal consolidation, and in external conflict for the conquest of the extension of the *orbis*. He then wondered how to establish a law that would constrain war and peace, and that could be imposed on the sovereigns from the outside. Since then, the law of nations, the law of peoples, has continued to progress and to become a majestic edifice which at times, in fact, succeeds in preventing conflicts and in maintaining peace. It does not succeed by eliminating war, which is rightly considered not to be a fatality willed by the gods or something flowing from the dispositions of nature but a means, an instrument, to be codified by a law which would resolve differences by force, in Grotius' formulation.[9] War thus becoming a juridical act of sovereignty, its codification enters naturally into the codification of peace. Looked at this way (which has not prevented world conflicts breaking out in spite of the progress of law and the creation of world agencies of regulation),[10] peace is posited as a quasi-impossibility, or, in any case, as

9. Grotius, *Le Droit de la guerre et de la paix*, I, 1.2.

10. League of Nations. The prevention of the outbreak of a third world war was not the doing of the United Nations. Rather, it was because the alliances had nuclear weapons that Europe avoided the outbreak of a war on its territory.

a contradiction—the contradiction of a constraint-law that is impotent to constrain. In this sense, the law of peoples would be, as Grotius put it at the end of his great treatise, the mark of a civilization (Europe's) where peace was not sought in order to make war, but, on the contrary, where war was waged in order to gain peace.

Henceforth (in the present world), we have to acknowledge that the contradiction of the law of peoples is only such for those who hold sovereignty—this contradiction does not flow from the nature of the *jus gentium* but from the nature of sovereignty, for which it is peace that is contradictory. The peace of law thus requires another foundation than that of sovereignty, and this foundation is to be sought today in the civil multitude itself, that is, in the federativity of the plural humanity of Europe.

It is not a paradox to say that the peace of law (not the simple suspension of war) is possible only if there exists an historical disposition towards peace (not a simple disposition of human nature). Certainly, human beings desire peace. In fact, those whose desire for war is absolute are non-existent. But we cannot found peace itself, and its legislative apparatus, the law of peoples, on such a desire. It is because of this that peace founded on the desire to enjoy it consists of wanting it as an end. It is not as a hoped-for end that human beings want to enjoy peace, but in their present lives. Peace as an end is destined to remain a pious wish if it remains an end. Peace is not desired for the end of battle-strewn history but in the present of the historical, in human existence in the present. For peace thus lived as opposed to simply desired or wished for is not a meaningful given, commonly experienced by human beings. And that is especially true of European humanity. We are not condemning the wish for peace as such. On the contrary, by marking it as something that remains just a wish, we are seeking to establish the conditions of a concrete peace. Peace as end is not a satisfying goal, since the given present is the present of war. Thinking peace must see that though such a desire belongs to human beings, peace itself cannot rely on such a desire to produce its pre-conditions. In any case, peace for me cannot be limited to what I can be allowed to expect or hope for. The (philosophical) elucidation of peace does not rest on considering what human beings want, but on a consideration of what it is possible for them to attain. Such is the paradox of peace. It does not reject desire, but highlights the fact that it is not only a question of desire and that men do not satisfy all their desires in their lives—and cannot. In this world, more human beings have suffered war in their lifetimes than have lived in peace. It was the same for past generations. The issue is not about peace as an end but about its possibility in the present. From this point of view, we have remarked that Europe is at peace, even if only at the moment a peace which is the absence of war. Negative peace, however effective, and above all, durable peace, inscribed in things if still not inscribed in law. It is no longer just suspended war, as when the present given of things is itself pregnant with conflict. What is important, then, is to move from peace as a state of things to peace as a state of law. This passage from the given to the juridical presupposes, so to speak, the substantial advent of the conditions for such a passage. In other words, there is no guarantee for the state of peace, if this is precisely only a state, a state of things not conscious of itself because it has emerged, so to speak, spontaneously out of chaos, not yet achieving clarity in thought. If human beings do not accede to the concept of peace, they do not enjoy it fully and only endure a state in which they find themselves, a situation into which they have fallen. It is as if peace were chanced upon, a consequence of things turning out well. But this bit of luck, this happy outcome of things, if not constituted and conscious, exposes the humanity that profits from it to every form of covetousness and submits it to the deformations and interests of powers. And the same luck that brings about a beneficial state of affairs could return them to unhappiness. That would not be something new in history, since it is a matter of the very grain of history. That is why the substance of peace cannot be abandoned to chance or hope.

I have said that the substance of the peace of law lies in the civil multitude, in other words European humanity conscious of itself (constituted). A *law of European peoples* is, in this sense, the juridical form that must grasp the present state of European humanity at peace. Such a law is nothing but the expression of the *cosmopolitan right* of freedom, discussed above, considered from the point of view of the constitution of peace in Europe. This is merely a translation of the idea that it is no longer the principle of sovereignty that can found peace and its law in the present world, but the principle of *federativity* from which the notion of the civil multitude takes its meaning. It is not a matter of semantics here. In other words, I am not trying to give a dictionary definition of a word (or expression: federativity, civil multitude) but to conceive a theoretical object whose very reality is the European world. The principle of federativity is hardly something new for philosophy (or for history); on the other hand, its current form is, but in a way that means its content needs to be examined afresh. In fact, we will see that the concept of the federative as it takes shape in the philosophical idea of the republic of Europe finds new determinations today. Nevertheless, the first and most important determination, since it contains the rest, is to be found in referring us to our historical context of Europe here and now, in what makes possible the very existence of a federative principle that might inform a republic of Europe. The problem is this—if a republic of Europe is (philosophically) *thinkable*, then so is a form of federativity. In other words, it is a question of knowing what power of their own and what laws that they have at their disposal will lead Europeans (or, if not Europeans in general, then some of them) to become a federation, and, under what form. This is different from knowing what concrete forms a republic can or must take (anywhere in Europe) in its positive juridical apparatus, a question that belongs to pragmatism (to interests), not to philosophical inquiry. Nevertheless, even if interest and concept are not entirely foreign to each other, they are no less different, each having its own order. It therefore does not seem to exceed the capacities of inquiry to rest the pragmatic dispositions of morality on the general theoretical foundations that only philosophy can establish, or at worst simply glimpse, and which will be found at the end of this chapter.

To clarify matters, we have to go back to John Locke's *Two Treatises of Government* (1689). It is in this work, where, in reflecting on powers,[11] Locke discovers what he calls *federative power*. By this, he understands the capacity or power (right) that comes from nature and gives the right to every individual of the civil multitude (in other words, those who have emerged from the state of nature) to federate himself with any other individual, someone like himself. Having stipulated that in the republic (or State: *commonwealth*) there is a legislative power and an executive power, he establishes the existence of a 'federative power'. 'There is', he says,

> another *Power* in every Commonwealth, which one may call
> *natural*, because it is that which answers to the Power every

11. A reflection, which, we know, will be completed by Montesquieu. Elsewhere in my work, *Le Dieu mortel* (pp. 160–2) and *Discours d'Europe* (Chapter 5), I have already commented on Locke's discovery of 'federative power'; I give this a wider treatment here than when I reworked those books, notably because the notion of *European humanity* as I have constructed it here was not apparent to me at the time.

man naturally had before he entered into Society. For though in a Commonwealth the Members of it are distinct Persons still in reference to one another, and as such are governed by the Laws of the Society; yet in reference to the rest of Mankind, they make one Body, which is, as every Member of it before was, still in the State of Nature with the rest of Mankind. Hence it is, that the Controversies that happen between any Man of the Society with those that are out of it, are managed by the publick; and an injury done to a Member of their Body, engages the whole in the reparation of it. So that under this Consideration, the whole Community is one Body in the State of Nature, in respect of all other States or Persons out of its Community.

This therefore contains the Power of War and Peace, Leagues and Alliances, and all the Transactions, with all Persons and Communities without the Commonwealth, and may be called *Federative*, if any one pleases. So the thing be understood, I am indifferent as to the Name.[12]

To say that Locke's text has an exceptional importance in our concern here—the law of European peoples—is an understatement. Once *updated*, it makes it possible to represent how Europeans might be capable of opening up a new terrain of morality by virtue of the particular features of their current common situation on the continent. In this passage, in fact, Locke refers to the natural right that every individual possesses to federate with a stranger or a foreigner. This emerges from the

---

12. John Locke, *Two Treatises of Government* (Peter Laslett ed., introd. and annot.) (Cambridge: Cambridge University Press, 1960 [1689]), Sections 145–6, p. 365. As we will see below, Locke's conclusion from his discovery of the federative is singularly burdened by the fact that he places the exercise of such a power in the hands of the executive. See Conclusion *Respublica*, 'The Federative'.

reference he makes to the idea of the citizens of a State being individually, and in their body, in a state of nature in relation to mankind, that is, in relation to humanity as a whole. This is another way of stating what classical theory already knew before Locke—that sovereigns are, vis-à-vis each other, in a state of nature. But the difference that Locke introduces here is considerable, since it is to individuals that he assigns, by nature, the *right* to federate. Federative power is a *federative right* of humanity which is enjoyed by the universality of the individuals of the multitude, considered together in relation to the humanity of the *orbis*.

Nowadays, we cannot simply take up this assertion as such. On the contrary: in order to give it its full significance—and only the particular context of our time allows us to do so, whereas in Locke's time it was impossible, hence the fact that he ruined his own discovery—we must not follow Locke and found this power of individuals on the relationship the latter have with a humanity otherwise only thought in the indeterminate abstraction of the general. Since, in fact, such a humanity does not exist *historically*, the right that proceeds from it can only be a verbal fiction. If the individuals of the multitude are not foreign to each other, by reason of their natural right to federate beyond the border of the States they come under, this is true as ideal and as end. But that is only a theoretical proposition, because in the historical world they cannot do so. Locke knows this since he declares that this federative power is, in fact, exercised by the executive—it is sovereignty in action. It is not a question, then, in reality of a natural right that belongs to each individual but of a positive State right. No federation of humanity can be founded on this basis, since it is the very division into particular sovereignties that, far from ignoring the category of the foreigner, posits and perpetuates it. Which not only makes a human federativity between *peoples* impossible but, rather, generates war or, at best, the division of the multitude unto peoples that are foreign to each other. Making the citizens of these peoples into enemies or simply adversaries is what the *jus gentium* does from its own principles. In consequence, we can see that peace comes second in relation to war, which is, *de facto*, as we have already seen, the recognized and accepted means of achieving peace.

Locke's idea of humanity, like Kant's which follows it, must thus be corrected. It is not an indeterminate 'mankind' which is the concrete possibility of a law of humankind of peace. If the tradition cannot concretely think the right of humankind it is because its concept of humanity remains verbal and abstract. Locke's mankind is indeed altogether within the state of nature, that is at war—certainly the case during his time, and during our own until very recently. So in considering the present state of human affairs in the world, we can see that the European world is nowadays alone in being at peace. In this sense, and in the light of Locke, Europeans are the *historical reality* of what he designated—in his context: the thought of the federative—as 'mankind'. So, by a strange and unexpected turn of events, just when the already venerable European tradition of political right has revealed that the idea of humanity or mankind refers incontestably to the canons of European man[13]—which in history was the source of the (often armed) negation of the humanity of others—it is only after the long detour which the world has made them take, that Europeans finally face up to what they had not suspected: what they believed to be humanity was in the end only themselves, and the universalism of their mankind was their irreducible particularism. But it is also true, as we will see, that Europeans will only have full consciousness of themselves in the civil constitution of their own humanity.

13. See Chapter 1 in this volume.

If, as I have just said, living European (historical) humanity is the illustration of Locke's notion of mankind, this is because at least a part of the European population are no longer foreign to each other as individuals and as nations (even if they live as such empirically), still less adversaries. The *right of federation* exercised is, in fact, the action by which Europeans from many constituted nations elect their representatives by direct universal suffrage—the members of the European *Parliament*, where those elected in France, Italy, Greece and so on are not representatives of France, Italy, etc., but European representatives as such. The fact of sitting in a transnational assembly[14] brought together by the direct universal suffrage of millions of Europeans confers on this assembly (and on its members) a *federative power*, which has itself been conferred on them by the vote of the individuals of European humanity. Because there is no mediation through the national *within the precinct of their assembly*, the concept of this assembly is the concept of the federative. It cannot be objected that the European Parliament as a real institution has no such power. In fact, that is indeed its real condition. I am not talking about facts but about right and law in the sense of *in law*; the European Parliament is in law a federative parliament. If I said that European humanity had emerged from the state of nature and now finds itself at peace, though that is a given fact it does not *formally* constitute (in law) freedom because its formal constitution requires a recognized act of federation. Although such an act may not be recognized in Europe (the

14. It is not a question of a 'multinational' assembly as is sometimes said. The European Parliament was multinational when its members were not elected by direct universal suffrage. The assembly was thus a gathering of national assemblies: a simple geographical juxtaposition of delegates of national Parliaments, *en voyage* to the European assembly. By contrast, directly emanating from the multitude exercising its right, the European Parliament is obviously of a different nature in its *concept* (whether that is known, recognized, or misrecognized).

European Union and the other parts of Europe), this changes nothing. To paraphrase Locke, it is not a question of words. The reality is this—if, being at peace, the Europeans individually and universally exercise their right of federation and thus emerge from the state of nature. State to State and nation to nation they are no longer in a state of war, whether declared or not. This situation is absolutely unprecedented, not only in relation to each other but even more so in relation to the non-European worlds. And it is precisely in regard to such a situation that the morality or *freedom* of the new world is henceforth *thinkable* on a foundation other than sovereignty. Such a foundation is found in European humanity as the subject of a European *jus gentium* which the right of federation makes concretely possible. This will emerge clearly after a study of the proper nature of right and law.

On the Nature of Right

European humanity is not, however, fully constituted as the real subject of Locke's 'mankind'; it is only such *in potentia*. Its real constitution depends on its capacity to form a *world*, that is, to *think* and *act* as world. Only in this way can the new freedom that peace confers upon it be truly historical for it, that is, to say *real*. This means that the European constitution of a world cannot be reduced to drawing up a charter to regulate the distribution of powers and competences between partners and actors. This is a *literary* activity that individuals can devote themselves to in scholarly fashion and no doubt with great enjoyment. Everyone can put forward his subjective vision and experience and can offer his ideal. But it is not a question of a single individual or even several becoming constitution-makers or legislators for Europe. The constitution of the multitude in an entity as complex as a republic of Europe (or elsewhere) might turn out to be, must, in the first instance be, concerned with material necessity and moral obligation before being taken up, expressed and translated in the unified (systematic) body of a *text*. Necessity and obligation do not command the will because they are the result of a past and the sign of a present. What is important is just what cannot be produced by decision but only by a slow coming to consciousness, which the majority of individuals will reach only in the long term. It is then, and only then, that the elaboration of a text can be seriously considered, with no guarantee of the question of its nature and form being resolved. The constitution of Europe cannot in any case be reduced to its juridical aspect, that is, the internal coherence of a set of articles, because what is at issue is a historical problem. In other words, the idea of a *law of European peoples* whose end is the constitution of Europe as world—a world facing other worlds—is different from the idea of a charter or fundamental declaration to which certain States subscribe—those interested in cooperating in certain aspects of their collective life or those ready to declare their common attachment to certain moral or spiritual principles.[15] In contrast, a law of European *peoples* is the juridical system of European humanity existing as a moral personality vis-à-vis other worlds (externally) and vis-à-vis itself (internally), a system whose final end can only be its participation in the peace of the *orbis*.

The problem that now has to be faced is this: what is the nature of this *law*, what meaning can be given to the *jus* of this *jus gentium*? Even if the effective content of this law must be defined, that cannot be done now because it is first necessary to determine the nature of what we understand by law in general. Only then will it be possible to define concretely the law of European *peoples* and deduce its constitutive elements. In its most general sense, what we mean by law and right here is the *realization of the idea of justice*, so that what is held to be just becomes materially the case. We thus see that the definition of the right presupposes the concrete definition of the just—it is justice as the regulatory norm of a particular

15. If the *law of gens* were no more than a coalition of interests—material or non-material—then the Council of Europe or the Union de l'Europe occidentale or, better, the European Union itself, would be that law.

society, a particular multitude which, hence, gives itself its rules and laws and is organized as a civil form. We thus consider that right is immanent in every human multitude, whatever the level of development or sophistication of its rule of law. For example, children are playing in a schoolyard and their game is possible if and only if there are rules for it. In the same way, the United Nations, the ultimate source of the law of humankind for the *orbis* (whatever its effectiveness in this or that situation), testifies to the existence of a norm that regulates actors. In both cases, schoolyard or sovereigns of the *orbis*, there is a rule of law. And this law—about which one might have an opinion, might feel such-and-such or have an idea about the rightness of its application—expresses the norm of justice in force at the moment when the law is in force. I am not going to examine the nature of justice and its concrete substance, nor what it should consist of here and now (in Europe or elsewhere). This question, however, is indeed real (it refers to the real world) but it cannot be approached without first studying the phenomenon of law and its mode of effectiveness as rule. Which comes down to asking how law functions when it tells a particular actor, the subject of law and the subject of right, that he has the right to do some action (or not).

Law, as the collection of rules that connect human beings in specific relationships, from the micro-society of the school playground to the sphere of State sovereignties, relates actors who, without it, would remain isolated and solitary. Such an association or connection is not necessarily a civil association, since it might only connect singular individuals to each other (schoolchildren, for example) at the precise moment when they are playing; but once the game is over, the schoolchildren separate. Or, the connection might concern collective individuals (sovereignties), which occasionally play the United Nations game; but once the game is over, they return home. The substance of civility cannot be found in the simple *existence* of a law; all that is found there is the connection of actors whose interests are temporarily involved, that is to say, the *possibility* of civil life. This is the case because law makes actors play a role, and these actors, as such, are equal. Law is just that—it equalizes individuals by assigning them a role. If the law is thus the condition of the game (because it creates equal actors), actors nevertheless must want to play. Such a desire is not constituted by law but only by *politics*. The positive law of the schoolyard or the United Nations, then, cannot produce an authentic human society (even less a society of mankind) if we understand that to mean participation in a common justice—not the occasional, temporary shared engagement, performed out of interest and which finishes when the interest terminates. The phenomenon of law, considered in itself, as the regulation of relations (we will see later what the nature of this regulation is) does not entail that its regulation will be durable. On the contrary, what is proper to rules and laws (and with them the justice that rules and laws bring into reality) is that they last only for a certain period of time, precisely as long as the actors see an advantage in keeping them in force. Once the moment of interest and usefulness is past, the rules change—men change them. To put it another way, the content of justice—applied justice— changes with the law that states it, but the form of justice does not change, in that it is constituted by what human beings desire the most—peace and freedom. The desire to live in freedom (and peace) is the most widely shared desire in the world—even if certain people deliberately resort to war to attain it. Sometimes the recourse to war is necessary to live in freedom and to enjoy a just peace (and not simply the peace of an armistice). Whatever the case might be, if what I want the most (as a political animal) is to live well, that is in freedom and peace, then this desire is the basis of a society that is possible in principle. And such a desire is not transient or self-interested but constant and freely given. Freedom offers no remuneration; we do not seek it because it brings a profit, but because it is desirable in itself. That is why civility rests on the desire for freedom—which is the just. By contrast, justice changes with the body of the laws and rules (*the* law). There is often a violent conflict between practical justice and what is just. If this were not the case, there would be no social or political revolutions.

Let us say, then, that because (positive) law, as the body of rules and laws, regulates relationships between individuals, it is the temporary mediation that opens up the common ground between individuals (singular or collective), allowing them to recognize each other as individuals. Law is the mediation of the individual with himself and with others. This allows us to speak of a subject of law—this is the bearer of law, without which he would disappear as subject. Law is, then, the power of an individual without which he could not know himself either as power or as individual. The consequence of this point is that without law I could not know the other as other—not knowing myself as an individual, I would have no possibility of seeing in the other an individual who is like me and with whom I enter into relation. In fact, law is what enables the mutual recognition of individuals. Being at once both *mediation* (between myself and myself) and *recognition* (myself of the other and the other of myself), law is neither myself nor the other. Law is thus a *third*, a neutral and disinterested third, in Alexandre Kojève's excellent formulation.[16] It is the third term common to both A and B. In this sense, it is the arbitrator between the two and the common place of both. Both A and B can address the law in regard to the dispute and difference of interest that arises between them. Law is the judge of peace, without which there would be no peace. The servant of justice, law is what delivers justice to those who are to be judged, and this latter refers to the capacity of a subject that exists as such through law. Hence, what characterizes law, and even more so the judge who embodies it, is the quality of being disinterested. If this were not the case, then the judge would have to be A or B or C, but, in this case, he would have to take a position in the conflict between A and B, putting himself on one side or the other in an alliance. The

16. Of whose theory of law and right I retain certain features. See his theory as outlined in his *Esquisse d'une phénoménologie du droit. Exposé provisoire* (Paris: Gallimard, 1981).

judge does not enter into alliances and cannot maintain a friendship with the person who is supposed to be tried; if he did, he would lose the quality that made him a judge. Conversely, the judge—and with him the law that he states in delivering justice—can exist only because A and B make him exist, as judge and common third, who then makes A and B recognize each other. C is the judge (the law) who assigns them the same role and thus makes them equal—both of them have the role of those to be judged (plaintiffs) and in this role are equal before the law. It is clear, in fact, that if A has a complaint against B, A will address C for redress of damage only if C is capable of making them agree, which presupposes that B is himself prepared to submit to C's judgement. But C can bring them to agreement if, and only if, they recognize themselves as A and B and recognize themselves in him. So it is indeed C who makes the mutual recognition of A and B possible. What does 'they recognize themselves' mean here? This—that they *know* that they are individuals who can have access to the judgement of a third, accept it and abide by it. To recognize oneself, in other words, to know oneself as the subject of law, is to accept justice, to want it. If I do not accept justice, I do not exist as an individual because I am not recognized as such. If, then, it is indeed necessary that I recognize the judge by addressing him, this shows that in recognizing the judge I come to know myself. And to know myself is *ipso facto* to recognize the other. Law suppresses the solipsism of natural man, and suspends his solitude. There are, then, two, and only two, ways of coming to consciousness of oneself (whether an individual or a collective one): by conflict or by law.[17] And as men desire peace, they prefer law. Consequently, they want a judge. But law as such does not suppress

17. We cannot say, for example, that there is a third way which would be moreover the first: language. It is not possible because to do so there have to be two —for I do not have the notion of two that is of myself and the other if I am only a *myself* who does not know what *this* me is. In other words, one can only advance that the formal condition of the possibility of language is the existence of law, as *mediation*, language being then what gives body to (or materializes) the mediation in giving body to the mutual recognition of A and B.

violence, because law has no concrete force that it can oppose to violence; no rule can produce a ceasefire. As law is nothing other than disinterested mediation, it cannot prevent nor *a fortiori* interrupt the unleashing of violence if the actors *want* and resort to it. This is the reason why I said that law changes and with it justice—but not what is just, which always remains what is just. That is why the change of law is nearly always revolutionary, so much so that what we call 'revolution' can be defined as the moment where one law gives way to another.

We could advance the following objection—I said that the recourse to the judge has the effect that A and B recognize themselves through the intermediary of the judge. Should we not rather say that it is the dispute that produces the recognition? This is the case, in fact, because it is obvious that, in order for A to complain about B, there has to be an encounter between A and B prior to their appearance before the judge. But this is a recognition in fact, not in law. Which means that their relationship, as pre-juridical or a-juridical (we could also call it 'natural'), is not a relationship *between equals.* This means that one of them (rightly or wrongly) has to make a complaint about some damage. If there is damage, in fact, it is because the condition of one of them is unequal to that of the other. There is thus no *possibility* of a relationship between the two protagonists if it is not a relationship between two equals. There is only an encounter. And an authentic relationship is possible only if both accept a third as judge and together abide by his judgement. In any case, it is only by a relationship to a third that A and B are equal, because they then play the same role. In this sense, an unequal relationship is one that exists in solitude and not in society. Solitude is that situation of existence where I am not recognized by the other(s), which does not mean that I do not encounter them—I do not exist in society with them because only the law puts me in a situation of association with others. The situation where I merely have encounters (rather than have relationships) is not a situation that would be mine *ex hypothesi* in a state of nature, understood as the original condition of men prior to the formation of society. Solitude is not such an asocial state of pure nature; on the contrary, it exists fully within society and is precisely the condition of the individual who, among those who are like him, is nevertheless not in relationship to them. He is unlike them. However, the label 'state of nature' could legitimately be applied (and perhaps ought to be) to the condition of those who, in an organized society, are dissociated from that very society either by crime or by infraction (in that case, the courts are the laboratories where society, from its own point of view, becomes the judge of the state of nature); or because society, through its own injustice, expels certain individuals into the state of nature, for example the unemployed, those without work or residence permits or the homeless. In any case, only law makes individuals equal so that it *can* bring them into association. Because only those who are equal can come into association, such equality cannot exist in the individuals taken in themselves but only from the point of view of an impartial third, because only a third is disinterested—he has no personal interest in favouring A or B; both are nothing for him, and he is nothing for them. By contrast, the protagonists who encounter each other have every interest in not being impartial, because it is their advantage that is in play. A priori, it is not in A's interest to share his advantage with B. For benefits to be equal, a judge must make them so. So A and B recognize themselves and each other through law.

Law is thus the *transcendental mediation* of man and man, which turns man into either a political animal (which he is in fact) or, not being *political*, into a solitary animal, although he might live in bands for whom there is no difference between war and peace, life and death, freedom and slavery, or what is just and what is unjust. Law in this sense is the very essence of the *human* animal as *political* animal, deliberating on the nature of the just and the unjust. He *is* political, in fact, since he takes his being from his capacity to live according to a rule of law, or, more precisely, *by* a rule of law. So, if what is proper to the human is to live politically, it is because law exists only within a body politic—there is no law in nature.[18] What we call *natural* law is only the law of a political society that positive law challenges; when the state of nature takes its first steps towards society, in society itself (when society *is* the state of nature) its law must be modified. Hence, the revolutionary idea of changing it. In fact, what we describe as 'natural' law is just that—(positive) law which must be transcended by a new law.

If law is indeed this transcendental mediation of man and man, we cannot in all precision speak about the law but only about *laws*. And since humanity has access, so to speak, to itself only through law, and humanity is plural, there *must* be a plurality of laws. That is to say, a plurality of forms of justice within the humanity of the *orbis*. It is this question of a plurality of forms of justice—since law is the realization of what is just—that produces the division of humanity and with it the radical impossibility of a *single* republic of mankind. It is important, then, for whoever is seeking peace to know that the internal order of humanity is oriented towards dissensus, even war. Even if human beings desire peace, they generally find war. This is what experience shows. To find peace, then, it is essential to start from law as the condition of possibility of humanity, and not, as so often, from the will for human beings to want peace (or occasionally not). Such a will to want peace unfortunately reverses the order of things. If, as experience shows, human affairs are tendentially orientated towards war rather than peace, this is a consequence of the plurality of forms of justice, each *wishing* to impose on the other its own norm of justice which it thinks of as universal. However, to the extent that such a plurality is constitutive of humanity, we cannot see how it

18. Save by giving the name 'law' to the given state of nature, that is, to its internal regulating constitution by which fish swim and birds fly, lions eat gazelles and human beings speak and walk upright. For it to be the law we are talking about, it is necessary to show that these dispositions are manifestations of justice—not something that is easy to demonstrate.

would be possible for law to cancel its own essence and create a single justice within a human humanity. That is why what is just is only what is true, in other words concretely thinkable in the form of a plurality of versions of justice (the particularism of what is just), since humanity is not one but plural. The very cause of war among men is the *will* to unify them under some universal idea of what is just and of a single justice. But that is not an idea—simply an ideal which might be opposed by another equally as arbitrary as the first. The state of war rests on the existence of arbitrary ideals of what is universally just. The *possibility* of peace, by contrast, rests on the plurality [of forms of justice]; and where humanity confronts itself in a sort of civil war, of which Europeans have had repeated experience, it is important to conceive and elaborate a positive law of plurality. It is here that the old law of *European peoples* (extended to the *orbis*) reveals its limits and some passage must be effected to a federative law of European humanity.

The Old Law of Peoples *and that of the New World*

The world as it is still rests on the aristocratic law of *peoples* that was inaugurated in the seventeenth century, in the period when the major European powers—England, France and Spain—fought to conquer the *orbis*. It was the time when empires were formed. Until the United Nations Charter was adopted, it was the rule of an aristocratic law which, without paradox, created war among nations (henceforth known as 'international relations'). To think the law of nations (*jus gentium*) is to think the state of war, that is, the state of nature. If there is no paradox in seeing the advent of the law of the *continuation of the state of war*, it is because the law in question (the law of *peoples* or the law of nations) is thought of as the law of war whose aim is peace. Law as it was conceived from the seventeenth century onwards was a strategy of war with the aim of peace—the goal of war is to establish peace. Such a conception is in no way paradoxical, because it brings law to war, that is, it includes war as one human activity among others with potential benefits, one of which is peace. In seeing war not simply as a calamity of nature or the fatal manifestation of finitude but as a rational (calculated), if violent, human activity, Europeans brought war into the sphere of law. Mediaeval thinkers had already suspected that war could be just or unjust. Just war was that which brought the order of the world into line with the arrangements that God had envisioned for it and thus was thought of as an orthopaedic undertaking to re-establish divine order in a world that had temporarily forsaken it. A war was unjust if it did not restore this order but was merely vengeful, precisely because it was destructive of this very order. But in the modern idea of war it is no longer God's design for the world that furnishes the moral criterion for establishing the just nature of war, but conformity to rules. Such disseminated rules provide belligerents with the legitimation for recourse to the violence of war (*jus ad bellum*) in constraining them to some extent in the use of this violence (*jus in bello*).

In fact, what is at issue is the elaboration—under the sign of the 'law of peoples'—of the natural law of sovereignties to act in their self-preservation. The power of the State is equivalent to the natural right of the State to self-preservation. Hence, war is not a simple manifestation of naked violence but a manifestation of law. War as law, or law as war, is the revolutionary invention of the Moderns who embarked on the conquest of the extension of the *orbis* and confronted each other without limit as they did so. There is, in fact, absolutely no paradox in asserting, as I do here, that the law of *peoples* is the law of the state of nature, if we understand, as it is useful to do, the expression 'state of nature' to be another name for the state of war. What challenges this new way of seeing[19] is the purely rhetorical choice that the modern tradition formulates as follows—force or law, or in other words war or peace. Here we have the modern fable of the state of nature and the political state

19. Which breaks radically with the theological tradition to produce the juridical tradition— Gentilis and Grotius.

that succeeds it. However, law is not identical to peace in the sense that the reign of law would be that of peace. On the contrary, international law is constituted by articulating law as the formalism of war or the formalization of violence. The original European constitution of international law is the theoretical elaboration of war among nations under the category of the state of nature. And the essential characteristic of this state of nature is that the law that regulates it is the aristocratic law of the 'Great', their natural right. In fact it appears that in the language we use to describe war, the general actors are those superior economic, military and political powers that we habitually term 'Great'. The milieu of nations is where law is pronounced by the Great: these then have clients, confederates, protégés or allies, so that relations between the Great structure and order a world of aristocratic law which is the world as a state of nature. Modernity in the *orbis* is the time of the state of the nature because it is the time of the advent of the Great as actors in an international order ruled by law. The law of *peoples* is the law of this state of nature.

The best illustration of this revolutionary conception of law, that is, the aristocratic law of force as the essence of the law of *peoples*, is given by Carl Schmitt in *The Nomos of the Earth*.[20] This is a theoretically penetrating text that seeks to grasp the essence of the law of *peoples* (*jus publicum europeaeum*) in relating the elaboration of conceptual structure of the territoriality of the modern sovereign State to its European constitution. The European 'seizures of the earth' through war, in particular in the extension of the New World, are the driving force that permitted the development of international law, its concepts and its jurisprudence. Being a specific juridical order (the order of sovereignties), the state is first of all a territorial order, or, as Schmitt says, 'it constituted within and of itself a closed area with fixed borders'.[21] If Schmitt's thought is relevant here, it is because

20. Carl Schmitt, *The Nomos of the Earth in the International Law of the Jus Publicum Europeaeum* (G. L. Ulmen trans.) (New York: Telos Press, 2003 [1950]).
21. Ibid., p. 128.

it reveals the aristocratic and war-based nature of international law, which Schmitt seeks to establish—for him, sovereignty is dictatorship in war. Hence, the ultimate significance of international law, whose origins he traces from Vitoria to the aftermath of the Treaty of Versailles,[22] is the formation of a European world understood as a planetary order of sovereignties. Here the great powers, seeking to constitute themselves as empires, produce a law of conquest and appropriation of extra-European extension. This law becomes the law of every State sovereignty as such, which Schmitt unabashedly sees as a manifestation of the superior order of a superior humanity engaged in the conquest of its 'dialectical' other, the 'sub-human'.[23] Law is thus understood as what has been its truth in the modern course of the state of nature—the *nomos* of the earth, that is, the rule of appropriation through war and subsequent distribution of the spatial extension of the *orbis* in the legitimate constitution of empires. In trying to elucidate the nature of the law of *peoples* as modern Europe has conceived and put it to work historically, Schmitt thought he was making manifest the meaning of modernity. For him, modernity is the period of emergence from a Hobbesian state of nature, thanks to the appearance of law in Europe. Undoubtedly, his project completely overturned his intentions, as it revealed Europe's total immersion in the pure state of nature instituted through the law of *peoples* whose truth he understood—it was the aristocratic law of the war of sovereignties.[24]

Although it was used to legitimize empires, the aristocratic law of *peoples* of modern States is not simply a legalization of war—it is also the law of war and peace. But peace in this context can never be anything but the negative peace of the absence of war. We know that this is precisely Hobbes' definition of peace,

22. In which he wrongly sees the dissolution of the *jus gentium* of Europe.
23. On this subject, see Schmitt's unambiguous propositions about 'humanitarian ideology'.
24. One of the sources of Schmitt's blindness, if not the only one, is to be found in his pre-Bodin conception of sovereignty as 'dictatorship', which cannot mask his fraudulent use of Bodin himself and Hobbes on this crucial question of sovereignty. See Chapter 1 in this volume.

where the state of nature is not defined as that of singular individuals not yet subjected to the 'common judge', but, rather, as State sovereignties themselves. Philosophers after Hobbes have been right to say that the international milieu remains within the state if nature has war (declared or not) as its rule, because there is no common judge for historical States and nations. International law does not thereby lose its formal status as being this neutral and disinterested third that we discussed above; on the contrary, it is what allows sovereigns in conflict for empire to recognize each other as competitors and enemies in conquest. Law does not fail in its task of being the third that produces relations between sovereign individuals, which, in its absence, could not know themselves nor recognize each other as sovereigns. This is the ultimate significance of the *jus publicum europaeum*—to make competition and war possible between legitimate actors who are recognized as equal and sovereign, and hence as having the same rights. Law, we will see, is itself no stranger to force and even less to that force which can prevent the recourse to violence. If sovereignty is in itself the historical process of the production of collective identities, the form of the individuation of historical peoples and nations, then law is its language and, in this sense, the *logos* of history and not the *nomos* of the earth. The advent of sovereignty in Europe is the advent of an aristocratic law: it allows the strong to elevate themselves to the level of the Great in world affairs, as they determine the latter according to their own interests (security and self-preservation) and grant respect to defeated sovereignties, the modern little princes whose sovereignty is, in fact, recognized only if they give their allegiance to the Great. The most visible site of such a law, where, in the aftermath of empire, great and small nations sit together as supposed equals, is the United Nations itself. What we have here, making and unmaking law, are the thrones of the winners, the permanent members of the Security Council, around which gravitate the rest, absolutely sovereign however *impermanent in right*, subordinated to the Great who govern them according to the law.

I am not saying that the United Nations is useless. On the contrary, we must see in the United Nations, as the final and prime source of all *law of peoples* of the world as it is, the tangible revelation of law as well as the culmination of the law of sovereignty in modernity. The law of sovereignties as materialized in the United Nations attests to the emancipation of Europe and the *orbis* from an ajuridical age, as it were, the time of the *mundus* unified by different sorts of revelations and not the time of the *orbis* divided by law. A Europe that, after AD 1000, tried to form the *res publica christiana* of a people that comprised those baptized according to the law of a Church with universal pretensions, gave way to a Europe comprising a multiplicity of sovereign States. Europe has ceased to be the unified terrain of revelation to become the divided space of a particular humanity, the humanity of a law of *peoples* whose principal foundation was stated by Alberico Gentili as he enjoined theologians to remain silent on the question of the just war—*Silete theologi in munere alieno!* Subsequently, law has been profaned like sovereignty itself. The world of law, in the sense that a world is produced in history through the mediation of law (no longer in revelation by Providence), is a profane world, entirely dedicated to founding action, that is to say, to the effects of will. We can indeed find here (as philosophers often have) a significance that transcends materiality and thus claims to transcend the historical by the historial. But the work of law still remains that of the recognition of sovereignties, the formal proclamation of their equality in principle in the ordered conquest of the *orbis*, a conquest where, by definition, the strongest win, and the Great administer the conquest according to their natural law and right. In this sense, *peacekeeping* as the preamble to the United Nations Charter defines it (the organization's goal and aim) and it cannot be confused with the peace of law, understood as a just peace between equals where each *has the right to what he is due*. However, the United Nations cannot be simply regarded as a fictional organization for peace, because it bears witness to the existence of the mediation of law. It is in effect the regulation of the absence of war by law, in the absence of which peace would be like war itself, a space of non-law. In other words, it is Hobbes' distinction between two times, that of war and that of peace, which are both simultaneously the historical times of the state of nature. 'Warre,' says Hobbes, in a famous passage,

> consisteth not in Battell only, or the act of fighting: but in a tract of Time, wherein the Will to contend by Battell is sufficiently known; and therefore the Notion of *Time* is to be considered in the nature of Warre; as it is in the nature of Weather. For as the nature of Foule weather, lyeth not in a showre or two of rain, but an inclination thereto of many days together: So, the nature of Warre consisteth not in actual fighting, but in the known disposition thereto, during all the time there is no assurance to the contrary. All other time is PEACE.[25]

It would take three centuries for the significance of this famous assertion in *Leviathan* to be finally revealed in the United Nations Charter—if the time of peace is henceforward the time of law, that means that the time of law itself is also the time of war. From this point of view, peace is a category of war, and law is what distinguishes one from the other. Such is indeed the state of nature. The law of *peoples* of the *jus publicum europeaum* has always been the law of the European state of nature and then the world state of nature: the Great Powers, the victors, raised it to a planetary scale and crystallized it in the United Nations.

But the *European* world of the state of war is coming to its culmination before our very eyes. With the culmination of sovereignty, we also have the culmination of the law of *peoples* that it produced. What is at issue here, as we have seen, is the *European* world and not the world in general. The world in general is still in a state

25. Hobbes, *Leviathan*, pp. 185–6.

of nature and will remain so for as long as the Great Powers rule and their aristocratic law remains in force at the planetary level. This is not a situation that can be
anticipated to disappear in the foreseeable future. Save by postulating the ahistorical realm of ends in a constant re-invocation of perpetual peace in a cosmopolitanism of universally democratic republics, we have to acknowledge that peace
cannot be constituted through law alone. *Real* peace (really just peace) does not
come from pure law but from politics. Which is not to say that law (*jus gentium*)
must be relegated to the museum of the state of nature. It is to say that the efficacy
of law is weak (and sometimes non-existent) if law is only juridical and not *political*.
The politicization of law, in other words the political construction of what is just,
appears to be the only alternative to the impotence of law. If international law is
what distinguishes war from peace within the historical time of nature, then such a
distinction cannot simply involve law but must, first and foremost, involve politics.
For such a revolution—which law must express in its own language when the
moment comes—cannot be made to work through the voluntarism of States, even
if they are Great Powers. The politicization of law which is the foundation of a
republic is not aristocratic. Moreover, such a foundation of a republic can only be
thought (and, therefore, be possible) within a particular world whose moral structure, historical form and particular humanity are proper to its realization, that is, its
concretization. This world is the European world, Europe as new world.

The Politics of the 'New World'

In its concept, the just does not refer to a simple juridical elaboration, but, rather,
to a political constitution. Now as before, it is a question of bringing what is just
into existence within a *republic* of which it is the concrete manifestation of its particular freedom. Here we have the old problem of the passage from the state of
nature to the political and civil state. However, the difference between the ancient

world and the new one is that the state of nature today is altogether different from that of yesterday. There is a *European difference* that compels a redefinition of the philosophical figures of the fable of natural law. If my assertion here that European humanity has been pacified is historically true (which is very different from the Enlightenment assertion of perpetual peace), then the question of peace—and thus of politics (the republic)—is redefined not in general but by European humanity—it is the passage to cosmopolitics. Now by this word I do not mean the republic of the world but the European world as republic. The following chapter will explore this and bring the theoretical structure to a close.

The political and civil context of European *morality* as lived (experienced) by Europeans themselves is today marked by the irreducible novelty of peace. Hence, the thought of the free life must redefine its received certainties and re-examine them in order to bring to light certain fundamental constitutive principles of that very freedom. We could resume this novel horizon of moral thought by saying that it is a matter of elucidating the philosophical and historical conditions for the advent of European humanity understood as civil multitude, which comes down to thinking the possible foundations of a republic of Europe. As we know, this is not some arbitrary project but expresses only the culmination of a world, that of sovereignty. This does not mean that the State suddenly disappears as if by philosophical magic but, that in the European sphere of morality, the State no longer produces the historical *to come*. Nor does this does mean (as I have repeatedly stated) that the State is dead. The State is not dead in Europe or anywhere else; it only exists—in Europe only—as the inert guardian of the past morality of particular nations. As these have been constituted by sovereignty, which is the form of morality that modernity implanted among the European multitudes, the culmination of morality does not mean the material disappearance of the State itself but its erasure as actor and producer of the morality of the coming European world. The ultimate significance of this evolution is that, for the nations of Europe, the universal is no longer separated from the particular—it is, rather, in the knowledge of its particularism that each of the European nations lives according to its own particular morality. For the nations of Europe, the *just* that emerges from their history is not understood and recognized as a common form of the *just* to be imposed on all these nations in the coercive aspect of a common law administered by a common judge (which can only be an imperial State sovereignty, or, at least, an aristocratic one), but as each participating for itself in a common space of possible morality whose constitutive imperative is that no particular norm of what is just can claim to dominate another or impose itself on all the rest, or even envisage such a claim.

The free life of the European nations henceforth resides in the structural impossibility of empire, or simply of conquest, which amounts to saying that the particularisms of nations and peoples are recognized universally as the *tacit* foundation of the common morality of European humanity. But freedom cannot be simply content with a tacit foundation—it requires a manifest basis. The problem of freedom in effect is historically and philosophically the following—freedom is nothing without recognition. For European humanity philosophically to conceive its common freedom is to constitute itself as republic. In other words, it is to constitute itself as its own world, as its own world of morality, and as world for others beyond itself. These are the two orders of the common being of Europe (or of any other): being for itself and being for others. These two orders are inseparable like the two sides of a coin. In the present world, the morality (or free and peaceful life) of European humanity is only inchoate and not conscious of itself, and tacit—it is not manifested publicly because of the persistence and resistance of sovereignty. Only being able to produce the particular, sovereignty cannot allow Europeans to constitute what would be universal for them—their common morality. This, however, is present in their world—it is *in potentia* in European humanity, in germ, we

could say, in the confused form of the aspirations of peoples, a more or less conscious desire, a more or less hidden will. Europeans know, with a knowledge that is
confused because it is not articulated in *thought*, that they form a European humanity, if we understand by this the body of a future republic. They know it (and this
might lead them to reject a republic) and this knowledge comes from their experience of living in peace as they contemplate war (the state of nature) elsewhere.

It is because philosophy (here or elsewhere) only thinks what the historical
world gives it to think that it must think a republic of Europe, that is, a principle
of general federativity, which would bring European humanity into being as the
subject and object of common morality for Europeans. If philosophy discovers
that its concept of European humanity is impossible to think, in other words to
conceive as *idea* (not as ideal), then the historical world is not ready for the republic. Philosophy considers such a prospect with the greatest seriousness because it
is on the basis of this possibility that it takes the risk of thinking the republic *concretely*, that is, thinking its conceptual and factual determinations. We can state
the principles of the *idea* of a republic of Europe here, principles or first propositions that will feed into its later elaboration. There are three.

a) First principle. European Humanit*y is the unique foundation of a republic of
Europe—it is the subject and object of the* freedom *of the new world*
This proposition must be accepted if we agree that the current European project
of union is not arbitrary, that is, purely voluntary, because it expresses or responds
to a demand of historical necessity. By historical necessity we do not mean an
external revealed constraint but the material structure of the European present. In
this sense, and to the extent that *union* is an effective project and goal in Europe
today, Europeans cannot attain such a union without bringing into being its concrete subject. Such a subject is European humanity, that is, Europeans constituted

as such, in other words the *civil* and not the natural multitude which comprises the hundreds of millions of Europeans populating a region of the *orbis* corresponding to the name Europe. The civil constitution of the multitude is the first condition for any union understood as a political union aimed at producing the morality not simply of the particular nations of Europe, as such, but the common morality of all nations. If union is a project, then, by definition, it cannot be understood as the realization of what already exists, that is, the particular freedom of historical nations. As a *project*, union is necessarily superior to the particular freedoms of nations—such a union is rightly the advent of a higher freedom, since it is *common* to the nations. Such is European humanity understood as the object of freedom of the new world. As subject of the new world, it is the agent of freedom; as object, it is the goal and reason of freedom. Constituent and part of the human plurality, European humanity—civil and political, or ordered in a republic—thus takes a direct part in the free and peaceful life of the humanity of the *orbis* but at the cost of the previous constitution of its own freedom.

The problem in effect is the following: it is futile to think that Europeans can constitute their freedom in an egoistic way. That is, they could do so but only on condition that they limited their constitution to a technical modality of union, in other words, limited their union to a purely juridical constitution instead of transforming it into the foundation of morality, that is, a political constitution. This is the criticism that must be levelled at the multiple projects for a 'constitution' for Europe that flourish periodically and flow from the pens of those authors who are inspired by an ideal of a world as they would like it to be because, quite rightly, they do not like the world as it is. These are not constitutions but literature. If a constitution does not state what it means to constitute, that is, here, the subject and object of the morality of the new world, it is not a constitution of morality but a recipe book for cooperation. At best, it would be an outline for the construction of Europe—not its constitution. The construction of Europe is not its constitution; while the latter thinks its morality, the former organizes its interests. This does not mean that the two things are incompatible, but it does mean that they do not contribute with equal force to the appearance of a *common freedom*; and, while one promotes the civil and political multitude within a republic, the other aims at the natural multitude in the space of the market—not the citizen but the consumer.

b) Second Principle. *In Europe, the condition of the individual of the natural multitude (the consumer) is the state of nature and his natural right is the federative power to make his morality part of the morality of the civil multitude (European humanity)*

The peace that Europeans enjoy, the peace where the guns have fallen silent, means that they experience the state of nature in a novel way. In the old world, war is the lot of the state of nature. On the threshold of the new world, the state of nature is constituted by the market. The constitution of freedom is not limited to the freedom of the market. In other words, the market—the universal space for the exchange of commodities—is not a civil or political space, it is not the space of morality. Or, rather, it does not transcend the order of civility and is not elevated to that of morality. If the market is the state of nature, then, it is not because it puts agents into competition and transforms individuals into consumers who constantly seek to satisfy their needs but, rather, because the market cannot always provide the moral happiness of the free and peaceful life. What the market emphatically cannot procure is the *philosophical life* which is proper to Europeans, that is, the thought of thought freedom. The market cannot procure happiness; it is limited to satisfying the needs of subjects of law. It does not produce *common justice* in which individuals participate (because this is not its proper aim). On the contrary, since the market is structured by the competition of interests, it is orientated towards the elimination of common justice. The market is not a priori the place of justice, if we understand by this the equitable distribution of what is due to each person. The market is not the site of duty but of contract, the sphere of contractual equality and not equity. In this sense, the market is not a state of nature—for example, its workings throw entire social layers into poverty, layers of people who subsequently can barely satisfy their needs (and it is this that makes the state of nature visible). Also, it eclipses the natural right of individuals to associate *politically* with each other in a republic. This essential point is nevertheless rarely noted. This is because it is little noticed in nations in the process of formation. When sovereignty was doing its work in Europe, the moral sentiment that animated individuals was that of the transcendence of their natural individuality for the sake of citizenship—the assumption of the citizen, his direct participation in the 'people' which is his participation in common passions, made the individual (whether or not he was fully conscious of it) take an active part in the philosophical life. His *freedom*—which philosophy constantly defines—was the stakes of his life and action. At bottom, the natural right of individuals in sovereignty is to participate in the advent of common being and common justice. It is this effective participation (which includes war as well as peace) in what is common that was at work in the appearance of historical peoples and nations whose particular States were their armed limbs. Now that nations and peoples are fully constituted in Europe, individuals find themselves thrown into the solitude of need in the wonderful milieu of the market. So we do not find the enjoyment of the free and peaceful life in the political constitution of particular nations but in the advent of a republic of Europe, in other words the common political constitution of particular nations. This is the passage to European cosmopolitics.

c) Third Principle. *The idea of a republic of Europe states the form of the morality of European humanity organized externally according to a law of European peoples (cosmopolitics) and internally according to a federative right*

Considered from the moral point of view of plurality, humanity in the *orbis* is divided into particular peoples who all possess the freedom to constitute themselves into *nations* within a common order of cosmopolitan justice. In other words, every nation is in principle free to take its part in a common (cosmopolitan) order which transcends its own particularism and thus participate in the civil peace that a common order of justice realizes in the world. In the case of Europe, this principle itself is a political transcendence of simple European market cooperation so that this passage to morality is of two orders. Internally, it is the passage to the *republic* while externally it is the agent of peace in the *orbis*. This means that the project of a civil and political constitution in Europe does not consist of the closure of a territoriality but, on the contrary, of the production of an open juridical space. In this sense, the foundation of a republic of Europe does not, as formerly in the constitution of historical States, consist of the delimitation of the frontiers of a territory but the political definition of a juridical space at peace. The intervention of law as the substitute for territoriality consists of the statement of a body of principles in which the individuals of nations form a federation with each other (in particular, by elections of their representatives through universal direct suffrage) because nations mutually recognize each other. The specific character of law as a mediation between agents who, without it, could not enter into civil or political relationship (as we have seen) becomes clearly manifest here. In the same gesture, law functions as the mediation between Europeans in relation to each other, the movement by which they constitute themselves into a republic, and as the mediation of European humanity in its relation to others, the movement by which Europe participates in the peace of the *orbis*.

We can thus define two aspects of the same cosmopolitan law that we need to elaborate in view of the morality of the new world. *Federative law* is the law by which the nations of Europe establish a *common being* among themselves, with an aim of participating together in a common justice. The *law of European peoples or humankind* is the law by which the new world so constituted internally acts with an aim of external *peace*, and, with this aim, to associate with other nations and organizations of nations who seek to establish peace.

Europeans achieve federation through law (which is law as simple means) only under the conditions of their previous and past constitution into particular States (or nations). It is because they arrived at the particular civility of historical States that Europeans now find themselves in a situation when they can federate in reality. But such a federation transcends the State itself as the coercive apparatus of sovereignty, as the material framework of moral particularism. Even though the transcendence of the sovereign State is involved, this does not mean the elimination of nations themselves which are reborn in a new way, far from nationalism. A people does not abandon its nation when it federates with another people, because the nation is the moral element of the particularism of a people, the milieu in which a people lives out its particular passions. Whatever it is, within a cosmopolitan republic, the nation is liberated from the state of nature of its State particularism. In fact, in the absence of participation in the cosmopolitan space of a republic, where each is in common with all, nations live out their particularisms in an egotistical way—this is their natural inclination, so to speak. What we call 'nationalism' is precisely this movement of self towards self of a nation enclosed in State sovereignty. Such a nation can only exist, then, in the immediate particularity of its being, that is, within its bordered territoriality. In its essence, the state of nature of nations is thus not the simple absence of global or regional constraint (which cannot be put concretely to work because it would immediately become the prey of the Great Powers) but the absence of participation in the space of a cosmopolitan morality (cosmopolitan justice) that is nothing but the recognition of particularisms in the form of law. Which can be summed up as follows—the participation of the individuals of a people in universal freedom consists, as citizens of a particular (historical) nation, in their *federative participation* in the freedom of other nations.

This is what the second part of our final chapter will show in producing a synthesis of the philosophical determinations of the *res publica* of Europe, conceived as the form of European freedom as it exists within the cosmopolitan law of the *orbis*.

Res publica *or the New World*

1. Life at Peace

During the period when Machiavelli was planning the restoration of the republic in Florence, the question of the new, the *ordine nuovo*, was uppermost. The question is deeply inscribed into both his period and our own: Machiavelli's problematic—how to produce a new constitution of the world—is also our own. It may be that certain people do not see its relevance (or seeing it, reject it) but it is no less pressing. We could formulate it in the following way: is the patriotism of sovereign nations the element of the future morality of nations? This question is not addressed to the world in general but to this particular world—Europe. This is because the dominant figures of the fable of morality have become figures of a world since Europe has constructed them as *world*. To great military and philosophical astonishment, Europe discovered in 1492 the extension of the *orbis*, or the *orbis* as extension, a very different category from the *mundus* as creation. Europe turned this into a world, its own. In this fabrication of the world, it created modern nations, first and foremost those European nations that we belong to today. Their sole common element is this fabrication of the world through which Europe was itself constructed and identified as Europe (vis-à-vis what was not Europe). This process was absolutely unprecedented and revolutionary from the point of view of general history. In fact, Europe found its identity, its *being*, outside itself. It did not appear within the history of nature, as the *sui generis* emergence of a wholly constituted entity that found its place and role in the events unfolding on the surface of the *orbis*. No. What we call Europe is a process, a movement, the production of a world (which it constitutes as an *historical world* in reflection). In this sense, Europe is *nothing* that can be represented with a definite and discernible outline— it is *nothing* in that to be something is to be determined in time and space. True, you can trace an outline on a map of the *orbis* and say: 'This is Europe', because what you see there is not, for example, Australia. Such a designation, however, does not correspond to anything *historical* that might be *European*. All you are then saying is that Europe is not Australia—a pure geographical tautology. The comprehension of Europe's being is linked to the characterization of what is *historically* European.

Patriotism

From this point of view, there is no difference between Europe and any other corner of the *orbis* designated on a map. However, there is a considerable difference between Europe on the one hand and Asia, Africa and the Americas on the other. Only in Europe has the *patriotism* of the nations that compose it been the cause of the appearance of these very nations, and the effect of the transformation of *orbis* into *world*. The current constitution of the *orbis* is a European production—European trade, European wars and European laws in one form or another have been strewn across the *orbis*. In fact, that should be in the past tense, because from the point of view of the future—*which is beginning before our very eyes*—the world in gestation is not the European world. One world (the European one) is giving way to another, and nobody today knows what world that might be.[1] Be that as it may, it is *empire* that gave birth to the *world*—from the fifteenth to the twentieth centuries, Europeans produced themselves as Europeans through conquest, that is, through the conflicts that pitted them against other people beyond their frontiers (which were themselves provisional and fictional) and the civil wars within these frontiers that made the victors into masters of the defeated. Perhaps, then, the *patriotism* of the inhabitants of the European geographical terrain is a key to grasping what belongs to Europe, or, so to speak, its 'nature'. To know what Europe is (not the question initially posed here) might then consist of carrying out an investigation into the varieties of European patriotism: the patriotism of the Spanish, the Germans, the French, the Swedes, the Poles and the rest, from Italy to Estonia. A person feels himself to be German or French, for example, because at root the following assertion is made: a German is not a Frenchman, and vice versa. The being of the patriot exists only in the negation of the other. If I am French, the being of the German is that he *is not* French; it is the same the other way round. The paradox of patriotism (and of nationalism so understood) is that the ontology that founds it is contradictory—my being has its being only from the non-being of the other. The condition of my patriotism (*I am German*) has only a negative sense: *I am German = I am not French*. Patriotism, in its constitutive essence, contains an appeal to the other that we perceive as the negative and inverse of what we are ourselves—or, rather, what we *want* to be.

1. There are strong arguments in favour of an *Oriental* world that will put an end to the *Occidental* one.

The consciousness of particularism, the will to identity, is irremediably linked to patriotism. The patriotic *self* is capable of sacrificing his own self for the benefit of the *common self* of the fatherland (*patrie*), because he knows himself as an *I* through the experience of the encounter of his empirical self with the common self of the fatherland—an encounter that often enough happens in war. It is this identity-bestowing encounter that gives body and power to his declared and eventually militant patriotism. What I must do when I am a patriot is defend the (threatened) fatherland. This could not be otherwise. What would a patriot be if he did not have the desire to sacrifice himself in defence of the fatherland that forms the object of his patriotism? The patriot is not an intellectual for whom the world is only an ideal. For the patriot, by contrast, the world is an *idea* and this idea commands the world. That is why there are fewer intellectuals than patriots—the first reflect on the world only according to the ideal that they have of it (generally because the real world is insufficient) but they do not make it. The second, by contrast, are the individual agents of the *common self* and this common self is for them the nation, their fatherland. While the intellectual stays at a distance from the world, the patriot submerges himself in it. If some accept self-sacrifice, it is because the world belongs to them, it is theirs; in some sense, they are its proprietors. This is not the case with those who reject it. The *world* of the patriots is the nation—that is their good and they possess it. It is the common subjectivity of which they are a part and whose body, the living and mortal material, is the *people*. The patriot suffers with the people, engages with it; he is a fraction of the people whose passion is inflamed when the nation or the fatherland is in danger. And if an intellectual sacrifices himself for his nation, it is not as an intellectual but as a patriot. Just as if an intellectual is close to the people, because he shares their passions and espouses their ideals, then he thinks and acts like a patriot.

So the novelty of our period comes from the fact that—in Europe—the patriotism of sovereignty is no longer on the agenda of morality. It is a question of *morality.* The patriotism of nations (the nationalism of a people) is no longer a prerequisite for being European—to be European is no longer to be *German* or to be *French* or whatever. This is so because Europe has arrived at a stage of its particular history where the morality of particular patriotisms has been constituted. In the order of morality, particularism (particularisms) has done its work. Which does not mean that patriotism (here or elsewhere) has disappeared from the European world as if by magic. That sovereignty has reached its culmination in its principle (and as principle) *does not* mean that States will disappear. On the contrary, it means that this particularism is no longer the breeding ground of war because it is, by contrast, the foundation of peace, its *condition.* Or to put it another way, peace is possible in Europe because patriotism has reached its end and been achieved—nations are no longer things to be conquered, internally or externally.[2] The singularity of the new century lies in the fact that the European continent (or part of it) lives its free existence, or simply its coherence, in the face of external social groupings because of the particularism of its particular nations which are no longer drawn up against each other. For Europeans, this is absolutely unprecedented. Considered from this point of view, the revolution of our time consists of having transfigured patriotism, not having suppressed it.

Today's patriotism, or, rather, tomorrow's, belongs to constituted nations—patriotism ceases to be negative and becomes positive because it no longer nourishes bellicosity. The patriotism of our time is the form of the common property (*propriété*) of peace. The patriot self, the *citizen* of a particular nation, does not renounce his nation, his fatherland (*patrie*) even if he could do so. For him, the

---

2. We do not mean that every European nation is a complete and homogeneous moral entity—such things do not exist in nature or in history. There may be, here and there, tensions and claims, perhaps accompanied by extreme violence, coming mainly from suppressed or despised nations. But this point does not throw into question my general assertion that the nations of Europe are *tendentially constituted* both in relation to themselves and in relation to the others. It is just this tendency that makes Europe a *new world.*

nation is only particular, which is not to say that it is useless. In other words, he does not sacrifice his fatherland because at another time he would have sacrificed his life for it. When the nation in question was threatened, refused recognition and at war, he belonged to it in a substantial way. Now that the nation is known and recognized, now that citizenship no longer makes the citizen into a *soldier*, he remains a patriot because his morality is that of the fatherland, it is his moral substance but it is not the negative morality of threatened or threatening patriotism. Having discarded the soldier's uniform, he has nevertheless not given up his patriot's costume. Europeans remain who they are—Belgians, Italians, Austrians, Danes, etc. This sentiment of national belonging is not one of negation; on the contrary, it is one of reconciliation and propriety (*propriété*). Nobody gives up what is *his own* (*propre*). Today, everyone in Europe can say: *I am this* or *I am that*, meaning that he is in free possession of his own person, not only his body but his own culture, his everyday habits, his own horizon and sensibility;[3] at least, he is not separated from them. In this sense, for an individual of the European multitude, reconciliation is the very condition for ownership of himself; the other, the one who is for him still a *foreigner*, is not *destined* to be a threat. In this sense, the patriot has shifted from being the negation of the other(s) to full ownership of self. This shift is not just a spiritual satisfaction—it is a historical given whose manifestation is that from now on the patriot exists as a free citizen within a nation at peace. Henceforth, nations are owners of themselves, subjectively and objectively, and the *patriot self* of every one of them is such in the knowledge and recognition of being simply the singular self of a common self which is his own (he owns) with the rest.

3. True, we could object that in the *everyday life* of each individual of the multitude, and this goes not just for Europe, individuals are far from being completely in possession of their own person, of their own self. But here I do not consider (no doubt wrongly) this aspect of things, however essential, but limit myself to understanding the moral status of the citizen in the European framework of constituted nations.

This evolution is the passage from war to peace. Moreover, it is a *revolution* and it has not yet reached its culmination; indeed, it has only just begun. We are only at its announcement. In fact, the patriotism of particular nations, as we know, was established and developed under the yoke of the wars of sovereignty. War, it is often remarked, is the natural element of patriotism—war drives it to its truth, sacrifice. To understand the matter correctly, it is essential to survey the extension of Europe. It will be surprising to discover that the *perpetual peace* half promised in the Enlightenment by philosophy is in fact what Kant also designated, not without bitter irony, as that of the cemetery. In this matter, philosophy can only propose precepts and no philosopher would have the naivety to believe that men of action would follow them and *suffer* in order to re-establish peace among men. Peace is a historical affair, not a philosophical one. On the other hand, if peace is *in fact* installed in Europe, this historical fact can be the object of a philosophical investigation. If the reason for peace is not philosophical, it is because it proceeds from the disposition of things that are no longer ordered by war.

You would be right in finding this the most obvious tautology—there is peace where there is peace, which is a variation on Hobbes' version of peace as the absence of war. Peace is in fact tautological, but exactly because what provokes war no longer exists. In other words, if peace follows war, it is not in the way that enthusiastic liberals think that trade follows war, with the former the aim of the latter, its final cause. The reasons for peace lie elsewhere—it is in the culmination of the principle of sovereignty understood as the means of production of historical peoples and nations. After nations are constituted, their constitution being the stakes of war, war ceases.

We are asking, in effect: what is the ultimate threshold of patriotism? It is the constitution (and defence) of the fatherland (*patrie*). If the fatherland is constituted in itself, I mean in its general formal structure, as it is outside itself, that is, vis-à-vis other nations because these recognize it, then what is left of the patriot and of patriotism? The moral and political question of European peace leads to this unique question: *is a* cosmopolitan European *patriotism possible?* By cosmopolitanism I understand the *European world.* I can indeed declare myself 'citizen of the world' and an Indian or Chinese could do the same. We are nevertheless, in what concerns us, inhabitants of India, China or Europe, respectively. The idea in which the world would be identical to the *orbis* confuses what belongs to *cosmos,* to the given universe as natural totality, with what is historical. It is far from the case that the world is identical with the *orbis*—one is the work of men, the other is always there and abides, whatever illusions we have on the subject, beyond the reach of men. In this sense, a cosmopolitanism that is claimed without further precision and that appeals to the universal fraternity of humanity is, precisely, not an idea but an *ideal,* an intellectual ideal, even a philosophical one. Humanity is not single but multiple, and to wish it to be single is to start up the process that would reduce plurality to the norm of a humanity that declares itself enlightened and superior to the rest. This is why the cosmopolitanism of the natural world is not the cosmopolitanism of the moral world which can be apprehended by a plural and differentiated humanity. That is why the question of a European cosmopolitanism (or one of whatever name we choose) does not refer to the European ideal of the planetary world. It refers to the *concrete* idea of Europe as *world,* or, rather, to the—highly problematic—question of its capacity to constitute itself as one world among others.

It is remarkable to realize once again, as we have already emphasized, that the very name of Europe refers, in its truth, to nothing but the development of a power having appropriated the *orbis* in making a world for itself, its own. If what we currently call Europe is, in the mostly widely spread *doxa,* the geopolitical extension known by this name, there is no question here of the comfort of imprecise language. The geographical polemic about European identity is as nothing compared with the 'cultural' polemic—at least to the extent that it is not the same debate under different headings.[4] Europe is a *power* which from the fifteenth to the twentieth centuries constructed what it still calls 'the world', and in our time this power is discovering that the world that was European up to now is no longer so. This means that the Europe of our discussion is no longer what it was during the period we customarily designate as 'modern', precisely because *the world* of this period had nothing to do (in its languages and morality and certainly not in the structure of its *res extensa*) with the ancient and mediaeval worlds. In consequence, if the Europe of our times is *no longer* the Europe of modernity because the *world* that it created is *no longer* a European one, there remains for Europe only the theoretical possibility of constituting itself as *world*. In this sense, the time has come for Europeans to think of their common morality in the form of a republic of Europe. But if it is not for philosophy to decide on the historical composition of this republic,[5] philosophy must conceive the republic as goal and as *form* of the morality of the future, under the category of *European cosmopolitanism*. The capacity of Europe to fashion itself as world vis-à-vis other worlds, in relation to what is *no longer* European, is the condition of the freedom of its nations, that same freedom which the historical nations that compose it conquered through war, to enjoy in peace.

For half a century now, the patriotism of sovereignty has been slowly transcended by overcoming the limitations of traditional particularisms, not because

---

4. Which can be seen in the rhetorical question about whether Turkey 'belongs' to Europe or not (and thus of its 'candidature' for entry into the European Union).

5. This question—which European nations (today members of the European Union) are ready to form a European republic together—obviously has no philosophical solution because the solution relies solely on the moral calculation of each of them, which is for a nation, the evaluation of its *interests*.

this transcendence erases them but because, on the contrary, it opens up the ground of *European cosmopolitanism*. I say 'on the contrary' because it is inconceivable to think Europeans' freedom, their very morality, if such a thought were to deny the fact of nations. If, as we emphasize here, the very significance of the European world is to have established nations and peoples in their rights and duties through war rather than peace, then it is inconceivable that these same nations should now be sacrificed. Rather, such a possibility is rightly a radical impossibility, and is raised only by those who pretend to believe that peoples might bear the cost of a republic of Europe, peoples who elsewhere would be extension and nature. *Everybody knows* that a republic of Europe can be thought in its principle only by building on the national traditions that are the constructions and consequences of modernity. And this principle is *peace*. Europeans have come to expect the *peaceful life* from their association with each other, now that they no longer use war to achieve peace and their patriotisms are no longer the pretext for conquest and occupation of the *res extensa*, whether the internal extension of the continent or the populated extension beyond its borders.

I noted earlier[6] that what distinguishes the European continent, or, rather, that part of the continent associated in a European union (a union that cannot be reduced to a single market, even if this still remains the most developed common denominator) from the other great *political* units of the *orbis* is that only Europe has emerged from the state of nature. By that I understand that being at peace with itself, it is also at peace with the other parts of the *orbis*. We might add that the civil organization of the *res extensa* is generally advanced there even if the *civility of morals* is largely an internal conquest yet to be achieved. So, the sense of this assertion—Europe is no longer in a state of nature—does not refer to a state of moral or juridical development but to a moral or political condition experienced

6. Chapters 1 and 5.

only by Europe. While non-European groupings live according to the morality of the particular sovereignty of historical States, Europe by contrast, because it has completed the cycle of sovereignty, no longer has sovereignty as the foundation of its historical life. Hence, the historical times of sovereignty have ceased to be the modality by which Europe conceives its future which no longer belongs to the sphere of the state of nature—which is, in a word, the state of war. It is not the case, then, that Europe is no longer at war because it has suddenly become 'pacifist'.[7] Rather, its pacifism proceeds not from its will or its refusal to resort to force if need be but from the extinction of sovereignty (its figures and modes) as the engine of history. It is unnecessary to rehearse this aspect of European affairs—the culmination of sovereignty—that we have already discussed; however, it is necessary to keep to its spirit. The proposition that Europe is no longer in a state of nature should only be understood in this way. This means that the historical conditions of Europe and the other groupings that populate the *orbis* are not equivalent. The contemporary condition of the European world (a *world*, truth to tell, that remains to be made as it remains to be conceived) no longer has anything in common with that of the other historical worlds of the *orbis*.

This is highly problematic for Europe, not just politically (morally) but philosophically. In fact, to keep for the moment to the language of a world that no longer belongs to it, Europe is no longer in a state of nature—philosophically its present condition is defined in a radically different fashion—*its pacified life has become a new state of nature for it*, because the peace it enjoys is not politically organized. The political non-constitution of peace in Europe places Europe and the Europeans in a new state of nature, which shares with the old one the absence of a common law. We can see that the difference between the old order of things and the new is that the absence of common law in the old world was the cause of

---

7. As we hear said by those who live in our time *authentically* in the state of nature.

the state of war. By contrast, this absence of common law in the world of Europe at peace means that the peaceful condition of their lives faces Europeans with the unprecedented historical possibility of a European cosmopolitanism that has the potential to found a *res publica*. It is here that the notion of a *European cosmopolitan patriotism* finds its significance. The multitude of Europeans (Europeans as *civil multitude*)[8] faces, consciously or not, the necessity of constituting, and in facing this necessity producing, peace, which means constituting the republic.

Rousseau conceived patriotism (albeit not that of the republic of Europe, since he conceived the citizen as particular to a particular nation) as this love of self in the love of the fatherland:

> If for example they were early accustomed to regard their individuality only in relation to the body of the State, and to be aware so to speak of their existence as merely part of that of the State, they might at length come to identify themselves in some degree with this greater whole, to feel themselves members of their country, and to love it with that exquisite feeling that no isolated person has save for himself; to lift up their spirits perpetually to this great object and thus to transform into a sublime virtue that dangerous disposition that gives rise to all our vices.[9]

If, from the point of view of *morality* (our perspective here), the care that each bears towards himself is what turns the individual away from the consideration of the universal as it exists in the State, then morality must be limited to that experienced by the juridical self of the market as we have uncovered it as the subject of law. Rousseau's text is nevertheless interesting, not because it describes an individual (for him, a *child*) whose republican future is to transcend the self through love

8. See the preceding chapter.
9. Rousseau, *Discourse on Political Economy*, in *The Social Contract and Discourses*, p. 148.

of the great totality of the fatherland, but because it describes the state of nature of the individual of the multitude who is the subject of law, that is, interested in his own self—the subject of modern law entirely filled by *self-love*. The immense difference between Rousseau's European and the European of today is revealed by Rousseau's illusion. Today's European has been educated by war within a patriotism of the particular, while the citizen that Rousseau envisaged was trained by education in the school of the republic. The difference is capital and returns us to a paradoxical state of nature that Europeans understand as the current condition of their very existence at peace. The patriotism of war was the school in which numerous generations of Europeans learned civility (*civilité*); this is no longer the case in our epoch. However, peoples outside Europe are still educated by war, whether civil war or war with other states. In both cases, we are dealing with a state of nature; but, while for the first it is paradoxically a state of peace, for the second it is a matter of a classic state of war. The difference between the two does not come from education in school but from training by history.

The contemporary patriot in Europe is different to what he is elsewhere. In both cases, the individual is thrown into the market and looks after his own interests in a spirit of self-love. Should he turn aside from the egoistic interest that drives him to love only himself, however, the patriotism of the non-European will have, as the horizon of his action and his thought, the great particular totality of his particular nation. The patriotism of the European, on the other hand, will have the horizon of Europe as republic. The patriotism of the first is still caught in the state of nature, while that of the latter opens onto cosmopolitanism.

The Federative

What the condition of the individual in the state of nature reveals, according to the fable of natural law, is in fact only *the subject of law* of civil society. The participation of the individual in the universal which, according to Rousseau, is the advent of the citizen is in fact only the regulated access of the subject of law to civil space, 'civil society', that is, to the market. As we have seen, each person presents himself there as equal to the other and this equality is possible only because the sovereign formally (juridically) equalizes natural conditions.[10] The State cannot elevate itself above civil society because it is the latter's condition. There is thus no civil society without the State because there is no individual without law. Rousseau does not think the advent of political law, properly speaking, what is common to the *res publica* but the civil law common to civil society, the universality of the law within the essential particularity of sovereignty. The authentic passage from civil to political, from society to *res publica*, requires an exit from the state of nature very different from the passage to civil society. If human beings associate with one another in order to live in a better way, the fact of instituting sovereignty and its necessary corollary civil society does not mean that they are living in peace—it means that the citizen is a soldier. The formation of the modern State does not consist of forming the State in order to have peace between States but of pacifying the market, that is, introducing a civility of morals where the war of all against all is the rule. The introduction of civility among human beings, as the fable of natural law describes it (and to which Rousseau is connected, however much distance he takes from it elsewhere), in no way guarantees the peace of sovereignties. Rather, it makes war between States possible because it opens up the sphere of another state of nature. Thus the citizen of the universal whom Rousseau intuits and who is in effect formally the model of the pacified life must be revealed to be a soldier. The modern rediscovery of the citizen-soldier who was the object of Clausewitz's admiration during the European imperial wars was the discovery of the intimate logical link uniting the modern nation to war, the nation in which the individual as citizen was no less a soldier.

10. See Chapter 4, 'Once Again . . . the *Little King*'.

From this point of view, the great modern revolution leads to the foundation of nations through war and to the enthronement of their citizens, those little kings. In other words, historical republics did not create the *res publica*, just as the modern invention of the 'sovereignty of the people' does not provide the most perfect form of democracy. This is because the concept of the citizen does not include the requirement that *citizenship* (the public morality of sovereignty) involve being a soldier. To include being a soldier in the concept of citizen is a given of the history of the State, not a deduction from the concept, to the extent that the concept of citizen need not be exclusively defined by sovereignty. In fact, it is remarkable that, since his appearance in the semantic context of sovereignty, the citizen has been defined in relation to and through sovereignty (Bodin). The idiom of the 'natural law' theory sets out to define the citizen as soldier. According to its premises, the civil peace that the citizen enjoys within the sovereign State places a moral and political *obligation* on him to take up arms if the State so commands when the fatherland is in danger. A point that can be equally well observed is the well-attested historical fact that modern States are an effect of conquest (colonialism and appropriation of extension) and hence war. The production of the citizen (or subject) as soldier cannot be challenged within the axioms of sovereignty. Or, rather, as we have just observed in regard to the question of patriotism, we cannot see how the citizen of sovereignty can escape his condition as soldier. In theory and in practice, there is no legal order that constrains sovereignties, and it is in the nature of States that they find themselves in relation to each other in the 'state of nature'. And from this point of view, citizens are also soldiers. We are tempted to say that, for every modern sovereignty (democratic or not), what is most proper to a citizen is to be a soldier. It is in the context of the war he participates in, accepting that he will sacrifice himself for the salvation of the fatherland, that the citizen has the ultimate experience of his citizenship. Obviously, this is no lighthearted sacrifice because it is in most cases an imposed one (by the thinker of 'natural law' theory)—just when he discovers death, he also discovers the futility of the citizenship that he had thought to be the guarantee of his freedom.

If Europeans can now be organized into a *res publica* it is because they have experienced the limits of the citizenship whose exercise and benefit sovereignty has guaranteed them. Or, more exactly, it is because they have reached the limits of their historical republics within which their respective nations have been developed and established—which I have called the *culmination* of sovereignty. This is why, as I remarked earlier, Europeans are not 'pacifists' because they are peaceful. They love the peace they have won, but without discarding the possibility of war (or its possible necessity). The *political* expression of their new historical condition is the representation not of a simple civil or public space administered by a more or less liberal sovereignty—which they already enjoy—but of a cosmopolitan space, or *res publica*. The *apprehension* of this new order of things which, as we have seen, has replaced one state of nature by another, so to speak, opens up for the individual a new world which does not negate the old one but transcends it, or perhaps brings it to its completion. It does this to the extent that Europeans can only do what the realization of their past permits them. Without the existence of pacified nations, it would not be possible (in theory or practice) to seriously conceive the *idea* of a republic of Europe. In addition, it is precisely on this issue—the political union of Europe—that we find a difference with the traditional *ideals* of Enlightenment philosophy or enlightened men of action, who, throughout modernity and until very recently, *imagined* formulae for peace among nations whose essence however was that the existence of those very nations lay in preparation for war.[11] If a republic of Europe is thinkable today. it is not as the ideal of what it might be but because it is for the Europeans the *idea* of the epoch.

---

11. The major *historical* example of this contradiction is the ideal invention, not at the European level but at the level of the *orbis*, of the League of Nations (Société des Nations).

This is because it is historically possible for this idea to be philosophically conceived. We have already said that it is the idea of a European cosmopolitanism whose concrete reality as federative republic nevertheless remains to be justified by the examination of the role (and place) of the individual of the civil multitude. I say 'civil' since the historical republic is the essential determination of the individual from which we must begin. What is posed is the question of the *European citizen*.[12] He can only exist, in his concept as in life, in the *res publica* of Europe— within the context of a European cosmopolitanism founded on the federative. The *res publica* of Europe cannot be thought, even less be established, on the traditional basis of the historical republic because it is not a sovereignty. In consequence, the citizenship that it generates is not reducible to the citizenship of the sovereign State. In its concept, the sovereign State endows the individual with a *federative power (or right)* that he holds by nature and which authorizes him to federate himself with any other individual of the multitude of any constituted nation.[13] This

12. From the start, I discard the purely verbal rhetoric which has hitherto expatiated on 'European citizenship'. If the concepts have any meaning in the theoretical tradition that established them, the European citizen exists ideologically. But not politically—we have as yet never seen in known political history (theoretical or practical) fellow citizens being *at the same time* foreigners. This is, however, what we must understand in the definition of the citizen given in the project for the Constitution of the European Union: 'Every person who has nationality in a member State possesses citizenship of the Union' (Title II, Article 1, 8, 1), a proposition that is radically devoid of meaning save by considering that the members of the same body politic are *between each other* foreigners—an absurdity given what follows Article 1, 8, 1: 'Citizenship of the Union adjusts itself to national citizenship and does not replace it.' The extreme theoretical poverty of the current notion of 'European citizen' nevertheless has the merit of indicating what such a citizenship *cannot* be—a simple ideological ornament. What this phraseology reveals is the absence of a *political* conception of the Union (as we can see in the totality of the project for the constitutional treaty itself which does not designate the common being that the treaty constitutes), where the individual of the multitude can *only* be in the Union what he has been for years inside the historical nations—a pure and simple 'subject of law', one privileged by the 'Rights of Man', a juridical self of the great European civil society in process of formation, that agent of the market rigged out in the rags of a purely verbal citizenship.

13. See Chapter 3, especially NOTE 13, in this volume.

determination of the individual fully conforms to the general determination of the *subject of law* which we have said is the individual of the state of nature, the metaphor of civil society and the market. In effect, each person is determined to act for his self-preservation, so there is no conceivable a priori reason by which an *I* of civil society can be refused the right to federate himself with another *I* of another civil society. To be fully intelligible, this proposition (from Locke) must be understood in the historical context of constituted nations. This is how Locke understood such a 'right' or *federative power*. Subsequently, it is obvious how much this right attached to an *I* is the stake of the citizen of an historical republic, that is, a right of nature which established civil society concedes to its members. But this is especially obvious. According to Locke himself, the space of sovereignty of a historical republic cannot—without destroying itself as particular sovereignty—allow the citizen in question the right to exercise his power. When Locke then confers on the executive or government of the State (as he does explicitly) the task of exercising the federative, depriving the *I* of his natural right, in the same move he ruins his discovery. Incidentally, this discovery is not subsequently taken up by anyone else within the republic of natural law theory, since it goes without saying that the federative, the 'right' that Grotius describes as being a quality of the person, must be alienated to the sovereign with the array of other natural rights (as Rousseau says).

What Locke's blunder reveals is that sovereignty can only give rise to a republic conceived liberally, in the best of cases, as civil society. In other words, sovereignty (the State) and civil society are the substance of the historical republic, so that the federative power is excluded from it. On the other hand, the unity of civil society-sovereignty is substantially transcended and its limitations overcome as soon as the *I* of a constituted nation exercises his federative right—which is the very culmination of sovereignty. The beautiful historical unity of the citizen reconciled with himself overcoming the finitude of his singularity and raising himself to the superior order of the universal cannot resist the federative right of each. It cannot be objected that the exercise of federative right by the *Is* of the European civil multitude is a simple *Lockean ideal* and cannot be effective in men's lives, an observation that Locke himself certainly made. The objection is not valid because it forgets that nations are already constituted in such a way as to divide European humanity without opposing it to itself—which was not the case in Locke's time. The Lockean (federative) right to make treaties, manage alliances and so on, is a royal prerogative *in sovereignty* derived from the original convention by which individuals hand over their rights to the sovereign. But, since the last century, Europe has shown that the federative right—in its formal principle—is exercised periodically by Europeans in the course of electing by direct universal suffrage an assembly which represents them—the European Parliament. The philosophical and practical stakes in play here are the historical *possibility* of the *res publica* of Europe as the practical content of European cosmopolitan right.

As this inquiry endeavours to keep to the principle of things, it is important to redefine what we understand by *res publica* to the extent that, on a European scale, it is defined, not on the basis of a right of sovereignty (which already exists and by definition does not make the *res publica* thinkable) but on a cosmopolitanism of European nations at peace. This is the problem reduced to its proper terms.

2. The Free Life

The republic is *free* when the exercise of its *federative right* by each individual of the multitude is the foundation of citizenship, so that the space in which the exercise of this right takes place is what we call the 'republic'. We could in fact designate this space which is, properly speaking, the public space of the deployment of

GÉRARD MAIRÉT

a right, *the public matter*, since the universality of the *I*s exercising their federative right is the very substance of a common being which would not exist without this exercise. It is not this right or federative power itself which is common (or what is common) to the universality of individuals concerned. In fact, they do not have this right in common because each of them has it as his own but does not exercise it subsequently. So what they do have in common is the exercise of this right, that is, the actualization of what they only had as potential. The freedom of the *I*s does not reside in the power they would have to federate. Their freedom is *true freedom* if, and only if, they actually federate. In other words, what is proper to each individual is the power of federating with any and everyone, but this does not constitute freedom, only its possibility. Freedom is thus not what it is only possible for me to do but what I am in a position to do. For what I am in a position to do—join a federation, for example—does not depend upon my capacity or power (*puissance*) alone but on what my power is in a position to accomplish in common with the powers of others. This is evident in that, by definition, I cannot 'federate' with myself. If I dispose of this federative right, it is not as a solitary right, or, rather, as a solitary right it does not exist. The freedom that I have to federate is only complete freedom if it encounters another freedom with which it can be exercised. This means that my right to federate (or federative power (*pouvoir*)) has concrete meaning for me only if this right is exercised collectively as opposed to individually, so that its exercise requires a space or an extension where it can be unfolded. Extension here is both *res extensa* and *res publica*. From the point of view of federativity, in fact, these are the same thing. There is a necessary link uniting these three terms: freedom, extension, and republic. It is only on the condition that it enjoys (appropriates) extension that my freedom can be concretely expressed. And this condition exists only in the form of the republic. Only the public matter offers me the possibility of actualizing my potential (*puissance*). If I

300

do not dispose of a public space which is at the same time an extension in which to experience my freedom, then I am an *I* who only experiences his own private self. I can in these conditions indeed think of myself as a free animal, because I think, I suffer or I enjoy, but I am just that animal which is not yet known by others, my fellows. It is not certain that I am what I imagine myself to be (an *I*) because in these conditions I am rather a self. If it happened, *ex hypothesi*, that I were to come into the presence of another *I* (who himself is a *self*), then the experience of the other would throw into doubt what I represent to myself as my freedom. If such a doubt insinuates itself into my spirit, it is because the other and I have in common a space, an extension, that is the element of recognition, or at least of encounter. Here we come back to our starting point in the fable of the world, the fable of sovereignty—either I try and eliminate the other before he eliminates me, or fear makes me yield to calculating reason and I resolve to agree a contract with him.

The substance of my freedom, its concrete materiality, is the *res extensa*, that is, the republic itself. To put it in the language of the fable the choice is this—either nature or the republic. In other words, either the singular freedom of the *self*, the animal that thinks and who is not fully an *I*, or the common freedom by which the self of nature is the *I*, that political animal, of a republic. The passage to the republic leads me to the necessary extension without which I cannot be in common with others; it is necessary that a space be opened that contains me and my fellows. The republic is thus this opening of public space in which I experience my freedom in the form of federativity. Citizenship functions in the context of the appropriation of the *res extensa* as foundation of the *res publica*. The citizens of a historical republic, that is, the constituted nations of Europe or elsewhere, dispose of a common space, that of sovereignty. Modern political (and social) space is the space of sovereignty. We must thus consider that the citizenship of a State is constituted by federativity which is exercised in the form of civil association. Citizens, we could say, are federated with each other after the founding pact of sovereignty, so that the institution of the State would be this association of *natural selves* by their transfiguration into a *juridical self*. The space of sovereignty thus becomes a space of the market[14]—the encounter of the private interests of persons or groups. In any case, those in association freely traverse this space in which, in addition to their subsistence, they find the moral element of their citizenship because they periodically renew the contract by elections of their representatives and governors. The three dimensions of the political animal or citizen are confirmed here: freedom (i.e. he disposes of a portion of extension); extension (i.e. the element in which he exercises his federative right); and the republic (i.e. the common being of his freedom). Since the republic is not what I experience in solitude but what I have in common, it is the common part of my freedom, or, more precisely, the common condition of my freedom. It is worth saying that the 'contract' is what federatively institutes my freedom. In other words, freedom is of the order of the federative; it is the very order of the federative, so that it requires the recognition and juridical form that states it. *Sensu stricto*, there is no freedom in nature, for the well-known reason that natural freedom is a contradiction in terms—something the fable of sovereignty demonstrated once and for all. Freedom must be civil (political) or it is not at all—it requires the republic, which must thus be instituted.

At once the question arises: what freedom—the *exercise* of my federative right—do I have in the historical State, and what is its *extension*? Is sovereignty the form of federativity that makes my freedom possible? Is the citizenship of the modern State constitutive of my freedom looked at from the point of view of my federative right? When Rousseau demands that *all* my rights be surrendered to the general will, when he demands that the self be raised above its egotistical condi-

14. See Chapter 4.

tion to conceive the universal, is my freedom safe, and must I understand that absolute freedom is identical with absolute sovereignty? These questions reduce to a single one, which is in no way speculative: is sovereignty compatible with the federative? They would be redundant if philosophy could resolve them. For that, philosophy would have to be interested in questions that were not the agenda of thought, in only posing questions that had no relation (or only a distant one) to what was historical. If the historical is not open to philosophical questioning, it remains merely given nature where the elements of a thought of thought freedom are elaborated. But these circumstances are irrelevant to a philosophy that knows that there is no freedom in nature. (Moral) philosophy is determined as philosophy, or at least in the fable of the world that it tells the Moderns, in positing as its axiomatic basis that the *thought* of freedom is thought by breaking with the natural. And there is a further axiom, which makes the historical the key to freedom, because the fable rightly calls 'history' the historial procession of freedom, its accomplishment through the period designated 'modern' for that very reason: modernity says of itself that it *is* the freedom being brought about in and through the sovereignty of the historical State.

A 'Brilliant Error'

So perhaps it is not *unjust* to ask whether the sovereign republic is the free republic it thinks it is. It is not a question here of abstractly evaluating the freedom of the historical world by externally opposing a real (historical) freedom to an ideal (imagined) freedom. In fact, there are good reasons to think that parts of the present historical world are free, and likewise good reasons to think that freedom is absent from parts of the same world. In consequence, the philosophical question of freedom is posed in itself not as a-historical speculation but as a constitutive element of the historical world. There is a good reason for this. Philosophy forms part of the world. Philosophy transforms definitions even as it is transformed by the world. To think the thought of thought freedom as *res publica* is not to consider a pure and abstract freedom but the free life that is political freedom, citizenship lived in the historical State. From this point of view, the federative, understood as the fundamental power (*puissance*) to federate with others, the form of freedom, not only contradicts modernity but revolutionizes it. And this, even if an investigation carried out with the means of philosophy only turns out to confirm in the form of the concept what is manifest in actuality in the historical world, that is, the obsolescence of sovereignty. The thought of thought freedom does not operate in the imaginary of an ideal world while practical politics is not separated from the real world. Quite the reverse. The *idea* of a federative republic has philosophical sense because, from the concrete point of view of morality, the freedom of the historical State is effectively brought into being and cannot elevate itself beyond itself, that is to say, beyond its particularism. Such a point of view must take an interest in what, in the order of morality, constitutes if not the essence, then, at least the principle of morality of the world as it is—the principle of sovereignty. To think freedom or the free life is then necessarily to link these two objects—freedom and sovereignty not as the categories of an academic discussion but as the pertinent political concepts of the *res publica*, here and now.

The question thus posed is this: in what practical form does the federative right of the multitude become the political freedom of the *res publica*? We know that the modern tradition, as recounted by the fable, reflects on federativity in the form of association, which makes the federative principle disappear from modern discourse, above all by its absorption in the State executive. This is how the thorny question of the compatibility of sovereignty and federativity is resolved. The corollary of the disappearance of the federative power from the language of natural law theory is the elimination of the thought of public freedom, or morality, in the form of the *multiple*. On the other hand, sovereignty does not disqualify a form derived from, indeed endowed by, its institution in the so-called federal State. *Federalism* is the instrument that sovereignty uses to eliminate the *federative* as the foundation of freedom in the republic—it is simply the specific modality of sovereignty (the ordination of the multiple into *one*) when it is put to work over a vast extension. In other words, the invention of the modern republic, a republic that comes out of the association of represented individuals—the *people* in person—happened in the Americas in the beautiful expanse of natural extension—the wilderness—in the form of the federal State. Federal sovereignty is the modern production of the *one* by the multiple, the substitution of the *one* for the multiple in a territory that is vastly more extensive than that of the traditional State and is governed by representation. Sovereignty in its classic European and pre-republican form was the reduction of *number* to unity in the institutional framework of the (more or less) absolute monarchy. What was invented—in America—was the modern republic— first, by the mastery of the *res extensa*; then, by mastery of the instruments of representation; and last, by the restitution of sovereignty to the 'people'. To put the people in the place of the king in the system of endowed sovereignty, that is representation, is to claim to guarantee the rights of the individual, his freedom as person, individual or group. Against the whole tradition of modern thought about a 'free State' from Machiavelli, via Montesquieu to Rousseau, the American revolutionaries invented and bequeathed to the future the radical model of the republic as a *democratic regime* of individual rights. They asserted not only that a republic *extended* over an immense space, virgin, wild and ready for conquest was possible, but at the same time that there was an obligation to conceive the government of the extension *democratically* but avoiding the risk of dividing space and men in uncontrollable fashion into a multiplicity of belligerent monarchies or principalities. In the aftermath of Independence, after Thomas Jefferson had declared the bill of *rights*, the crucial question for the Americans was that of creating a body politic that could preserve these very rights.

The *metaphysical* assertion of the Declaration of Independence would have remained metaphysical and agreeably literary if James Madison and Thomas Jefferson, in particular, had not conceived the notion of the federative republic as a federal sharing out of sovereignty—the plural constitution of unity. Consciously opposing the theoretical *doxa* which stated that republican freedom was only possible within the narrow and limited framework of small city-state republics, Jefferson, claimed that *justice*—and in consequence freedom—can exist only in a republic of great extension because the representation of everyone's particular interests prevents a single particular interest from asserting primacy over the rest. This was a definitive response to the nevertheless philosophically powerful objection made by Rousseau, who opposed all representation of the 'will' of the people. Here, by contrast, the people—that is to say the differentiated multitude of a 'people' who nevertheless lacked elites and aristocracy—can only enjoy its rights[15] within the framework of a representative democracy. The key to the republic, that is to say to *justice*, thus resides in extension—something neither Montesquieu nor Rousseau had seen. 'I believe', writes Jefferson,

> that experience will disprove, like so many brilliant errors spread by Montesquieu and other political authors, the doctrine by which the republican regime can only suit small States. Perhaps one day one will see that to set up a just republic (and it is precisely in order to ensure our just rights that we have recourse to government) it is necessary that it be of sufficient extension that local egoisms can never attain the greatest part:

---

15. Let us recall in passing that Jefferson wanted the Constitution to include a Declaration of Rights—something Madison refused. Jefferson's demand made him the true inventor of the modern 'democratic' republic, which is only, as we have already observed, the (democratic) association of the subjects of law—in other words the 'republic' itself.

so that, on each particular question, we can always find in its counsels a majority exempt from particular interests and, in consequence, always giving preponderance to the principle of justice.[16]

The virtue of the representation of the multiple is that it annuls particularisms by majority vote and eliminates any interest superior to the rest. At bottom, the invention of the republic rests on a paradoxical situation, so to speak. If Jefferson and the other revolutionaries invent the modern republic, it is because at the moment of constituting extension, they find themselves facing an absence— that of the aristocracy. In other words, Rousseau and Montesquieu (and Machiavelli already) assert that republican freedom is possible only in a very limited spatial framework because they face the threat of the Great, the Magnates, who constitute a danger that their interests will have irremediable primacy over those of the little peoples of the multitude. The American solution is only republican because, at Independence, America lacks the Great. The modern republic that the Americans constitute is a republican monarchy that divides in order to rule as Madison explicitly wanted. *Sovereignty* in this sense is a 'shared sovereignty' (Madison), and, for Alexis de Tocqueville, the crucial element underpinning any understanding of American democratic equality.

The proposed constitution [writes Madison] far from implying the abolition of the State governments, makes them constituent parts of the national sovereignty, by allowing them a direct representation in the Senate and leaves in their possession certain and very exclusive parts of sovereign power. This fully corresponds, in every rational import of the terms with the idea of a federal government.[17]

16. Thomas Jefferson, letter to François d'Ivernois, 6 February 1795, in Thomas Jefferson, *Liberté et État* (E. Dumbauld comp. and introd.) (Paris: Nouveaux Horizons, 1974), p. 104.

17. J. Madison, A. Hamilton, J. Jay, *The Federalist Papers* (1798) (Harmondsworth: Penguin Books, 1987), Article 9, p. 122.

Tocqueville precisely put his finger on the central question of shared sovereignty:

> An initial difficulty must have presented itself to the minds of the Americans. It was a question of apportioning sovereignty such that the different states that formed the Union might continue to govern themselves in all that concerned only their internal prosperity, without having the entire nation, represented by the Union, cease to make up a body and to provide for all its general needs. A complex question, difficult to resolve.[18]

It is in fact a theoretically powerful coup to share out sovereignty in the State, and rightly call it a 'federal State'. It is thus the specific American context that allows the dissemination through the Old World of the new idea of a republic or representative democracy. The invention of the democratic republic, operating within the context of federalism, opens up the radically new idea of an extended republic which the old European monarchies could not imagine, never mind establish, given that they were all marked, by definition, with the elitist stamp of aristocracy. The American republic, nourished by European political and moral philosophy, brings into being the realm of the *sovereignty of the people*, an idea that Rousseau produced but which could not be realized because of its very radicalism. It is thus America that demonstrates the truth of Rousseau's definition of the democratic principle but at the cost of sacrificing the element that this doctrine posed as condition—the impossibility of representing the will of the people.

The other sacrifice, though not perceived as such, was that the introduction of representation as the form of shared sovereignty, in instituting the federal State, radically removed the federative principle. If, as Tocqueville says, in democracy in America 'the people reign over the American political world as does God over the

---

18. Alexis de Tocqueville, *Democracy in America* (Harvey C. Manfield and Delba Winthrop trans., eds and introd.) (Chicago: University of Chicago Press, 2000 [1835]), I, 8, p. 107.

universe. They are the cause and end of all things; everything comes out of them and is absorbed by them',[19] then the republican model has become the Atlantic model. There is no difference of substance or principle in the structure of republican sovereignty (where the people are sovereign) on either side of the Atlantic. The differences are not of essence but of realization, and they emerge because Europe had an aristocratic elite and a class of nobles. Their absence meant that the American Revolution occurred without sound and fury, and without crime. By contrast, the French Revolution had to put the whole of Europe to fire and sword, and France itself took two centuries to arrive at universal suffrage.

The Atlantic model of the republic—sovereignty of the people and representation—could thus be defined as the system of sovereignty where the federative principle understood as federative power, federative right, is handed over to the executive. The Atlantic model is the articulation of 'three powers', as Montesquieu says, among which only the Executive power *is* invested with the federative power, eventually producing the federal State. Be that as it may, every State is endowed with the federative power, generally understood as the capacity of the sovereign power to engage the State in alliance, war or peace. Thus the essence of the Atlantic model is to be found not in the Legislature, where the will of the people is represented, but in the Executive, where the federative power is incorporated. It is because the *people* is the foundation of the republic that the free life, justice, defines this people in a particular way—the free life is thought as the particularity of *the spirit* of a people. The particular dimension of the common being of a people is to contemplate its own collective self. Being in constant subjective identity with itself constitutes the spirit of the people, or, rather, it is through this feeling, the passions that it experiences in contemplating its own self, that the people experiences its freedom. Sovereignty, we know, is the historical modality of a peo-

19. Ibid., I, 4, p. 55.

ple's freedom, a freedom made in the movement of collective passions seeking self-assertion. Because the people is the central character in modern morality, it is the assertion of self in the State and it is the radical assertion of its *being* that the State produces when it calls on the citizen to vote or don military uniform. It protects the life of the people, its very substance, and administers it through force in a perpetual and constantly renewed gesture of sovereignty, faced with a menacing outside. As guardian of the *collective self*, the modern State is, of necessity, the holder of the federative because its juridico-technical system, like its thought, is ordered through the preservation of the people's freedom as what is particular and singular to it. The Executive that holds the principle of force and the right to resort to violence is from this point of view the natural element of the federative.

However, the question of the Atlantic republic could be considered in an opposite movement—the sovereign State is the instrument that the multitude makes use of in order to become a people, that is, to live according to an accepted norm of justice, according to its own freedom and morality. A people does not exist spontaneously constituted in nature, and it is *politics* that brings the people into being as *this* people and not another. However, this just leads us back to our starting point—sovereignty and its federative dimension put to work, by the State, with the aim of preserving the particularity of a people. So what we call here the Atlantic republic (or democracy) is marked by the concept of political freedom which has the people as authority. Moreover, we know that one of the claims of the present inquiry is that European nations are now so formed that the sovereignty that produced them no longer needs to engage in the task that preoccupied it throughout modernity. This is confirmed by the fact that the historical world of contemporary Europe paradoxically experiences a new state of nature because there is no law common to Europeans that would make them citizens of the same public space. However, this situation—of non-constituted peace—throws an unexpected light on the Atlantic republic—it brings about its culmination in producing an essential rupture within Atlantic freedom. Against what constitutes the very meaning of their past history, the States of Europe have been engaged in the cosmopolitan reform of their morality. Europe has no aim for the *orbis*; on the contrary, having come back to itself, and fully occupying its own extension, Europe thinks itself as *world* and cannot avoid conceiving its freedom as that of a new world, that is, as the republic of Europe. When we say that it cannot avoid this future, we are not being prophetic but are determining the concept of freedom of a world (the European world) after which this freedom cannot be thought as the sequence of particular freedoms of historical peoples. It is because the Europeans no longer live their freedom as particularity that the European world has become separate from the Atlantic republic. In this sense, a *schism* within Atlantic freedom is being produced in the current mutation of sovereignty in Europe, which appears not as the condition of the republic of Europe but, rather, as its effect. In other words, if the political constitution of Europe is the necessary effect of the culmination of traditional sovereignty, then, so too is the schism in Atlantic freedom.[20]

We cannot grasp the sense of this proposition if we take 'the freedom of the Europeans' to mean the negation of the obvious fact that Europeans do not renounce their freedom as Germans, Italians, British, etc. If the freedom of the Europeans leads to such a negation, we will not understand the nature of their

20. We cannot seriously consider a 'constitution' that is more a neo-classical treaty of international law organizing a space of the market accompanied by minimal socio-political measures. A political constitution of Europe would have to institute a cosmopolitan space (or *res publica*) no doubt limited to various founder members who have decided to work for the advent of a community sovereignty on the basis of a principle of *federativity* (and not of simple federation). This means that the Atlantic schism of freedom follows a division within the European Union itself as it is organised by the current treaty or 'constitution'. The next decades of this century will probably be occupied in tracing out the new lines of demarcation and division. On the theoretical bases of *federative freedom*, see section in this chapter, 'On the constitution of the free life'.

attachment to a particular quality, what they think of as their own, the feeling that makes them think of themselves as Germans, Italians, British and the rest. The durability of this sentiment is incontestable and will no doubt take a long time to be overcome, but this does not lead to the impossibility of a republic of Europe, whatever form it might take. On the other hand, what is an unsurpassable moral given is that this national sentiment is *no longer* constitutive of the nations themselves. In other words, the current mutation of freedom in Europe comes from the fact that, because they have been constituted, these nations are no longer historically motivated to found that particularism of freedom. The freedom that Europeans live and which they must constitute lies beyond the foundation of their being as Germans, Italians and the rest. The reason for this, we have said many times in the course of this inquiry, is that the foundation of each nation's self, with its own morality and the particularism of each nation's *spirit*, has been achieved. It seems difficult not to recognize this fact, unless we say that Europeans are once more ready to kill each other in the name of their homelands. Given this is not the case, as we think, we must acknowledge that the very *nature* of their freedom has been transfigured, hence the adjective cosmopolitan that will characterize it from now on—my freedom is no different from my neighbour's. This sole fact is itself the bearer of a political revolution, if revolutions have as their intention and goal (which they often pervert) the introducion of freedom where it is lacking. This is not to say that Europeans are slaves who must be freed from tyranny; it is to say that they are discovering a different substance to their freedom than the particularism of the nation, or, at least, this means that their freedom is, and will be, different to what they are used to.

Thus the first sign of this novel introduction of a new world of the republic is Europe's separation from the Atlantic model. Europe sees America moving away from the sphere of freedom that it has begun to discover for itself as the new possibility of living in the extension of a new territory whose outlines remain to be explored. It is the status of the *federative* that manifests the rupture with the traditional model of the republic as invented beyond the Atlantic. Since the States of Europe are no longer in a state of war, even if in a new state of nature, the federative still linked to the executives of these States is no longer oriented towards particular freedom. On the contrary, the European horizon of the federative is linked to the constitution of a common space of freedom which no longer rests on the venerable and traditional category of the 'people'. The latter is the bearer of particularism, as is the morality which is proper to it.

The breach with the Atlantic model occurs because there is no European people, and there cannot be one because there are can only be *peoples* of Europe, the very ones created by a war-ridden European history. On the other hand, what exists in Europe and does not exist in America is the civil multitude, that European humanity in the process of being born, in the process of being constituted. The difference here is substantial—it is essential and a matter of principle. If freedom is acquired in the Atlantic tradition by the confrontation of freedoms, the confrontation of sovereign peoples,[21] the subject of freedom is no longer 'the people', that supreme figure of sovereignty, but the multitude, that is, Europeans as citizens of constituted nations. Thus, the republic understood as the space in which the federativity of the Europeans unfolds does not found its morality and law on the 'sovereignty of the people' because the people no longer exists. Thus Europeans are finding the sources of a new patriotism which is not that of historical nations but a cosmopolitan patriotism, which you can give any name you like. As the problem is not verbal, the name is unimportant. Nor is it important from the philosophical point of view adopted in this inquiry, that the federative is not

---

21. A confrontation aimed at what is just as Jefferson understood it, and which he also knew the new American extension would be exempt from, and for good reason—in America there were only colonists, slaves and Indians who did not *a priori* form part of a *number*.

in our time realized by the executives of the historical States. We could regret this fact or rejoice in it, but this is not what is changing the nature of things that can *in right* be expressed as follows—the freedom of the universal (the federativity of European humanity or civil multitude) is morally superior to the freedom of the particular (the sovereignty of the people).

On the Constitution of the Free Life

What the previous analyses and deductions have allowed us to establish can perhaps be presented under four headings. The first is that philosophy must think the freedom of the *plurality of worlds* and of the advent of the European world as new world. The second is that the effective subject of the new world is *European humanity*. The third is that the civil organization of the free life consists of the exercise of federative power instituting the *federative norm* of a transnational democracy. Finally, *cosmopolitan law* is the foundation of the freedom of the republic as the transcendence of Atlantic freedom. These are the four *theoretical sites* where we can trace out the philosophical coordinates of the territory of the new freedom that the European culmination of sovereignty obliges or compels us to think, or, better, to constitute.

True, we cannot present a constitution in a form that would be valid for Europe and would be more just than those imagined in the past or envisaged in the present. In its empirical form, a constitution is the law of the distribution of powers, rights and obligations, within a common being (or *res publica*) whose expression or historical manifestation it is. We cannot then write a constitution that would bring a republic into existence, for the very reason that it is only when the republic is *possible* that its concept can be formulated. What we call a 'constitution' is only the public statement of the concept of the common being of a republic. This is why constitutional work, as we have observed, is not reducible to the editorial activity of an individual or assembly. The Americans did not produce a constitution for themselves, thus inaugurating the era of the Atlantic republic, because they had talented political writers (in fact, the ones they had were European) but because the historical American world was pregnant with a republic at the moment of its independence. In this sense, it is not a text that founds a republic; it is when the republic is possible in reality, because the historical world requires a new form of freedom, that a constitutional text can be drafted[22] and which makes the general spirit public. We thus have to go over these four philosophical sites and make a synthesis of them, in order to give account of the new constitution of freedom.

The Plurality of Worlds

The idea of the world must be philosophically recognized and politically established to make the free life under the peace of law possible. In other words, a world is not constructed through the magic of law, but, rather, the *res publica* is established in the world and as world by historical political action. What is proper to our time is not the globalization of the world in making it *one*, so that it can be governed from a single centre, which (past and present) experience shows will then fall into the hands of a group of magnates or a single ruler. 'Globalization' in this sense rests on a widely accepted cliché, but is no less a poorly crafted fable nourished by a fantasy of omnipotence. If globalization is the universalization of the reign of the commodity, then, indubitably, it has nothing to do with the question of morality we are concerned with here—the free and organized life. Put another way, the *freedom* of the world cannot be reduced to the universal reign of

---

22. As we know, it is not at all necessary for a text to be written—it is enough that a constitutional tradition, visible in the numerous texts spread out through time, regulates the *res publica* (as, for example, in Great Britain).

the commodity. I am not a free individual (singular or collective) because I am free to produce in order to buy, and sell in order to produce. My rights are not guaranteed or preserved by the globalization of the commodity; they can be guaranteed only within the framework of my belonging to a world at peace that can be given a norm of common justice. The question of freedom, then, is this: is there a world capable of accepting a law common to all those who compose that world, a law expressing the freedom of each and every person? A world where individuals (collective or singular) are satisfied? A world where the interest of all is to preserve the interest of each? A world where those who live in it, whether persons or States, have equal rights and duties and are *cosmopolitans*?

We have to reply to these questions in the negative. Morality, which is the *system* of freedom, does not presuppose the fantasy of 'globalization' but the perception of necessary particularity and, with it, the division of the *orbis* into a plurality of worlds. I do not mean by that some differentiation between developed and underdeveloped states. This difference does indeed exist,[23] but what is at issue here is the particularity of moral systems which are in no way reducible to a common universal model. And even if the sovereignties of the planet do not form differentiated systems of morality (in their essential, particular form, most of the historical States of the *orbis* are identically structured by sovereignty), they also no longer refer to a common model. This arises from the fact that sovereignty works on cultural and historical substrates which make their reduction to the same morality impossible. For example, most States have included the protection of the 'Rights of Man' in their constitutions, but this concession to liberal ideology remains for the most part merely verbal because it is precisely a State power to sovereignly interpret what is to be understood by the 'protection of the Rights of

23. And this fact alone disqualifies the term 'globalization' as the master term of current neo-liberal ideology.

Man'. By definition, sovereignty allows for semantic interpretation or latitude in definitions.

If, on the one hand, we consider the criterion of sovereignty and on the other the differentiated forms of morality, we can see that there is no single world but a plurality of worlds. In this context of a plurality of worlds, it is evident that Europe presents a particular configuration owing to its unique relationship to sovereignty —sovereignty was born there, as we know, and reached its culmination there. It is this culmination that puts Europe in a novel situation—that of being at peace with itself and with the non-European worlds. In this sense, *peace* is a radical novelty in history that structures a European world. Where philosophy dreamed of bringing peace to Europe (by good will or cosmopolitanism) and where the powerful attempted to unify the continent under the peace of Empire, it is after all from Europe itself that peace has emerged. Neither law nor will nor force brought peace to Europe, but the extinction of war, the culmination of the works of sovereignty. Since war is over in Europe, a new world (Europe as world) is made possible.

In consequence, if we consider Europe's novel situation as world, it is obvious that this new world is separated by its reality from what was once the New World. Similarly, the existence of new sovereignties emerging from the collapse of empires during the last century and the civil and economic development of the other continents or parts of continents divide the *orbis*, which, far from being 'globalized' under the peace of the commodity, offers the spectacle of war provoked by the new determinations at work in the plurality of worlds populating the *orbis*.

We can see a new problematic of freedom being traced out here—the genesis in Europe of a peace founded on the culmination of sovereignty makes room for a cosmopolitan foundation of peace whose condition is the republican institution of European humanity. As peace (and freedom) in Europe can only substantially exist in relation to the plurality of worlds, Europe as *res publica* can only find another solid foundation for its existence in its effective contribution to the peace of the *orbis*.[24] It is thus essential that the plurality of worlds be known and recognized and that Europe is constituted as a new world.

European Humanity

It was in the utterly novel context of the nascent Atlantic republic in the aftermath of the American and French Revolutions, while Europe was setting out for the modern republic and war, that Kant stated the philosophical idea of a 'cosmopolitan right (and law)' which would be the foundation of a peaceful order of the world. This was not the world as a republic of cosmopolitans but as a union or association of the free States—'republican' as he put it—of the world. We should observe that the world involved here, the world of the republic-world, is the *orbis* and its inhabitants, 'humanity'. Kant's idea rests on two premises: the first is that sovereignties cannot be transcended, and the second is that the *European* world (America is still rooted in the wilderness) is the whole of the world. In his eyes, the European continent is called upon by 'nature' to guide the other continents. We must regard these conditions as prejudices of the times, and we cannot remain attached to them two hundred years after Kant. In this sense, Jürgen Habermas' initiative is worth looking at given its attempt to overcome Kant's prejudices even if it does not quite manage it.[25]

24. It is an illusion to want to found the republic of Europe, an obligation where it would be the Europeans who gave body to their common being in a *republic of Europe*, under the constraints of globalization, indeed as we sometimes hear said, as a 'response' to such constraints. If Europe can, in fact, constitute its own freedom, it can only do it in the same act in which it associates its own freedom with that of others and with *peace*—not the planetary extension of the market.

25. Jürgen Habermas, 'Kant's Idea of *Perpetual Peace*, with the Benefit of 200 Years Hindsight', in James Bohman and Matthias Lutz-Bachman (eds), *Perpetual Peace: Essays on Kant's Cosmopolitan Ideal* (James Bonham trans.) (Cambridge: MIT Press, 1997), p. 113–54.

In his rereading and updating of Kant's 'cosmopolitan right', we can see a critique of the insufficiencies of the strictly Kantian point of view in relation to the needs of our times. Habermas' critique essentially turns on the idea, which Kant rejected or simply did not see, that cosmopolitan right is less concerned with sovereign States as subjects of international law than with individuals themselves. Why would individuals be directly concerned with cosmopolitan right without the intermediary of the State to which they belong? The answer comes from the original postulate (already made by Kant) that individuals have, by nature, inalienable fundamental rights, not reducible to the freedoms conceded them by the sovereignty that rules them. In other words, the transcendence of the 'Rights of Man' by the positive rights of particular historical States makes cosmopolitan right into that right which makes the rights attached to the individual human person universally effective. At bottom, cosmopolitan right as Habermas conceives it expresses the universality of the Rights of Man stated in and protected by a universal republic of the *orbis*. This does not consist of a world Super State of particular States, he says, but a universal juridical system such as a radically reformed United Nations. Thus Habermas' critique of Kant is that the latter, while he rests internal right and cosmopolitan right (and law) on the inalienable rights of the human person, still requires the good will of State sovereignties to respect these rights, since he holds that the principle of sovereignty cannot be transcended either in the civil or cosmopolitan order. This is in effect what Kant demands when he posits that one of the essential conditions of 'perpetual peace' in an association of States is that the States of the association must be politically organized according to a republican constitution—in other words, that of a free and sovereign State which would guarantee those rights.

Behind Kant's assertion of the Rights of Man and Habermas' critical 'revision' of it lies the same common foundation—humanity as such is the subject of cosmopolitan right. Thus, the rectification, the 'revision of fundamental concepts' as Habermas describes his engagement, concerns the *humanity of the world in general*. But what is at issue here is an abstract humanity of an abstract world. With Kant, world humanity is that of Europe; with Habermas, that of the planet. Neither of these propositions stated two centuries apart can found a cosmopolitan order at peace because of the inconsistency of their concept of the 'world', at least in this context. In both cases, the world of cosmopolitan right is apprehended as empirical given material. This is what I call the *orbis*. The substance of cosmopolitan right cannot be reduced to the extension of the (European or planetary) *orbis* for the simple reason that, as such, the *res extensa* can be neither politicized nor moralized and as it is given empirically—it is simply given extension. As such, the extension is *wilderness* and state of nature. Extension must become *world* for this world to be potentially organized for peace. It is important that a concept of world—a common being—be forged for cosmopolitans (individuals or collectives) to associate. It is not enough to determine the previous conditions[26] for the common being of a world to spring forth. Kant's representation of perpetual peace followed a certain necessity—it was world peace. But the French Revolution was putting that 'world' to fire and sword, in the process giving birth to a new European world which would replace the old one, an absolutely inchoate world at that point but the very world from which we are only just emerging two centuries later. When Habermas conceives a cosmopolitan order of the world, which he designates as 'planetary public space', he has in mind the given empirical world that the history of the last century has bequeathed to him. Thus his critique of Kant's text suffers because of his starting point, which is limited to rectifying the empirical world (there are today, he notes, a great number of States sitting at the United

---

26. 'Republican' form or acceptable budgetary deficit. These are certainly necessary conditions that correspond to a determinate necessity which nevertheless are altogether insufficient to bring about the *common being of a republic*.

Nations who do not respect the 'Rights of Man'). What is important is to formulate the *concept of the world* appropriate to the cosmopolitan state to which he appeals.

The *world* of cosmopolitan right cannot be pared down or reduced to the *res extensa* that I have before me. In consequence, it is as much about the 'world' (or *orbis*) as the mankind (or 'humanity') that inhabits it: to be absolutely empirical, it nevertheless must involve entities that are purely and simply abstract. Their abstraction comes from the fact that this 'world' and this 'humanity' are constructed with the aim of producing a right whose substance they are meant to be. This is what Habermas seems to intuit, and he undertakes, following 'political science' he says, to distinguish three worlds.[27] But this distinction is itself empirical, or rather sociological. There is a developed world (which is free), a world in development (authoritarian and prey to fundamentalisms) and finally a 'third world' of a new kind, socially and civilly destructured. It is obvious that these categories cannot in themselves found some cosmopolitan right: right or law in general is mediation between *equals* and it is obvious that (*ex hypothesi*) a right or law that would be common to these three 'worlds' would ratify absolute inequality. And inequality of world founds war not peace.

So the concept of the world must be constructed for a (cosmopolitan) right—the right expressing this world—to be possible. Here again we must recall that law is *impotent* to found common being and peace. Law does not found a world, only politics does that. Only political action is foundational. Law is only the mediation which expresses what is politically conceived and established. Our thesis is that there is only one place that constitutes a—politically conceivable—world that can be thought (and organized) according to cosmopolitan right and law: the European world, Europe as world. This is because sovereignty has reached its cul-

27. Habermas, 'Kant's Idea of *Perpetual Peace*', pp. 133–4.

mination there and this very culmination, in bringing a world to an end—the universal world of the *orbis*, the world of sovereignties and their state of nature—opens up the possibility of another world, a particular one, the only one of its kind, the European world. In this sense, contemporary cosmopolitan right can take shape only in the form of the *law of peoples of Europe*—as the realm of a republic of Europe, and the norm of the free life at peace of its particular humanity—European humanity. The *morality* of European humanity is thus to be thought as the humanity of a particular world that has obligations vis-à-vis the humanity of the plurality of worlds. The wars and disorders of the *orbis* are an effective moral constraint on European humanity. Moreover, it is in this *constraint or compulsion*—which is exercised on a humanity finally at peace with itself when it observes the spectacle of the wars and poverty of the *orbis*—that Europe finds the most solid foundation for its constitution as a republic (so long as it does not refuse it).

If it were necessary (and indeed it is) we could think this morality as the morality of the Rights of Man, even if that cannot serve as the unique foundation for a cosmopolitan right extended to the humanity of the *orbis*: that must be the just peace that a European world at peace can help to build. By definition, the *orbis* is the sphere of the plurality of worlds where the state of nature reigns, and it would be to yield to an illusion to say with Habermas that it is moving towards a cosmopolitan state.[28] The illusion here is, in fact, to think that the *orbis* forms a world, or, in other words, that the world as it is can be governed by (cosmopolitan) law. The Europeans of our time (the time of the culmination of their past world) are beginning to understand—that there is no *single* world, but a plurality of worlds. They are finally grasping this truth because it is theirs. As we have said here many times, they have constructed a world which they know is not *one*, a sin-

---

28. The contemporary world situation can be understood in the best case scenario as a period of transition from international to cosmopolitan law' (ibid., p. 130).

gle world; it is not a 'world' and therefore cannot be the material for a single law or the place of 'perpetual peace'. And what differentiates European humanity *tout court* is not that one form of humanity has another essence (which many have wanted to believe and some still do) but that it has another history—that of the impossibility of a *single* world and its 'perpetual peace'.

The Federative Norm

The modern concept of democracy is that of the 'sovereignty of the people'. So the theoretical problem of (European) federative democracy must be formulated as follows: since the will of the people is by very definition a particular will, how can we conceive of a democratic principle appropriate to a *res publica* whose civil substance is that of many historical nations and peoples? We cannot resolve the difficulty by positing a priori that the federative republic ('federative' in a mode yet to be defined) in federating a group of peoples who are already civilly constituted is the space within which a new people (or a new nation) could be produced by the fusion of particular peoples. This solution—which means that there could be a European people—is philosophically unacceptable, because it rests on the paralogism that reduces the new to the old. In effect, it says that, in a democratically governed federative republic, the coalescence of the particular wills of peoples into a single will occurs only at the moment when a single people is formed out of these multiple peoples. A federative democracy of Europe would thus be—if we postulate the possible existence of a 'European people'—a democracy on a grand scale founded on the sovereignty of the people by the production of the general will. This approach encourages the project of a complete political union of Europe and, more widely, *mutatis mutandis*, the idea of a pacified world (the *orbis*) organized as a cosmopolitan (world) democracy in which the United Nations would be a sort of world parliament.

The crippling difficulty of this way of thinking—with regard to our problem of a *res publica* of Europe—is that it does not take account of the culmination of sovereignty since it tries to reproduce the latter's schema by imagining the creation of a 'European people'. The contradiction here is that if the federative democracy of Europe is structured in the form of sovereignty, it would require the negation of the particular sovereignties that it nevertheless takes as its model. And such a negation cannot found a 'democracy' because it gives rise to its opposite, empire. We have already said that the condition of a democratic *res publica* of Europe is that the historical nations and peoples form the civil and moral basis on which it must be built. There can be no other foundation, since the process of the emergence of modern historical nations (under the banner of sovereignty) resulted in the birth and development of these particular peoples. In other words, no 'European people' or 'European nation' is philosophically *thinkable* or historically possible without recourse to the violence of empire.

The paradox of federative democracy as it can be thought in the European framework of constituted nations and the culmination of sovereignty is that such a democracy does not emanate from the people but from the *multitude*. And by 'multitude' I understand Europeans considered according to a transversal principle of civility, by which, as I have said, they *de facto* individually dispose of a federative right whose regular exercise by means of universal suffrage allows a federative assembly to be established—the European Parliament.[29] There is a paradox here only to the extent that our traditional political understanding is structured by the founding equation democracy = sovereign people. This idea was perhaps correct in the context of the modern State but has ceased to be so in the context of post-State democracy. Understanding this paradox allows us to discard the presupposition that is implicitly invoked when democratic government in the *res publica* is

---

29. See 'Life at Peace. *The Federative*'.

founded on the presumption of a European people. In so doing, we presuppose that the supersession of States (particular sovereignties) to the benefit of a European political union requires the dissolution of particular peoples as the site of the will. The corollary of this implicit presupposition is that every democratic *res publica* of Europe would take the form of a federal political and administrative centre of decision that aimed to constrain particular sovereignties for as long as it took for the remnants of the historical States to become the relay of the European *res publica*. In this context, the legitimacy of such a centre is conferred on it by the (democratic) will of the European people—the new, superior general will. Its condition of existence, however, is unarguably the elimination of particular peoples and nations. We thus see the rebirth from the ashes of a new State, now called 'Europe', which presents itself as democratic and has, over time if not immediately, the attributes of classical sovereignty—power and territoriality. Internally, the power of this European State would articulate a principle of civility, a norm of justice; and externally, it would act as the subject of international law. No doubt, we have to convince ourselves that the result (if not the intention) of such a democratic system, by dissolving particular wills in favour of the will of a single people, would *ipso facto* dissolve the freedom of each into that of empire, eventually adorning itself with the ideology of the 'Rights of Man'. We can see that the problem thus revealed is that the idea of federative democracy, which rests on historical peoples and nations, does not found its will on that of a sovereign people.

That is why the European idea of a federative democracy has little to do with notions that emerge from 'political law' or the law of sovereignties, and everything to do with cosmopolitan right—not the general will of the people, but the *general spirit of nations*. It is not a question here of re-establishing the already discredited notion of a European 'spirit' but of using this term to discern what the passage of Europe from (national) politics to (transnational) cosmopolitanism produces to make the federative constitution of democracy possible.

Montesquieu was the first to define the general spirit as an ensemble where 'climate, religion, laws, the maxims of government, examples of past things, morals, manners'[30] form the historical particularity of a nation. It is the same for the general spirit as for the spirit of the laws—the spirit of a thing is the concept of that thing. It expresses the form that presides over its nature, what defines it in what is proper to it. Therefore the general spirit does not refer to who knows what psychology of nations and peoples to authorize its characterization. The general spirit in expressing the form of what is given in history does not aim at fixing an essence which, rightly, would escape to becoming. For the author of *The Spirit of the Laws* (1748), it is a question, rather, of grasping the fundamental original structure by which nations take shape, the institutions that develop—a question of grasping what makes the collective existence of a 'people' or 'nation' possible, what makes them specific entities that cannot be reduced or interchanged. In what conditions and according to what determinations can a human multitude constitute itself into a republic, that is, form an ensemble according to the dispositions of its laws, morals, traditions and past? If the general spirit is a form, it is the form that differentiates one nation from another. More than the fundamental form of sociability, the general spirit is the name of what produces civil orders and differentiated politics among human beings. Thus, the general spirit does not refer to the beginning of a people or nation but to what founds it in forming a common being. In consequence, it is only once in history that it is established that the common being of a people can comprise its own form. That is to say, the general spirit shows the particular form of freedom that a nation is endowed with in the course of its history. The foundation of its freedom can thus be grasped through the form that expresses it as a result, in the sense that a free nation does not spring forth com-

30. Montesquieu, *On the Spirit of the Laws* (Anne M. Cohler et al. trans. and ed.) (Cambridge, Cambridge University Press, 1989 [1748]), XIX, 4, p. 310.

pletely formed from nothing. At the base of Montesquieu's idea lies the profound idea that common being is constituted historically.

This detour through the general spirit leads us back to the idea of the federative democracy of a republic of Europe in making manifest that the latter is philosophically possible and historically realizable only on condition that historical particularisms become the material of a cosmopolitanism of freedom. A *res publica* of Europe is a federation of freedom—not of peoples. And the federative foundation of freedom requires a democratic principle whose foundation would be the general spirit of the Europeans. In effect, the notion of the general spirit allows us to resolve the major difficulty presented by the idea of a federative European democracy—the reconciliation of the particularism of peoples and nations with the constraint of a common being, that is to say, a higher freedom than that of the particularisms themselves.

A new question in turn arises: how to express the general spirit of the Europeans and to found the common being of a republic upon it? I repeat: the recourse to the notion of a general spirit (replacing the general will of a 'people') is relevant because the concept refers to the historicity of freedom and freedoms, which do not spring forth *ex nihilo* from the multitude become 'people' but from laws, morals, experience, religion and so on. These things are not the fruit of pure will. On the contrary, we have to consider duration and memory. The first is the fabric of patience necessary to establish freedom, while the second recalls that the present of a world for a people is the permanent result of the past. It is so as not to deny what is most important about European history—the experience of suffering produced by its extended civil war—that the common being of Europe can take shape as a republic if, and only if, this *spirit* of particular freedoms, proper to nations forms the material of a common freedom. Thus the expression of this spirit must operate through the exercise of the federative right of all.

To examine the matter concretely, that is, the effective procedure by which Europeans constitute their common being in conformity with their general spirit, we will define two complementary founding actions. The first is the determination of a constituent power (*pouvoir*) and the second is the determination of the federative norm as the *law of the* peoples *of Europe*.

I understand by *constituent power* the power that sets up the republic, which states the fundamental law (the constitutional norm). Since the republic of Europe can only be a federative democracy, the constitutional norm can only proceed from a body capable of expressing both the democratic dimension *and* the transnational dimension. We have seen that the democratic dimension cannot be reduced to the 'will of the people' since this people does not exist (I say again that the 'people' in the modern sense would only reintroduce what has been superseded: sovereignty). The *demos* of this democracy can thus only be the multitude, or, put another way, the Europeans of historical nations or the universality of individuals. We know that the right of the multitude is the federative right and we know too that its regular and legal exercise is to elect the European Parliament. We have already demonstrated that the power enjoyed by the European Parliament as such, that is, when it deliberates in assembly, is *by right* a federative power—even if, we know, the positive law in force does not *de facto* recognize in it such a right. It remains the case that the assembly, the representative of the multitude (because of its election through universal direct suffrage), is the depositary, not of the general will (because the multitude is *not* the 'people') but of the *federative will* of the Europeans.

In effect, there is no power without will, as constituent power is itself composed, first of all, of a federative will that it formed in the federative body of the European Parliament. Another element of constituent power is required which allows the principle referred to above to be satisfied, that is, the principle by which the general spirit must express the particularism of historical freedoms as they exist within the nations of Europe. In consequence, I propose that constituent power is itself formed if and only if the national Parliaments are represented at its heart. Subsequently, constituent power takes the form of an assembly (or a congress, if you prefer) that brings together the representatives of the national Parliaments sitting with the European Parliament—a sizeable majority of seats will naturally belong to the European Parliament elected by Europeans alone and not by particular nations.[31]

The constituent assembly is only empowered to state the *federative norm*: this consists of stating the clauses that would set up a *res publica* of Europe, as part of a *jus gentium* of Europe (a *law of the European peoples*). There are six of these, if we confine ourselves to the philosophical formulation of their principle, as we do here:

Clause 1: *The* law of the *peoples* of Europe *is the European form of a general cosmopolitan law whose aim is peace.*

Comment: this clause is more a principled foundation that the constituent assembly would make its own in declaring that the *res publica* of Europe is an arrangement of affairs made possible by the law of the peoples of Europe. Properly speaking, then, the first principle of the *res publica* is:

Clause 2: *The* res publica *of Europe brings together some of those Europeans from the historical nations who have adhered to the law of the peoples of Europe and who*

---

31. It might be useful to specify that the formation of a constituent congress, the sole holder of constituent power whose fundamental and essential core would be what I have just described (we can complete this congress provided that its principle remains), requires as a matter of urgency a profound reform of the procedures currently in force for the election of the European Parliament. Most obviously, it would require that electoral laws be made uniform over this terrain.

have renounced the exercise of their sovereignty with regard to international politics and defence, and accept the harmonization of their politics as regards social, economic and educational matters, as well as research, health and public security, on the basis of objectives and programmes defined by common agreement.

Within the res publica *of Europe the federative norm has primacy over every other internal norm.*

Comment: a) this clause rests on the two essential determinations of cosmopolitan law as I understand it here. First of all, it is the determination of a continental territorial space; the territory of a *jus gentium* of Europe thus might include Russia and Turkey. The aim of this arrangement (which is in no way reducible to a 'federation' or 'confederation') is to constitute a common world of European peace. Secondly, it is also the determination of a *federative political space* within the continental space. Cosmopolitan law begins then with the constitution of the European world, and hence can act so as to put the cosmopolitan law of the *orbis* into concrete practice (see below), and (b) in order to avoid possible ambiguities, it would be useful to explain here that the extension of the *res publica* does not necessarily require the extension of the European *jus gentium*. In fact, the *res publica* is constituted by and composed of just those nations, otherwise party to the *jus gentium*, who accept that certain traditional prerogatives of sovereignty (diplomacy, defence, etc.) be held in common. The *res publica* thus does not require the *jus gentium*; rather, the latter would be the formal condition of the former. Emerging from the *jus gentium*, the *res publica*, once constituted, is thus neither the effect of sovereignty nor the institution of another sovereignty.

Clause 3: European citizenship *belongs to any person regularly resident in the territory of the* res publica *of Europe, who has a regular activity that confers on him or her a status that creates a right to social protection. It makes it possible for any person so entitled to vote or be elected or engage in the political life of the* res publica.

European citizenship is independent of nationality. A person who satisfies the above conditions can keep his original nationality and enjoy European citizenship.[32]

Comment: by this clause, what is manifest is that *any person* (born in Europe or not) satisfying the defined conditions is entitled to European citizenship without losing their original citizenship.

Clause 4: Federative democracy *is the form of government of the* res publica *of Europe. It guarantees the fundamental rights of the person. Its rules and laws conform to the arrangements of the law of the* peoples *of Europe and to the general political arrangements outlined above. Any nation of the* res publica *is free to organize itself democratically (at the local or national level) and to enter into relationship with the other nations of the* orbis *provided that its action in these domains is not contrary to present arrangements.*

Clause 5: *a* Court of Justice *that specifically examines the complaints of individuals linked to the exercise of European citizenship and a* Constitutional Court *empowered to oversee the compatibility of European and national laws with the federative norm will sit permanently.*

Clause 6: *the* res publica *of Europe enjoys the status of moral personality: the federative norm is compatible with international treaties.*

Cosmopolitan Right and Law

The six theoretical clauses stated above in tracing the outline of the European *res publica* open up the field of cosmopolitan law to the extent that the law of the *peoples* of Europe is a regional political form of the latter. We have already comment-

---

32. Citizenship is the most obvious *sign* of the extension of freedom. This is thus not fully guaranteed by the anticipated arrangements of the Constitution currently under discussion in Europe. See NOTE 12.

ed that the weakness of pure law is that it only has force of law, an assertion that it is difficult to contest. *A fortiori*, a pure cosmopolitan law—a planetary law of a planetary public space—is doomed to impotence if it is manifested only in a set of written dispositions to which nations and States subscribe without involving a substantial community (in particular as regards the fundamental rights of the person) and with no relation to civil and economic development.

The *free life* of the nations of the *orbis*, the peaceful and organized life, must be made possible—regardless of our pessimism about its attainability in some foreseeable future—by a cosmopolitan law whose reality would be different to the everyday confirmation of its impotence. The materiality of cosmopolitan law cannot be reduced to the resolutions of the United Nations, whether or not they are respected, or those armed men, those 'peace troops', which the United Nations sends to areas of conflict without the right to intervene militarily. Everyone can see how much international law, far from becoming cosmopolitan law (whose cosmopolitans would be the universality of the individuals of the *orbis*), is, on the contrary, either prey to the Great Powers or one of them. This is because the sovereign order of the world is the very one which, in the middle of the last century, presided over the foundation of the international order and its law, whose *incipit* was the United Nations Charter. But the time of sovereignties has comes to its end, if not in the world then at least in Europe. And it is because Europe can constitute itself as a republic—indeed must do so—that it is in a position to give body to a cosmopolitan law whose first stone would be the *jus gentium* of its nations.

In effect, Europe's constitution *in potentia*, emerging from the *jus gentium* (and not from the procedures of sovereignty) gives cosmopolitan law the force of a revolutionary renovation of international law. If the constitution of Europe as a *res publica* is the sole means currently available—because *possible*—to clear the path to a cosmopolitan law, endowed with sufficient power to establish a just and balanced international order, and with a capacity to act, it is because the European republic is, in its founding principle, the *body politic*, not simply a juridical one, of cosmopolitan law since, following the theoretical propositions developed here, it proceeds from a (European) international law, a *jus gentium*. Law ceases to be purely law if it exists in the form of a body politic, in the absence of which there would be no law at all. But considered from a properly juridical point of view, the republic is a figure of the *jus gentium* and, for that reason, a regional modality of general cosmopolitan law. Contrariwise, a constitution of Europe in a mode of sovereignty, even if in a republic, would entail it closing in on itself, according to its own self-positioning. In consequence, in positing its particular freedom by a political act open to the freedom of all—a European *jus gentium* conceived as part of the cosmopolitan law of the *orbis*—Europe, as new world, irresistibly separates itself from the New World, thus putting an end to the Atlantic freedom that the latter founded. At the same time, it opens up the sphere of peace to the plurality of worlds of the *orbis*.

Europe is embarked on a different road of another freedom. In the course of this process which remains to be completed and which cannot take place outside the foundation of a republic where the civil multitude exercises its federative right, in terms of the procedures that only history can reveal in the course of action, a revolution approaches. The probability that this revolution would take place in the sphere of the Atlantic republic is high because it could only be produced under these conditions, that is to say in the form of a schism bringing an end to what had been a common foundation of freedom. The two sides of the Atlantic might have moved apart from one another; on the other hand, it might be the occasion of a new *rapprochement* because of the very novelty of contemporary events. Philosophy is not prophecy, and makes no strong claim for the latter here. Philosophy is limited to discerning what perhaps is at work in history and to proposing its concept so as to know it. This is what I have tried to do here.

We would be mistaken if without further investigation we thought that the *idea* of a republic of Europe, the political space of Europe as *new world*, is the fruit only of a moral or historical optimism, or both. What we have here is philosophical optimism, that is, the optimism of the concept which has no *weight* in the face of pessimism based on the historical. Who would assert that humanity always and everywhere perceives the *good* that it nevertheless desires? This is why even the best despair to some extent at the obvious corruption of freedom in the organization of the nations of Europe. I am not talking so much about the corruption of *political personnel* (though this does exist) as I am about the corruption of the *system*. Moreover, political science might show us that the corruption of one proceeds from the corruption of the other.

So, the following does not seem unfair. Europe at the beginning of this period seems at times seized by a madness which makes us career erratically, compelled to act but ignorant of what actions to take. Whether it involves matters of the European Union or national affairs, the spectacle of this madness, which makes governments and countries reel, is not at all rare. This is made extremely obvious when governments, whether because they are deaf and blind to the demands of the people, or because the governing class is simply bought off and corrupt, embark on a path that the immense majority of people refuse to follow. We thus reach the summit of immorality when the issue is the choice between war and peace, undoubtedly the most serious matter that a people has to consider and its governors to *think*. To choose war when the people want peace (not always and everywhere: if the people are peaceful, they are not *pacifist*) is to negate democracy and to corrupt the freedom of the republics. This *madness* overtakes some but involves everyone. The madness, in a certain way, also overtakes the people—they do not overthrow their corrupt leaders. They become either resigned or demonstrative but they do not unleash an insurrection.

Who can say that the corruption of freedom and contempt for democratic morality are not the signs of that madness which has become embedded in various European States because Europe is looking for the path to follow? Could it be after all that Europe simulates madness because it refuses to see the way opening up in front of it, as it faces the worrying world of the *orbis*, and, even more, faces itself? It might be that Europe simulates madness when faced with the necessity, which Europeans grasp in a confused way, of breaking with the Atlantic republic. Europe is perhaps that tragic figure who simulates madness because his duty is intolerable since its fulfilment, he thinks, is beyond his powers. If Europe is seized by madness in these times of transition and revolution in the offing, it is no doubt because it fears the future that seems so different from the past.

The cost of freedom, for sovereignty first of all, then for its popular version, the Atlantic republic—universal war of each nation against all—truly belongs to the past. The freedom that thus emerged was bought at such a price that it is difficult for the Europeans who have paid it to embark on the new road of a freedom. This is especially so, since this freedom remains to be defined—its philosophic definition is rudimentary, since its definition, properly speaking, can come only from history and practice. They hesitate because no one knows what the future will bring. They are ready to step back and re-engage with the Atlantic model, maintaining it, even at the cost of the stagnation (or worse, cancellation) of a freedom which would remain riveted to past tradition, to each nation's territory, the internal space of its sovereignty, the meanderings of those *common selves* that are the outcomes of war, and which is at risk in a peace that comprises consumption without aim or risk. Europe might still refuse an open cosmopolitan freedom, a refusal stemming from the exhaustion that finitude produces. However, that would not efface the freedom at work within contemporary European humanity, because freedom *is* the felt necessity of a revolution inscribed in things at the very moment they seem to discard it.